New Approaches to Religion and Power

Series editor: Joerg Rieger

While the relationship of religion and power is a perennial topic, it only continues to grow in importance and scope in our increasingly globalized and diverse world. Religion, on a global scale, has openly joined power struggles, often in support of the powers that be. But at the same time, religion has made major contributions to resistance movements. In this context, current methods in the study of religion and theology have created a deeper awareness of the issue of power: Critical theory, cultural studies, postcolonial theory, subaltern studies, feminist theory, critical race theory, and working class studies are contributing to a new quality of study in the field. This series is a place for both studies of particular problems in the relation of religion and power as well as for more general interpretations of this relation. It undergirds the growing recognition that religion can no longer be studied without the study of power.

Series editor:

Joerg Rieger is Wendland-Cook Professor of Constructive Theology in the Perkins School of Theology at Southern Methodist University.

Titles:

No Longer the Same: Religious Others and the Liberation of Christian Theology
David R. Brockman

The Subject, Capitalism, and Religion: Horizons of Hope in Complex Societies
Jung Mo Sung

Imaging Religion in Film: The Politics of Nostalgia
M. Gail Hamner

Spaces of Modern Theology: Geography and Power in Schleiermacher's World
Steven R. Jungkeit

Transcending Greedy Money: Interreligious Solidarity for Just Relations
Ulrich Duchrow and Franz J. Hinkelammert

Foucault, Douglass, Fanon, and Scotus in Dialogue: On Social Construction and Freedom
Cynthia R. Nielsen

Lenin, Religion, and Theology
Roland Boer

In Search of God's Power in Broken Bodies: A Theology of Maum
Hwa-Young Chong

The Reemergence of Liberation Theologies: Models for the Twenty-First Century
Edited by Thia Cooper

Theological Perspectives for Life, Liberty, and the Pursuit of Happiness: Public Intellectuals for the Twenty-First Century
Edited by Ada Maria Isasi-Diaz, Mary McClintock Fulkerson, and Rosemary Carbine

Decolonial Judaism
Triumphal Failures of Barbaric Thinking

Santiago Slabodsky

DECOLONIAL JUDAISM
Copyright © Santiago Slabodsky, 2014.

All rights reserved.

First published in hardcover in 2012 by PALGRAVE MACMILLAN® in the United States—a division of St. Martin's Press LLC, 175 Fifth Avenue, New York, NY 10010.

Where this book is distributed in the UK, Europe and the rest of the world, this is by Palgrave Macmillan, a division of Macmillan Publishers Limited, registered in England, company number 785998, of Houndmills, Basingstoke, Hampshire RG21 6XS.

Palgrave Macmillan is the global academic imprint of the above companies and has companies and representatives throughout the world.

Palgrave® and Macmillan® are registered trademarks in the United States, the United Kingdom, Europe and other countries.

ISBN: 978–1–137–52028–9

The Library of Congress has cataloged the hardcover edition as follows:

Slabodsky, Santiago, 1977– author.
    DeColonial Judaism : triumphal failures of barbaric thinking.
      pages cm
    Includes bibliographical references and index.
    ISBN 978–1–137–36531–6 (alk. paper)
        1. Decolonization. 2. Political science—Philosophy. 3. Civilization, Western—Jewish influences. 4. Judaism and politics. 5. Jews—Politics and government—20th century. 6. Other (Philosophy) I. Title.

JV151.S53 2014
325_.3—dc 3   2013050468

A catalogue record of the book is available from the British Library.

Design by Newgen Knowledge Works (P) Ltd., Chennai, India.

First PALGRAVE MACMILLAN paperback edition: May 2015

10 9 8 7 6 5 4 3 2 1

To my abuelas/abuelos

Gita/Arnoldo
Clara/Santiago

East/South
Socialist/Radical
Cosmopolitan/Laborer

Jews
Latin Americans
Barbarians

Contents

Acknowledgments

It is customary to start this section in a straightforward manner acknowledging the writer's networks of support. The responsibility is to extend gratitude and exculpate extraordinarily generous individuals and institutions of the mistakes contained in one's volume. I learned from the history of barbarism, however, that co-conspirators are usually blamed for *culpas ajenas* (foreign transgressions). While a civilized gesture would be to exculpate my interlocutors, my barbaric impulse impels me to do the contrary. Since this book responds to challenges my comrades presented to me over the years in four continents and no intellectual contribution is made in isolation from a community, I show my gratitude by making them co-guilty in this enterprise.

First of all I would like to thank/blame people who have been on call throughout this process. Over ten years ago Marc Ellis, pioneer of Jewish liberation theology, enlisted a peripheral Jew as a junior conversation partner and since that time has served, for me, as a model for twenty-first century Jewish committed intellectualism. Rachel Gostenhofer is the primary individual responsible for the sophistication of this text, editing (and re-editing) my Spanglish bringing it to a level that could not have been achieved without the skills and commitment of a superb scholar and longtime friend. My peers in Berlin, Chicago, Vitoria/DC, and Gronigen, Manuela Boatcă, Robert Smith, Michael Marder, and Stefania Travagnin, walked with me through different steps of the process offering not only scholarly encouragement but also warm humor that made it possible to overcome the obstacles such an endeavor inevitably entails. My doctoral students, Ann Hidalgo, Drew Baker, Yi Shen Ma, and Chris Carter were and continue to be an incredible source of vitality. Ann wonderfully edited my first drafts and with Drew, Yi Shen, and Chris have been a continuous epistemological challenge, making my Claremont years a fruitful intercultural and inter-religious experience.

In the second place, I would like to thank/blame senior scholars who supported my work when I was conducting research and writing this book. They entered into conversations with me, published my work, invited me to lecture and teach in their institutions around the world, and/or offered me wonderful advice about the publication of this book. I owe a substantial debt of gratitude to Robert Gibbs, Walter Mignolo, Vincent Wimbush, Ramon Grosfoguel, Enrique Dussel, Eric Meyers, Nancy Bedford, Malachi Hacohen, Ivan Kalmar, Kurt Anders Richardson, Lewis Gordon, Salman Sayyid, Nelson Maldonado-Torres, Paul Myrhe, Jonathan Judaken, Fernando Segovia, Victoria Fontan, Luis Rivera-Pagan, Samuel Pagan, Mitri Raheb, Miguel de la Torre, and Elizabeth Conde Frazier. A special thanks to the editor of *New Approaches to Religion and Power*, Joerg Rieger and the blind reviewers, editors, and team members at Palgrave including Burke Gerstenschlager, Caroline Kracunas, Devon Wolkfiel, Rachel Taenzler, and Madeline Crum.

In Claremont wonderful colleagues made it possible for me to navigate the first years of my life as a young professor even when my incurable barbarism inevitably posed its challenges, as well as caused me to create imaginary ones. I would like to thank/blame all the faculty and staff and name close friends including Helene Slessarev-Jamir, Grace Kao, Frank Rogers, Marvin Sweeney, Roland Faber, Richard Amesbury, Najeeba Syeed-Miller, Monica Coleman, David Jamir, Sheryl Kujawa-Holbrook, Lynn O'Leary-Archer, Dennis McDonalds, Kathy Black, Gamward Quan, Duane Bidwell, Jeffrey Kuan, Martha Barcenas, Donna Porras, and the soul of the institution Sansu Woodmancy. Forming part of my extended institutional network and a continued source of inspiration, I would also like to thank my Latina/o Wabash cohorts including Angela Tarango, Jacqueline Hidalgo, Chris Tirres, Cláudio Carvalhae, and Gregory Cuellar as well as my social organizers/public intellectual comrades Paulina Gonzalez, Mario Brito, Carolina Fuchs, and Clara Takarabe.

This book could not have been completed without institutions that collaborated with my research, either providing generous funding and/or a nurturing space to develop my ideas. They include the Wabash Center for Teaching and Learning, the Centers for Jewish Studies and Global Studies and the Humanities at Duke University, the Chicano/Latino Studies Program and the Department of Ethnic Studies at UC-Berkeley, the Center for Intercultural Dialogue in Spain, the University for Peace in Costa Rica, the *Centres* for the Study of Religion and Jewish Studies at the University of Toronto, St. Thomas

More College at the University of Saskatchewan, the Department of Religious Studies and Center for Jewish Studies at the University of Cape Town, the Latin American Rabbinical Seminary in Argentina, the School of Social Sciences at the University of Buenos Aires, the Roosevelt College-University of Utrecht in the Netherlands, and finally the Rowlett Fund and the dean's office at Claremont School of Theology.

Initiating my conclusion, I would like to thank my family for their unconditional love. Even though learning to hug, smile, and cry by skype is not the easiest task, they have always been my primary source of spiritual guidance and wisdom. My parents Mabel and Jorge taught me the value of responsibility in times of despair and permanent struggle in moments of certainty. My sister Silvina is the source of inspiration for my struggle in Jewish Latin America and my sister Deborah my accomplice in the subversion of global networks while entrenched in eminently local problems. My nephew Alejandro and my niece Nahiara taught this parachute uncle how love can fundamentally defy and defeat both spatial and temporal distances. My uncle Daniel and my aunt Julia initiated me in alternative readings and have been models for committed intellectualism.

Lastly, I would like to thank my wonderful *caminante con camino* (co-walker), Elly Gong-Hee Rhee. She stormed into my life with a passionate unbalance of energy, care, enthusiasm, and patience. Without her unfailing love and tenacity this book would never have been possible. We share a life thinking in Korean and Spanish within a predominantly Anglophone setting. It was only thanks to our common life in translation that I understood the Caribbean-French recommendation of Aime Cesaire about completing the prayers of Marxist German/Polish Jews. So I start this book by problematically exclaiming: barbarians of the world unite!

Santiago Eitan Slabodsky
Buenos Aires, Argentina/
Berkeley, California
October, 2013

INTRODUCTION

The Past Was Worse
(and We Miss It)

Barbaric Rubble

I was so immersed in the book that I became unaware of the desolate setting in which I found myself. But another young Argentinean Jew grabbed my shoulder and shattered my reverie: "Please Santiago, snap out of it" she pleaded "don't you realize you are sitting atop the rubble of a library nearly reduced to ashes? We have only a few hours to *save* hundreds of other books!" My comrade was right. In the years to follow I would locate more traditionally inspiring places to read a good novel from the Global South. I remember encountering Isabel Allende in an edgy library in Jerusalem, Chinua Achebe in a smoky Marxist cafe in Havana, and Salman Rushdie in a sunny public garden in Paris. This time, however, I was attempting to read a Tunisian Jewish decolonialist in the remains of a building that only weeks before was incinerated by a car-bomb attack. Though the setting was sinister, I was unable to part with the book. The novel did not have covers, was missing over thirty pages, and contained more dust that my allergies could tolerate. Perhaps the tattered covers made the rallying cry of Albert Memmi even more evocative and resonant. While comparing the elusive temptation of European civilization with the life of Global South Jewry, he proclaimed: "I am an incurable barbarian."[1] It is this statement that prompted the question I intend to answer in this book.

This was not the first time I read a radical Jewish manifesto in a dusty and dark room in Buenos Aires. My hometown is not only home to the largest concentration of Jews in the South, but it is also well known for her old bookstores that serve as functional libraries and loci of leftist congregation. If one spends enough time plotting impossible revolutions with radical activists, one could be invited to hidden storage spaces behind second walls that were constructed when reading was considered a crime. During the convoluted 1970s, South American military dictatorships besieged a generation of revolutionaries who went underground with their books and the incendiary proposals they contained. The dictatorships were instigated and supported by Western powers during the Cold War, allegedly for the purposes of defending Christian civilization against its barbaric enemies. The Argentinean dictatorship (1976–1983) was not only one of the bloodiest of these genocidal systems; it also found in the Jewish community one of its central targets. Of the total number of people "disappeared" (kidnapped, tortured, and murdered without leaving a trace), Jews represented over twelve percent when they comprised less than one percent of the entire population. In the late 1970s and early 1980s, these Argentinean Jews were cast as a threat to civilization. Perhaps reading Memmi in a dark and dusty room in the South was an ideal place to reflect on the affirmation of Jewish barbarism after all.[2]

I read the Arab Jewish social theorist, however, in a different dark and dusty room of Buenos Aires. I formed part of a cohort of young Jews whose mission was to retrieve books buried under the rubble. In 1994, the Jewish headquarters that hosted the library were destroyed by an attack whose perpetrators are yet to be found. The car bomb transited the same streets from which seditious Jews had been kidnapped by the genocidal forces of civilization only twenty years before. The dominant narratives of both events, however, clashed in one major respect. According to the reading that rapidly came to predominate, the attack was perpetrated by an unholy alliance, held together only by their timeless and irrational hate for the (now) "Judeo"-Christian civilization: international Muslims and local Neo-Nazis. Soon thereafter, the unholy alliance was transformed into a profane trinity, as regional Marxists were added to the list of antagonists. After 9/11 this unlikely front of "new barbarians" became an almost normative portrayal of the global threat to civilization. In South America this Manichean dualism was reproduced, even as Jews appeared to have ceded their pride of place to the new instantiations of late twentieth-century barbarism. The narrative of eternal anti-Semitism may have persisted, but the rationale was modified: while in the 1970s Jews were attacked because they were perceived as a threat to civilization, two decades later it was their civilized status that rendered them victims. Reading Memmi in a dark and dusty room in 1990s Buenos Aires made me realize that Jews (even in the South!) may have found the cure for their incurable barbarism.[3]

I was able to encounter Memmi in Spanish because local Jews had already explored their elective affinities between his Maghrebi decolonial theory and Latin American struggles.[4] The records of the experiences of the two Global South Jewries not only concurred in their Third World re-evaluation of Marxist theory but also corresponded in a historical turn. In just a few decades, both went from being victims of the portrayal of Jewish barbarism to being complicit in a narrative of new barbarism, often questioning their historical loyalties. Some Latin American Jews, explicitly influenced by Memmi, penned decolonial works of apologetics explaining to perplexed revolutionaries how former friends were now enemies and vice versa.[5] Memmi himself would eventually acknowledge Jewish ultimate integration into Western society and abandon the barbaric project.[6] Twenty years after their re-affirmation of barbarism, they largely reproduced and advocated a geopolitical design that strengthened the civilization that had hitherto victimized them. Were I a cynic, I would argue that Global South Jews were co-opted by an imperial design that benefited the North (including its Jewry) to the detriment of the barbaric relationship between local Jewries and the South. For now (and just for now) I will suggest that some Southern Jewish voices were among the last to fall in a long, systemic process of racial reconfigurations that required Jews to be civilized and shorn of their alleged barbarism.

A Decolonial Judaism is a study of resistances; provocative, powerful, problematic, and unsuccessful resistances, to this systemic change. It is an analysis of intellectual Jewish projects that emerged during the ultimate re-articulation of this transformation spanning the late 1940s and late 1980s. I focus on social theorists who inverted and fundamentally reconceived the Manichean dichotomy that had racialized Jews, among other barbarians, until this period. These projects did not draw from nuanced deconstructionist persuasions, but they rather combated the dualism by imagining of themselves as belonging to an alternative community, often times consciously barbaric in self-conception and orientation. Furthermore, several of them challenged the dualism through recourse to Southern epistemologies. Unfortunately they ultimately became prisoners of a systemic change that isolated them from the barbaric collective. As a consequence, their projects suffered from conceptual limitations, the persuasiveness of which became especially circumscribed in their post-9/11 legacies. I argue that an analysis of these Jewish proposals can shed considerable light on the possibilities and limitations of both colonial designs and decolonial resistances. Since regnant racial dualisms are presumed to be immutable, the analysis of a community in historical transition between two exclusive poles exposes the cruel nakedness of the design and the difficult ambiguities associated with a resistance thereof.

Civilizational Construction

A Decolonial Judaism is a reading of modern Jewish experiences through the optic of the Manichean civilization/barbarism dualism. For most of the modern period, European discourses portrayed Jews as non-Westerners. While the descriptions varied depending on geopolitical context, normative descriptions of Jews often oscillated between assimilable primitivity and irremediable barbarity.[7] The specific narrative of Jewish barbarism proved particularly persistent across time, space, and ideological persuasion. Even champions of liberal values—Spanish humanists, English deists, French *philosphes*, and German idealists—considered Jews a threat to civilization and permanently interrelated them to other barbarians of the Mediterranean and Atlantic including Muslims, Subsaharan Africans, and Amerindians.

These discourses regularly posited Jewish masterminding of and participation in plots to destroy European civilization, whether defined as Christendom or capitalist imperialism. The irrational desire to regress the forward march of history challenged a core component of the modern project, its reified teleological nature. This accounts for the persistence of such narratives, which still resonate powerfully today. Following 9/11, but with antecedents in, for example, the Jewish headquarters in Buenos Aires, Euro-American discourse combined the adversaries of the Second World War (Nazism), the Cold War (Marxism), and the War on Terror (Islam) into a single barbaric front, reproducing one of the most enduring narratives of Western history.

The construction of Jewish barbarism, however, deteriorated following the Holocaust and during the formal postcolonial period. Throughout the transitional period the civilizational portrayal became normative. This process, however, was not completely novel, immediate, or uniform. As we shall consider below, instances of Jewish "aspirancy" to civilization are in evidence throughout the modern period, especially after the last quarter of the nineteenth century. In this period, a minority of Jews were extended civil rights and/or appointed as intermediaries between colonizers and colonized. While some of these processes immediately precipitated backlashes and obstacles, others eventually reinforced the normative re-articulation after the 1940s. This progressive change does not perforce mean that all Jews were converted immediately or unambiguously. This book canvases instances of intracommunal discrimination that accomplished a re-racialization of, especially, non-Europeans Jews. Some of these voices, which range from Argentinean activists to Israeli Black Panthers, developed resistances that put in question this systemic change. Perhaps the alternatives were not limited to the Global South or Fourth World but could explain Jewish overrepresentation in the United States and Europe during the civil rights movement, anti-Vietnam war protests, or the uprising of 1968. While the process was not new, uniform, or immediate, it progressively transformed the normative portrayal of Judaism. In the twenty-first century, the refusal to accept (or the inability to be indentified with) this reified civilizational identity results in accusations of parochial self-hatred, historical anti-Semitism, and, in more extreme cases, straightforward denial of Jewishness *tout court*.

Over eighty percent of global Jewry is concentrated in North America, Europe, and Israel/Palestine, and they are typically (and uniformly) portrayed as integral members of Western civilization. In the United States, the largest diasporic community in the Northern hemisphere, Jews became integrated into a civilized white society in order to reinforce racial binarisms in the post-war era. In the twenty-first century, when Latinas/os and Muslims (or Afro-American Jews?) challenge this dualism, organized communal Jewry can hardly be distinguished from the myriad declining mainline white Protestant denominations.[8] In Europe, homeland of the old majority, Jews often became token spokespeople, used in the service of challenging the social adaptation of immigrants from Asia, Africa, and Latin America. Today public intellectuals in the largest metropolitan areas, such as Paris or London, support racist and xenophobic discourses that disempower immigrants of the Global South. Ironically this represents a permutation of the same narrative that racialized their grandparents and even parents until as recently as a few decades ago.[9]

This new portrayal also takes place in Israel, today home to over forty percent of world Jewry. The Jewish state is largely portrayed as a civilizational force that, allied to Western powers, was able to create the "only" democracy of the Middle East. As most Occidental replacements, it is important to point out, Israel achieved her political status by racializing non-Westerners including natives (Palestinians), foreign workers (Subsaharan Africans and South-East Asians), and Jews (*Mizrahim*/Orientals and *Beta Israel*/Ethiopians). This enterprise, far from challenging her credentials, reinforced her normative portrayal as a triumphant, if besieged, Western enclave, engulfed by the forces of barbarism. The widespread support among European and American Jewries—now integrated into local mainstream societies—for political Zionism as a constitutive commandment of faith further, if not anachronistically, naturalizes global Jewry and Israel as eternal Western formations. This portrayal effectively becomes a self-fulfilling prophecy of the utopian dreams of the founder of the central European branch of the nationalist project. In his seminal manifesto (1896), Theodor Herzl had clearly affirmed that the ambition of the movement was to create "a rampart of Europe in the Middle East" or, more precisely, "an outpost of civilization as opposed to barbarism."[10]

Herzl's program represents but one of the several intellectual precursors of civilizational Jewish projects analyzed in this book. These antecedents are not, however, limited to European Jewish aspirations. They also include the experiences of a limited number of non-European Jewries who interfaced with colonial designs and became associated with settlers shortly before and after Herzl's manifesto.[11] These experiences are not accidents in an otherwise streamlined history of Jewish barbaric victimization. In hindsight, they are on the historical vanguard of a position that steadily increased in persuasiveness until it achieved normativity. Such antecedents, furthermore, catalyzed new historical processes. Following the Holocaust, Herzl's project was instantiated. Israel became not only a force in the normativization of civilizational Judaism but also a keystone in the global alliance against post-war barbarians. Jews associated with settlers fled the postcolonial states. In Euro-America they were predominantly integrated into mainstream societies and, as outlined below, strong voices within these communities employed a narrative of barbarism to oppose immigration and/or neo-colonial policies. In Israel/Palestine, their experiences were forcefully reinterpreted to support a portrayal of the irrational and timeless hatred of Muslims for Jews and the West, a sine qua non of post-9/11 narratives of barbarism.[12]

Though the new normative portrayal of Jews as civilized subjects found support outside a European Jewish constituency, it was conceived as a response to a particular event of European origin. The integration of normative Jewries into the positive side of Manichean dualism served as a guarantee that there would be no second Holocaust. Some analysts have argued that the process of transformation could be explained by the Western need to assuage its guilt. Indeed, in recent decades, several scholars have pointed to the existence of a new "ecumenical deal" in religious and political secular forms that enables Western Christianity to expiate her sins incurred from her ideological and material complicity (or leadership) during the Holocaust.[13] The outcome of the new Judeo-Christian project, dissident voices argue, goes even further than ethno-religious exculpation. It has enabled the West to perpetuate the same civilizational atrocities by, ironically, justifying their reproduction with the excuse of protecting its former victims. In this way Jews became re-inscribed into the same dualistic paradigm that was responsible for the annihilation of one-third of their population during World War II.

In the new configuration, the normative Jew is portrayed as *the* quintessential victim of history disattached from other experiences of racialization. This universalizes European history as world history and a very specific narrative of European Judaism as world Jewry. Notwithstanding the fact that Jews (including and especially pre-Holocaust European Jews!) were largely victims of civilization and not of barbarism, the West portrays itself as the protector and liberator of the now-civilized Jews (first from Auschwitz, later the Iron Curtain, and now the nuclear threat of Teheran). In some cases, such as the 1994 attack in Buenos Aires, all the barbarians allegedly attack in concert. Western discourses conflate all such enemies, freezing them in a science fiction-esque recapitulation of the Second World War. Imperial actions of the West are justified as an attempt to dissuade the barbarians from perpetrating a new Holocaust. The irony is that the same Western narrative responsible for perpetrating the first Holocaust has assigned itself the role of pre-empting a second. Western civilization, tragically, uses the memory of some of its past victims to justify the perpetuation of the same dualism that annihilated them. Many Jews, most Jews perhaps, joined the new normative portrayal. Some courageous Jews have resisted. While resistances have been growing in the twenty-first century, it has become increasingly difficult for protesters to object outside the rubric of humanist dissident of a civilizational project. Once barbarians among other barbarians, Jews progressively became naturalized as part of Western civilization.

Southern Lenses

A Decolonial Judaism is set during a transitional period. I focus on Jewish political projects that reformulated the Manichean dualism during the last articulation of the normative passage from barbarism to civilization and that, while failing, left a conflicting legacy in the post-9/11 world. In this text, I will take three methodological risks that will hopefully stimulate further conversations about the prospects for a diverse and robust decolonial Judaism. The first risk this project entails is with respect to area studies. Instead of limiting myself to the study of the geographical Third World, I will consider the Global South, a source for an epistemology, that can disrupt hegemonies by reinterpreting the North as well. Second, I will not a priori assume that permanent deconstruction is the only option for subverting colonial dualisms. Instead, I will explore the possibilities and limitations of a re-imagination of dualisms as an epistemological enabler of alternative modalities of thought. Finally, I build upon the superb research undertaken by cultural theorists who reject the equivalence of critical thought with philosophy. I will, nonetheless, conduct a sociology of Jewish thought, emphasizing the role of intellectuals, organically understood, in the construction of a Jewish decolonialism.

This book is thus not a work in area studies. It would, nonetheless, be illuminating to select a number of cases emerging from Global South locations and grant them epistemological privilege to understand the especial features of colonial dynamics. Throughout this book, we will explore compelling scholarly proposals which have deconstructed Global Jewry in aggregate explaining that some Jews—from, say, the Middle East, Latin America, the Maghreb, or the rest of Africa—underwent experiences that do not conform to a general narrative arc modeled on the European historical experience.[14] I am sympathetic to their political objectives and have followed this path elsewhere.[15] In this book, however, I will not follow this line of thought for two reasons:

First, the discursive resistances I will explore presupposed the relationality of Jewish histories and I resist dismissing them with an anachronistic framework, at least before their analyzing. I prefer to understand the possibilities and limitations within their own (certainly questionable) decolonial logic. Second, since the field of Jewish thought has been largely resistant to non-Western epistemological challenges, my proposal would be read as a reduction to an *exotic* experience of a peripheral minority. That is, according to the best possible outcome, my project would be cited in an obscure footnote, and glossed as an exception in the sweeping history of Jewish thought that would still privilege the historical questions emerging from a location that is impervious to the extremes of imperial discourses that have affected them. Since I write this text in Spanglish the possibilities of assimilation of my *picturesque* exception as a neutralization of the difference increases exponentially.

In this book, I argue that the colonial narrative of barbarism affected multiple Jewish networks throughout the world, including in the North. My case studies, therefore, go significantly beyond analyzing Southern

Jewries. Sensitive to the aforementioned historiographical critique, this work does not intend to account for the totality of global Jewry—I will explain my Southern Atlantic frameworks in a mere few paragraphs. I intend to include a diversity of voices from the provincial North, the Global South, and the in-between. I insist, however, that Southern inhabitants usually experience the most extreme consequences of the colonial narrative. As a result, they have the potentiality to acknowledge, recognize, and theorize its centrality and outcome in a more lucid and poignant fashion. For this reason I emphasize the need to employ Southern epistemologies to analyze a phenomenon that affected networks across the globe.

My intention is to engage in the disruption of intellectual hegemonies. If Eurocentrism forces the analysis of the Global South with the theoretical formulations of the globalized North, a decolonial epistemology can accomplish the provincialization of the North through the use of Southern frameworks. Instead of dismissing histories of racialization because they took place at geopolitical centers, I reintroduce them within a broader framework, reclaim their legacies, and problematize their resistances. In this work, therefore, I interpret multiple spatial legacies to show the benefit of employing Southern epistemologies to analyze Jewish projects, as well as to challenge the monopoly of current Eurocentric epistemologies to even analyze sources that today (and only today) are considered as part of the European canon. In other words, I will interpret barbarism with barbarism, even if we need to venture inside the geographical gates of civilization without first knocking on the door.

In the second place, this book will not follow the deconstructionist tendencies prevalent not only in Poststructuralist and Postmodern theory but also in contemporary Postcolonial studies. Since Said published *Orientalism* (1978) and Bhabha popularized the concept of hybridity (1994), this has been one of the most provocative contributions of Anglophone Postcolonialism.[16] Oftentimes the dismantling of polarizing imperial discourses is the only means by which to critique and, more importantly, escape vicious circles. Not to engage in deconstruction exposes one to several risks. One could, for example, inadvertently ratify the agenda imposed by polar identities presupposed by colonial discourses and/or finish defending essentialist politics of identity that reproduce ideal Nativisms. This enterprise, unless one engages in a dual critique, may trap the discourse in vicious circles and/or reify, for example, sexual politics as ontologically uncontaminated and authentic proposals.[17]

While I do draw on Anglophone Postcolonialism–especially Said, and less Bhabha— I do not a priori assume that a permanent deconstruction of the narrative necessarily represents the only or best manner to confront and overcome imperial constructions. This follows historical lessons learned from a conceptual study of the employment and deconstruction of the dualism between barbarism and civilization. Since the sixteenth century, some European and American dissidents have tried to deconstruct normative Manichean dualisms. Unfortunately, this project actually has helped undergird the power of these constructions by either naturalizing a difference that justified (religious/secular) evangelization or disregarding alterity and thereby justifying an idealist Humanitarianism which ignores the material consequences already structured by the dualism.

As a result, some critical intellectuals have forged an alternative approach. They either applied the concept of barbarism to the empire, deeming the West as barbaric or, more interestingly, re-appropriated the concept, endowing barbarism with a positive valence. This re-imagination of the dualism, I will argue in the next chapter, does not re-enact the narrative. In the contrary it engages in a dual critique by simultaneously acknowledging the world created by the dualism and exploring the colonized identity as an alternative to the reified asymmetry. I explore this strategy to unveil not only its decolonial originality, but also—especially toward the end of the book—its limitations. Fortunately, I am far from the first to do so among Jewish voices. For example, during the transitional period, racialized Jews–especially of Asian and African extraction—reclaimed pejorative accusations to define their struggles (i.e., *Mizrahim*/Orientals or *Schorim*/Blacks). While currently the most articulate and persuasive works in the field problematize this re-appropriation, opting for complementary—yet interrelated— strategies, the record serves as a welcoming antecedent of my retrieval within re-racialized voices of the transitional period.[18]

Third and last, this book is deeply informed by cultural theory, but still explores projects emerging from organically conceived intellectual proposals. This decision is, in the first place, professionally and biographically dictated. I am a sociologist of knowledge trained in Jewish and Global South social theory who was a political activist in a neocolonial society where reading and writing were categorized as crimes. Intellectual labor, based on the framework I will soon describe, is not an armchair enterprise confined to the ivory tower, but a barbaric act of community organizing that could put one's life at risk in the service of a revolutionary outcome. Second, this is also contextually appropriate for the following analysis. While intercommunication among cultures is ubiquitous in human history, the period canvassed in this book (i.e., 1940s–1980s) witnessed a veritable explosion of intellectual interchange among cultural critics throughout the world. As I will detail below, Jews and (other) decolonialists met in this period and meaningfully collaborated. My intention is to richly texture this practice, and prove that the conceptual construction I am trying to elaborate is based on existential (material and historical) conditions that, despite their limitations, challenge the traditional way of interpreting works that are otherwise universalized as European philosophy (or provincialized as parochial Third World literature).

In this book, therefore, I do not shy away from strategically polemic decisions. I embrace them with the hope of generating more discussion and apprehending the limits of my own formulations. It is in this spirit that I will employ Global South epistemologies to analyze projects of Jewish resistances in the provincial North, the Global South, as well as the interstices thereof and therein, risking the possibility of not truly escaping the normative centers. I will invert and re-imagine dualistic narratives at the risk of ending up in discursive dead ends. And I will understand Jewish thought as organic intellectual enterprises at the risk of not fully opening decolonial thought to alternative sources of knowledge. This book does not intend to write an encyclopedic summary of Postcolonial Judaisms. A further analysis of Global South Jewries, the challenge to polarizations, and the exploration of other sources of knowledge are critically necessary to construct Jewish resistances. But I will avoid the seduction of objective systematization hoping that this book will help my work enter into conversation with others who are more capable of tackling the issues, regions, or ambiguities I am not able to cover. This book is, therefore, a proposal that intends, from a position of self-conscious partiality, corrigibility, and incompleteness, to collaborate in a critical reflection of barbaric resistances to geopolitical racializations of Judaism.

A Chronicle

A Decolonial Judaism is divided into three parts, each containing two or three chapters. The first part, including chapters one and two, introduces the problem. I analyze the historical and conceptual overlaps between Jews and other experiences of colonization, which enable a decolonial interpretation of Jewish barbaric resistances to imperial narratives. To do so I explore both the relationship between Jewish thought and Postcolonialism as well as the Western narrative of barbarism. The second part, comprising chapters three to five, delineates three Jewish counter-narratives of barbarism, one from the provincial North, one from the Global South, and one from the interstices. I explain how these Jewish projects, written during the transition, ultimately reconceived the dualism between barbarism and civilization and insisted on an alternative locus for Jewish projects of resistance. The last part, chapters six and seven, is a contemporary engagement with the counter-narratives. I broadly outline both the limitations of these resistances and their currency in the post-9/11 context, especially among Global South intellectuals. The epilogue explores the possibility of a Jewish barbarism for the twenty-first century and beyond.

In the beginning and final parts of the book, I engage in diversity of sources including highly developed Jewish studies of American and Israeli/Palestinian provenance. In the substantive core of the book, which canvasses the three aforementioned counter-narratives and assesses their currency in the Global South, I will be guided by a Southern-Atlantic perspective and my analysis will focus in a triangular fashion among Latin America/Caribbean, the Maghreb, and Europe. I made this decision for three reasons. As I will further detail in the first chapter, this is where the networks of re-appropriation of barbarism developed throughout the second half of the twentieth century. Secondly, as I will show in the last chapter, this is the frame of reference and general orientation to which theorists in the twenty-first century are heirs. And finally, in the interest of being explicit about my own subject position, this represents the precise connection to my own background that was present when I first formulated the problem years ago amidst the rubble. Since my temporal and geographical lenses are circumscribed, I do not aim for comprehensiveness. I intend, rather, to enter a conversation with other scholars, and complement the studies they are currently undertaking in different geographical contexts and/or with alternative theoretical, methodological, and definitional paradigms.

In the first chapter, "Jewish Thought, Postcolonialism, and Decoloniality: The Geopolitics of a Barbaric Encounter," I elaborate a framework for the exploration of Jewish decolonial proposals. I start by explaining the contributions made by the Anglophone branch of the field. In particular, I outline their contributions to the understanding of Jewish racialization, in relation with other experiences subject to the patterns of domination I will soon define as coloniality. I detail how this field can be conceptually extended, in the interest of realizing the varieties of decolonial Jewish resistances to hegemonic imperial designs. In order to do so I bring the historical engagement of Jews with decolonialists that were interconnected in the French and Spanish branches of the field. I explain how certain historical and conceptual frameworks can effectively respond to possible objections raised from both Postcolonial and Jewish studies.

The second chapter, "The Narrative of Barbarism: Western Designs for a Globalized North," explores a key narrative undergirding Western imperialism. That is, I investigate the social, political, and economic conditions surrounding the construction of barbarism, particularly in the modern period. The onset of modernity coincided with the first global deployment of barbarism to denote non-Westerners who were "naturally unable" to overcome their condition. I show not only how a multiplicity of communities among Jews, Muslims, Natives, and Africans were embraced by this category but also how this association formed the basis for a potential epistemological alliance among these newly conceived barbarians.

The second part of the book, beginning with chapter three—"Negative Barbarism: Marxist Counter-Narratives in the Provincial North"—considers the first Jewish counter-narrative pertaining to barbarism. I demonstrate how this counter-narrative was mobilized by a European Jewish Marxist tradition that reached its high watermark during the Frankfurt School's 1940s exile in the United States. I contend that this radical tradition represents an accusation of barbarism in reverse, using the category to critique Western imperial formations, and exculpating Jews (*inter alios*) of barbarism in the process. Within this context, barbarism retains its negative valence, and applies it to European discursive reifications (Christianity, Imperialism, Fascism, etc.) that were responsible for regressing history. I end by discussing the extent to which an intra-European critique leveled without the presence of the Global South can actually subvert the colonizing narrative.

Chapter four, "Transitional Barbarism: Levinas's Counter-Narrative and the Global South," considers the encounter between Jewish intellectuals and Global South thinking. I study the thought of Lithuanian philosopher Emmanuel Levinas subsequent to his acquaintance with Argentinean Enrique Dussel in the 1970s. Starting from a classical understanding of barbarism, Levinas demonstrated his openness to "barbaric thinking" after his initial encounter with Dussel and later familiarization with the bourgeoning sub-field of "barbaric philosophy." Levinas made his own contribution to the topic, deploying Talmudic texts in the service of a new decolonial framework that included Jews. I study the possibilities of this intellectual turn and end by identifying its most important limitation: the integration of Jews into a decolonial community through an entity he calls "Israel" just months before the first Intifada.

The final chapter in this section, "Positive Barbarism: Memmi's Counter-Narrative in a Southern Network," considers a third counter-narrative of barbarism. I explain how Tunisian Memmi made a radical gesture by affirming his Jewish Maghrebi identity and self-identifying as an "incurable barbarian." I portray Memmi's re-affirmation as a Jewish proposal within Third-Worldist thinking that explores the role of Jews within a myriad of decolonial voices. Following national liberation models Memmi decides to integrate Jews into a decolonial space through the State of Israel. I explore the possibilities and limitations of this move and the reasons behind his abandonment of the barbaric project. I argue that his resignation follows an acknowledgment of a re-positionality of Jews in the last decades of the twentieth century.

The third and last part of the book opens with "Barbaric Paradoxes: Zionism from the Standpoint of the Borderlands" (chapter six). It offers a deep exploration of the possibilities and limitations of the counter-narratives. I start by analyzing the decolonial features of the proposals and argue that the positive projects result in a difficult tension. On the one hand, they sustain the need to integrate Judaism into a barbaric community. On the other hand, they propose to do so through a particular political project that portrayed itself as reproducing the narrative of barbarism, rather than its subversion. I return to Anglophone Postcolonialism to show the limits of the narratives, and I turn to Hispanophone Postcolonialism to explain the conceptual reasons underlying the tension stemming from the re-positionality of normative Judaism.

The concluding chapter, "After 9/11: New Barbarism and the Legacies in the Global South," offers a recapitulation of the counter-narratives in the current context, especially Jewish voices from the Global South (Maghreb and Latin America). I argue that given the normative reconfiguration of Jews in the twenty-first century, the heirs of the counter-narratives finish supporting a new narrative of barbarism reproducing patterns of domination and naturalizing the relation between Judaism and Western civilization. I intend to disrupt the uniformity of voices by retrieving the contemporary legacy of the negative counter-narrative, while simultaneously arguing that it is necessary to recover some decolonial features from the abandoned positive barbarism. The epilogue explores the possibility for the analectical emergence of an alternative Jewish thought in discussion with the same narrative that currently enjoys normativity.

CHAPTER 1

Jewish Thought, Postcolonialism, and Decoloniality: The Geo-Politics of a Barbaric Encounter

The publication of Edward Said's magisterial *Orientalism* (1978) heralded the beginning of Postcolonial studies in the Anglophone academy. This field's engagement with modern Jewish thought, however, was slow to develop and is still in its initial stages. On the one hand, the limited cross-fertilization between the two fields comes as a surprise. The historical experiences of Jews and other collectives affected by colonial discourses have exhibited remarkable overlap. For the last five hundred years, Western discourses have established a common set of patterns of domination applying analogous tropes and stereotypes to Jews as they have to Muslims, Africans, Amerindians, and others. The end result of Jewish racialization was nothing less than a tragedy. As a result of the Holocaust and political colonialism, between the 1940s and 1980s, over half of world Jewry suffered systematic displacement and/or annihilation. During this period, Jews from around the world wrote penetrating accounts confronting the existential conditions of racialization and faced imperial narratives in parallel to other collectives affected by colonial discourses. Their prescriptive systemic proposals, however, have rarely been studied under a postcolonial optic and correlated with other anti-imperial struggles.

On the other hand, the scarcity of postcolonial Jewish thought should come as no surprise whatsoever. In the twenty-first century, only thirty years after the emergence of Postcolonial studies, the normative racial portrayal of Jews has undergone a radical inversion. Long seen as a threat to the West, Jews have been seamlessly integrated into a new re-articulation of the Judeo-Christian civilization. They are largely perceived by the formerly colonized as loyal, if not zealous, Westerners. Jews are frequently associated with Global neo-colonial policies and accused of perpetrating the same racist atrocities they themselves suffered in the past. American and European xenophobic discourses, moreover, serve to deepen the cleavage among colonized communities. Local Jewries are extolled as model communities of successful integration and assimilation in order to undermine the legitimacy of Muslim, Latin American, and African immigrants or minorities. This discursive reclassification of Judaism, with antecedents throughout modernity but with a last re-articulation and normativization after the 1940s, militates against investigating the decolonial aspects of their conceptual programs or correlating their historical resistances to imperialism with contemporary anticolonial struggles.

The field of Anglophone Postcolonial studies largely reflects this underlying tension. On the one hand, the field recognizes the persecution of modern Jewry. From the outset, Postcolonial theorists have acknowledged discourses on Jewish racialization as intimately connected to colonial discourses. Said himself not only associated Orientalism and European anti-Semitism but also critiqued the re-racialization of non-European Jews, including Arabs and Latin Americans.[1] In the last fifteen years, and following this early openness, disciplines in the humanities and social sciences (e.g., literature, cultural theory, history, and sociology) have increasingly focused on the Jewish existential conditions affected by colonial discourses and the patterns of dominations that emerged from them.[2] On the other hand, established Postcolonial theory has more difficulty in recognizing discourses of Jewish resistance as decolonial proposals. Scholars who emphasize the study of resistances sometimes employ Jewish critical intellectuals as theoretical records. On most occasions, however, they identify the eurocentrism or the ignorance of racialization among these proposals and ultimately reduce them to Western internal critiques of modernity instead of decolonial proposals. While this helps avoid the universalization of the Jewish case, it also raises the following paradox: the prototypical Jew is acknowledged as a historical victim of colonial discourses, but his/her systematic attempts of decolonialization go largely unrecognized. There is, however, a rich tradition in Jewish decolonial thought that seeks to address colonial narratives and programmatically confront them.

Some of the most provocative Jewish scholars confronted this paradox and have offered correctives to central aspects of the field. These studies either tend to re-evaluate the area's sweeping generalizations or, conversely, its excessive narrowness. *Mizrahi* studies follow the former trajectory, which is perhaps best exemplified by the pioneering work of Ella Shohat. The field acknowledges that while some European Jews did benefit from colonialism, often times they did so at the expense of non-European Jews. The colonial divide, however, is veiled by a Western historiography that subsumes Jews within a single, undifferentiated European experience. This trend serves to correct the reproduction of this all-encompassing discourse and enables the decolonizing potential of Jews with origins in the Islamic world.[3] Intellectuals of Levantine and Maghrebian provenance, such as Ammiel Alcalay and Gil Anidjar, have formulated groundbreaking accounts of a Postcolonial turn that could eventually radicalize Jewish thought.[4]

A second trend is well represented by intellectual historians of modern Europe, and is especially in evidence in Susannah Heschel's incisive work. While this field acknowledges that Jews significantly reproduced colonial discourses such as Orientalism, it also recognizes the way in which certain Jewish circles creatively interacted, re-imagined, and sometimes even initiated the discourse, employing it to critique the West and not merely as a racial construction of an imagined East. The field thus criticizes narrow interpretations and insists that what Postcolonialism may disregard as a colonial discourse can in certain instances be better construed as a European Jewish subversion of colonial narratives.[5] Critical theorists, moreover, have complemented the work of intellectual historians. Daniel Boyarin and Sander Gilman, just to name two leading voices, consider post-Saidian developments of the field. They further explore not only the possibilities but also the limitations of Jewish discourses especially in central locations like the United States, Europe, and Israel. Such historical and cultural critiques challenge many presuppositions of both Jewish studies and Postcolonial theory.[6]

These two scholarly trajectories have fundamentally different objectives. Consider Shohat' and Heschel's contributions. The former represents a dialogical qualification of several major tenants present from the outset of the field while the latter is a thoroughgoing criticism of some of these central locations. Putting both projects in dialogue is productive as it enables an opportunity and the formulation of one question. In combination these critiques bear witness to the existence of innumerable Jewish experiences—sometimes in overt rivalry with one another—that can be re-analyzed and/or unveiled by one of the most provocative fields of current scholarship. The tension between the two proposals, moreover, invites us to consider whether current Postcolonial studies is the only framework within which to study the decolonial features of modern Jewish thought. The fact is that even Shohat, a pioneer in the study of Jewish Orientalization, is of the most lucid critics of contemporary developments of the field.[7] This book, deeply influenced by recent studies of Jewish resistance, intends to offer a complementary locus of analysis. There exist a set of decolonial frameworks that, for conceptual and historical reasons, offer another illuminating platform to investigate overlooked resistances to racial re-classifications.

This book seeks to complement the contributions made by Anglophone Postcolonialism. This branch of the field will be crucial for this project. For example, I will mobilize English-speaking sources to explain modern racialization in the next chapter and to illuminate the limits of Jewish decolonial discourses toward the end of the book. Nevertheless, to explore my core interest, the formulation of a Jewish decolonialism, the reader will find limited references to well-known categories employed by contemporary Postcolonialists including, for example, Homi Bhabha's hybridity and Gayatri Spivak's subalternity. In its place, and influenced by other Jewish resistances, she will find alternative categories such as *pensamiento fronterizo, filosofía de Liberación* and especially *barbare* (border thinking, philosophy of liberation, and barbarism) developed by intellectuals such as Walter Mignolo, Aime Cesaire, and Enrique Dussel.

My decision to draw from conceptual frameworks and terminology at the intersection of Hispanophone and Francophone decolonialisms is inspired by the very Jewish theorists I detail in this book.[8] During the period of my study (late 1940s to late 1980s) some Jewish decolonizers grounded their programs in a thoroughgoing engagement with Spanish- and French-speaking decolonialists. If Tunisian Jew Albert Memmi was influenced by the Afro-Caribbean thought of Cesaire, Lithuanian Jew Emmanuel Levinas changed his perspectives on decolonization after his engagement with the thought of Latin American Dussel. It is precisely the historical encounter between Spanish- and French-speaking Postcolonialism and Jewish thought that enables some Jews to offer a programmatic resistance against their re-classification as a Western population. And it is in this very tradition that *Decolonial Judaism* is located.

Barbaric Encounters

Most of the conceptually and theoretically innovative work I cite above is born of dialogue. Memmi encountered Cesaire in the 1950s, Levinas meet with Dussel in the 1970s. As a young scholar in the early 2000s, I was part of another encounter. I was visiting for the first time the University of California, Berkeley—not far from the location twenty-five years earlier Said had written *Orientalism*. During a conference, the leading Latin American decolonial theorist Walter Mignolo challenged me with an intriguing question. "What language does the *barbaric* Jew speak?" I paused before answering the question, reflecting about why a scholar deeply sensitive to the geo-politics of racialization was relating Jews with barbarism, commonly associated with seditious perversion and rejection of rationality. What at first seemed like a confusing question succeeded in penetrating the very essence of a lengthy and over-looked collaboration between Jewish theoreticians and Spanish/French Postcolonial theorists: the re-appropriation of barbarism.

Mignolo belongs to a provocative tradition of decolonizers who problematize the regnant dualisms of imperial discourses, and reinvest traditionally pejorative terms with positive valences. While Western thought defines the barbarian by her/his incapacity to achieve rationality, the barbarian herself/himself affirms that there is an alternative to the monopolistic rationality of civilization. This affirmation affords the barbarian an epistemological advantage defined as a double register. She/he is acquainted with regnant understandings of civilizational rationality given that it was imposed on the colonized as the only acceptable framework of thought. But her/his experience within her/his community enables the barbarian not only to understand the dark outcomes of the system's rationality but also to imagine alternatives that arise from discarded thinking. This critical engagement with her/his double register is what constitutes Mignolo's conception of "barbaric thinking." The South American semiologist, who in his work *Local Histories/Global Designs* (2000) identified a large number of Jews as barbarians, was simply challenging me to discern the barbaric alternatives within Judaism that meaningfully confront Western rationality.[9]

"Aramaic!" I belatedly concluded without knowing I was not the first to answer the question. For Aramaic was the language of rabbinical literature, which was predominantly written during moments in which Jews faced imperial subjugation, forced to accept the tragedy and humiliation of exile. Given these cultural and political circumstances, rabbinical texts exhibit a deep knowledge of host imperial nations and bear witness to the Jewish struggle to retain its local distinctiveness and particularity. They react to what they experienced as the repressive behavior of ruling societies by emphasizing ethical community living and theological metaphors to articulate an alternative power that surpasses that which oppresses them. Jews write with a double register when confronting their subjugation and re-claiming their community as an alternative source of rationality. Aramaic, I argued then, furnished a compelling paradigm for Jewish barbaric theorizing.[10]

A few hours later, however, another conversation partner would articulate an alternative to my formulation. "I start from [Biblical] Hebrew," Dussel, the prolific and influential founder of the school of Liberation Philosophy explained. While Athens and Jerusalem have served as symbols of two antithetical modalities (i.e., reason and faith) for over two millennia, Dussel expanded this notion beyond the symbolic to encompass language itself. For while these Greek imperial categories, developed and elaborated by conquistadors, preempted the possibility of "slave emancipation," Biblical Hebrew, a vocabulary developed by the vanquished, enabled "the possibility of the revolution of the poor." To philosophize from Latin America, a continent of "colonized, humiliated, and dependent" peoples, it was necessary to begin with the categories developed by the historically defeated who were symbolically represented by Jerusalem. Dussel, who uses conceptual categories of Biblical Hebrew in his seminal *Filosofía de la Liberación* and *Etica de la Liberación* (1973 and 1988), told me he learned the power of this language while working as a laborer among Christian Palestinians in Israel/Palestine in the 1960s. He further extended his decolonial orientation after encountering Levinas, a Talmudic interpreter who—as we shall see later—refers to the rabbinical Aramaic text as "Hebrew." Dussel added that the orientation of Levinas and the biblical Hebraic categories enabled him to start elaborating a "barbaric philosophy."[11]

While Medieval Aramaic guaranteed the continuity of Jewish barbarism, Biblical Hebrew represented the Jewish influence on other barbarians. What impressed me was not Mignolo' and Dussel's alternative formulations; what I found particularly striking was their underlying similarity. Both Spanish-speaking intellectuals—one a semiologist and one a philosopher, one living in the United States and the other in Latin America—considered the Jewish people among the colonized. Jews not only belonged to the underside of history, but the interrelation between them and other racialized collectives seemed to find a natural point of convergence in the decolonial re-appropriation of barbarism. Here were two leading Latin American decolonialists who not only found a place for Jews within their frameworks but also associated them with the barbaric resistance.

Spanish-speaking decolonizers, however, were neither the first to re-appropriate the concept of barbarism nor the only ones to relate it with

Judaism. Before the flowering of Postcolonial theory in the English-speaking world, the French-speaking decolonialism in the Maghreb and the Afro-Caribbean had made the connection. Both Albert Memmi and a Cesarian influenced Frantz Fanon considered Jewish life to be an experience deeply affected by discourses of colonization. Early in the post-war process of decolonization, Memmi became a leading voice in this emerging field, publishing the well-known *Portrait du colonisé, précédé du portrait du colonisateur* (1957). In addition, his abiding interest in Judaism led him to write his landmark *Portrait d'un Juif* (1961) and *Juifs et Arabes* (1974). His early auto-biographical novel, *La statue de sel* (1953), considered the affinity between Jewish identity and decolonial epistemologies. The novel's Jewish protagonist, Mordechai Benillouche, offers a particularly penetrating observation. He attempted to achieve a Western conversion but soon discovered he could only engage in mimicry because he was "a native in a colonial country, a Jew in an anti-Semite universe, and an African in a world dominated by Europe." He follows this reflection with an acknowledgment of a "self-evident truth." When he faces the Western and non-Western identities, those "ancient and monotonous melodies" of his Jewish African quarter and "all the great music of Europe," he cannot help himself in feeling "far more deeply" for his "African" Judaism. He has, then, no option but to declare himself an "incurable *barbarian*."[12] As an alternative to later deconstructivist Postcolonialism, an Arab Jew identified himself with a barbaric decolonial aesthetic, challenging preconceived cultural conceptions of colonial European universalism.

This identification of Jews with geo-political challenges was thus accomplished by Jews themselves as well as by some of the most iconic figures of the French-speaking decolonial struggle. In Algeria, for instance, the Martinican social psychologist Frantz Fanon discerns a natural affinity between Memmi's "barbarians" and Jewish people. In his celebrated *Peau noire, masques blancs* (1952), Fanon elucidates the history of suffering and resistance that connects Jews to other colonized peoples, including the inhabitants of the Antilles. In this seminal text Fanon recalls his teacher, Cesaire, in a very explicit formulation. Cesaire had written that the Holocaust was a European extension of racializing practices in the colonies, and he wrote a poem, "Barbare" (1943), in which he, like Memmi, manifested the utility of the re-appropriation of barbarism for the decolonial struggle.[13] Fanon, the student, assimilated both lessons. First he recalled his "professor, a native of the Antilles who one day reminded me of the fact that whenever you hear anyone abuse the Jews, pay attention, because he is talking about you." And later, mobilizing similar phraseology, he defined "the Jew" as a partner in a struggle and a barbaric "brother in misery".[14]

During the process of Jewish racial re-classification, with antecedents throughout modernity but with a final re-articulation and normativization after the late 1940s, Spanish- and French-speaking decolonialists identified Jews as a source of resistance against epistemological colonization (not free of paradoxes, as we shall see). English-speaking Postcolonialism has offered profound explorations of colonial discourses that include Jews. In general, however, it does not advance in the decolonial re-appropriation of barbarism, one of the key encounters between Jews and decolonizers. This is not to say that Jewish voices or themes are absent from the celebrated "trinity" of Anglophone Postcolonialism. Anticipating ill-intentioned critics, Said relates anti-Semitism with Orientalism and recognizes the re-racializations of non-European Jews. He also praises a "small handful" of Jews who opposed the treatment of Palestinians, including Noam Chomsky, Judah Magnes and Marc Ellis and a number of "cosmopolitans" Jews who disarticulated European identities, including Shohat, Adorno, and Sigmund Freud.[15] Spivak selectively applies Benjamin's philosophy of history and earned early renown for her translation of Jacques Derrida.[16] Bhabha prefaces a compendium on the relation between modernity and portrayals of Jews describing the Parsi, his own ethnicity, as the "Jews of the East."[17] Yet, as far as I know, they have not retrieved the long dialogical historical/conceptual construction of resistances that include Jews via the epistemological reclamation of barbarism.

Barbaric Racializations

Spanish and French decolonialisms emphasized the inclusion of Jews. In these discourses the subversive use of the term barbarism became a usual strategy. Memmi, an Arab Jew, referred to himself as an incurable barbarian, and Dussel, a Latin American, elaborated a specifically barbaric philosophy. Cesaire, an Afro-Caribbean, associated barbarism with the pathos of revolution, and Mignolo, an expert in Andean culture, elucidated the logic of barbaric theorizing. Communities that prior to the onset of modernity had limited contact were now developing relational projects to subvert one of the most powerful rhetorical tools for imperial designs (i.e., the narrative of barbarism). The reaction to barbarism, therefore, became a rallying point among colonized peoples. We will explore the origin, development, and role of the term barbarism in the following chapter. I will begin by reflecting on the importance of the term in the re-casting of Jews as another group among those affected by colonial discourses.

Throughout modernity Western discourses oscillated between two broad descriptions of the colonized. They were either blissfully welcoming or irrationally violent. While the former predominantly described them as easily assimilated or purely uncorrupted, the latter presupposed a natural inferiority and either limited or complete incorrigibility. Since colonial discourses were never a closed system, the two poles intersected in the middle of the oscillation.[18] But the description of the barbarian was largely placed at the latter end of the spectrum. This association was not necessarily new. Since the Western world conceived of itself as heir of the Greco-Roman, it reified its own history by re-appropriating central features of what understood as its classical model. For most of classical antiquity, the barbarian was defined in incommensurable opposition to civilization and associated with the rejection of natural law and the perpetration of political, sexual, and economical perversions. Prior to modernity barbarians were, in the preponderance of cases, either a latent or actual threat to the reified understanding of civilization that informs Western history. Classical Athens accused the Persian Empire of barbarism. Late antique Occidental Rome and medieval European Christianity did likewise with Germanic collectives and, later, Muslims. The strength of these alleged barbarians and the relative symmetry of powers they shared with their civilizational counterparts made them more than merely an imagined menace.

In the process of fashioning their own self-understanding, modern Western powers re-appropriated the ancient narrative. Let me here clarify that I do not analyze every modern use of the term. I will rather texture a long-standing narrative that obscured its genocidal practices with a discourse that balanced a civilizing mission (Christian, evolutionist, developmentist, nationalistic, or democratic) with an asymmetrical portrayal of the barbarian as a candidate for annihilation. During the Renaissance, Europeans identified the powerful Ottomans as barbarians and following the Reformation Catholics employed it to portray rival Protestants. The term would soon thereafter come to denote colonized populations including (but not limited to) those found in Atlantic locations such as Natives and Latin Americans, Africans and Blacks, Muslims and Arabs, and finally Israelites (not Israelis) and Jews. In all of these cases, the use of the term was deeply asymmetrical since the European resources significantly exceeded most of their rivals. While this inequality was interpreted as a result of divine or natural choice, it was actually a consequence of imperial designs that developed an original capitalist accumulation by conquest, expropriation, subjugation, and/or enslavement.[19] This marked asymmetry led to unfortunate consequences for the barbarians, ultimately rendering them candidates for annihilation.

This phenomenon was the product of a triumphalist philosophy of history that would eventually be described as a rhetoric of permanent progress. According to normative Western accounts, history is a teleological march toward the final liberation of humanity. European discourses, reifying their superiority, arrogate to themselves the moral exigency to redeem the non-Westerner. This teleology, however, veiled a theodicy. If history was to advance, those in actual or imagined opposition were to be eliminated as an obstacle to human fulfillment. The barbarians would not be annihilated as a cruel choice; they were collateral damage in the noble pursuit of universal liberation. This narrative of barbarism, then, helped Western discourses to police dissent and create a justification for profitable enterprises that enabled accumulation and further deepened global material asymmetries. It would simply take a mere pretense of opposition to civilization to qualify a population as barbaric. Its destiny was either annihilation or subjugation under the threat of annihilation.[20]

Genocide was one of many possible violent outcomes. Since the process itself depended on a civilizational rhetoric, large groups of barbarians were often forcibly brought into the system and sometimes converted or made candidates for assimilation. This emancipatory discourse denied the alterity of the other intending to exterminate any alternative to the unfolding Western system. Yet the forced inclusion of the barbarian rarely guaranteed the overcoming of her or his natural sub-humanity, inferiority, and/or limited corrigibility. The reproduction of the barbaric features naturalized a fixed hierarchical order that served to police further dissent. In early modernity, for example, this narrative was used to pacify and subjugate a variety of barbarized populations and make them a disposable commodity under Christian rule or ownership. Conversion, however, would not save them from permanent suspicion, continuous surveillance, and especially, socio-economic enslavement or servitude. Beginning in the sixteenth century, the simultaneous assertion that there was only one path toward salvation and the insistence on the natural limitations of barbarians opened the path for actual or threatened genocide.

In some later accounts, as another example, intellectuals created evolutionist accounts of history situating barbarians in a pre-civilized historical stage. In most evolutionist accounts the primitive was identified as able to transcend her/his corrupted status insofar as she/he followed the footsteps of an allegedly universal European path of development. But in some evolutionary schema even the barbarian was included as a nominal candidate for assimilation; some Humanists may be inclined to think that the construction of these accounts opened a space for secular barbaric redemption. Nevertheless, the definition of the barbarian during times of cultural or scientific racism did not undermine developments underway since early modernity. In general, the barbarian would still be suspected of having natural limitations and constituting a threat to civilization. While evolutionists forced barbarians to abandon their communal resources in order to become candidates of assimilation, the racial narrative they reproduced predominantly fixed their role, made them live under permanent suspicion of being a menace to civilization, and heavily regulated their access to civilization and even humanity. One of the central features of the narrative, the incorrigible opposition to the only path toward development, made barbarians candidates for annihilation and, on some occasions, victims of genocide.

Writing after the Holocaust it would hardly be a surprise to contend that Jews fulfilled a barbaric role in the Western imaginary. By exploring this reading I neither imply that the history of Jewish victimhood is the only possible account of Jewish lives nor that all possible Jewish histories culminate in a largely (though not uniquely) European event. I rather suggest that given the geo-political conditions created by imperial expansion, the Western narrative created networks of barbaric portrayals that included Jews from the fifteenth to the twentieth centuries. This history, which symbolically spans the Jewish expulsion from Spain and the Final Solution during the Holocaust (1492–1942), may not account for the totality of Jewish experiences. (No account does.) But it does describe the relational experiences of a large number of Jews in the Atlantic framework I presented in the introduction. In the last chapters, I will further explore this interrelated character and I will explain that the same construction did not end in the Holocaust. It was reproduced in Palestine and Israel in the second half of the twentieth century.[21]

The inclusion of Jews among barbarians represents a key difference between medieval and modern Western accounts. In medieval narratives, deeply influenced by an Augustinian persuasion, Jews were treated as witnesses to the truth of Christianity. The Hebrew Scriptures had already anticipated Jewish disbelief in the Messiah and, paradoxically or not, their refusal to accept God's incarnation was proof of the validity of Christian claims. While Jewish survival was a testament to divine mercy, their dispersion and misery was also understood as a form of punishment. Jews, in this context, could have been accused of deicide, stubbornness, legalism, and ritualism. Many times they were reduced to a state of misery, expelled from their homes, and murdered by self-righteous mobs. For most of the medieval era, Jews could transcend their allegedly corrupted nature. It would only take a conversion to Christianity to integrate them without the permanent suspicion that Jews confronted in the following centuries. Though an early attempt to eradicate difference, this homogenization did not presume any incorrigibility on the part of the barbarian; it was a pre-eminently local endeavor, in competition with other projects, which lacked the global implications it would later acquire.[22]

The situation, however, started to change in early modernity when colonialism guaranteed the primitive accumulation of capital justified by incipient stratifications that in time morphed into racial classifications. All historical turning points are post-facto constructions and unhelpful for understanding the *longue durée* of most phenomena, including the varieties of Jewish persecution. There is a strongly recursive nature to Jewish mistreatment throughout Western history, and isolated instances of suspicion of incorrigibility, as well as comprehensive redemption, exist throughout previous centuries.[23] Generally speaking, however, the advent of modernity represents a watershed—while Jews were largely corrigible prior to the modern era, normative European discourses continuously challenge this possibility in the modern age. A few years before the turn of the sixteenth century, the Jews who inhabited the recently colonized South of the peninsula were forced to leave the first modern empire unless they converted. Some left, settled in more welcoming Muslim environments and, deeply transformed native communities in the Maghreb and other regions under Islamic rule. However, the converts that either stayed or fled to the Americas suffered the consequences of the incipient constructions with which they would come to be associated. *Conversos/Marranos* (former Jews) along with ex-Muslim *Moriscos* were unable to shed their alleged immutable features according to *Pureza de Sangre* (Purity of Blood) legislation and the Inquisition.

The laws of Purity of Blood differentiated Christians with a Catholic heritage from those of Jewish and Muslim descent. They significantly circumscribed access to residency and/or social advancement for anyone who was not an "Old Christian." These social limitations, however, was just the ground for a persecution that shows the limitations of Jewish corrigibility. The Inquisition exercised social control by persecuting new converts who presumably practiced their Judaism surreptitiously. As the Inquisition had selectively conflated Jews and Muslims, this hybrid creation would then be associated with other racialized groups. In the Americas, Natives and Africans were accused of being barbarians who practiced Judaism. Furthermore, as we shall see in the next chapter, several people burned at the stake had been accused of being part of a Jewish-Indian-Black cabal to expel the Spaniards from the Americas. Jews, in this context, were incorrigible barbarians plotting with the colonized against the empire.[24]

The Western identification of Jews with incorrigible barbarism continued after Spanish imperial dominance and was translated into every dominant European language. From the seventeenth to the eighteenth centuries, Jews were accused of barbarism by some of the most important champions of liberal freedoms: the Deists in England and the Enlightenment revolutionaries in France. In the nineteenth century discourses about barbaric incorrigibility featured prominently in the debates on the Jewish Question in Germany. From the discussions regarding social emancipation to the rise of anti-Semitic parties, Jews as a race were seen as incapable of shedding their barbarism and persistently involved in conspiracies to overturn European dominance and destroy empires, nations and/or civilization itself.

While this accusation was not the only modern description of Jews, it became one of most powerful portrayals throughout modernity in general and in the years preceding the Second World War in particular. In the 1930s, the Third Reich rose to power in Germany, likely the Western nation where Jews had apparently been more successfully assimilated. Considering Jews to constitute an incorrigible threat, however, they exterminated one-third of global Jewry. Jews suffered the same objectification in other regions in the Maghreb during Vichy and German occupation and in Latin America during several waves of military dictatorships. So conceived, the Holocaust, today seen as the turning point of modern Jewish history, was not an extraordinary irrational action of fanatics on the continent. It was the consequence of the long-standing colonial rationality that employed the modern narrative of barbarism as one of its central tools. This narrative portrayed Jews, among others, as incorrigible threats to civilization and candidates for annihilation—in other words, Jews were barbarians.

Exploring Limitations

The study of Judaism through this framework helps to illuminate several aspects of modern Jewish experiences. In the first place, it demonstrates how colonial discourses have applied the category of barbarism to both Jews and other colonized peoples. Second, it traces the conceptual strategies employed by decolonizers to find a place for Jewish thought within their own attempts to subvert colonial discourses. Finally, and most significantly, it provides an alternative structure for understanding the historical and conceptual responses to racialization on the part of Jews. Properly conceived, this literature should be understood as decolonial proposals. This exploration highlights the need to complement the canon of Postcolonial studies and unveil the barbaric connection between Jews and decolonial projects. It is important, however, to acknowledge that this enterprise, as any intellectual exercise, faces obstacles. I would here like to name a number of possible objections to the framework I explore here. My intention is not necessarily to undermine these factors, but to show how *A Decolonial Judaism* will account for these challenges throughout the book.

The first challenge is the interrelation between existential conditions and epistemological creativity. If it is true that Jews have undergone a racial re-classification, can they still represent a challenge to the same structure that now welcomes them? In other words, can Jews still be a compelling source of decolonial proposals? Scholars in both Postcolonial and Jewish studies might be hesitant to answer in the affirmative. The Postcolonialist would likely protest the use of decolonial tools for a people whose history is normatively portrayed as an intra-European discussions and who are seen in the current context as white and Western in North America, civilized in Europe, and as colonialist settlers in Israel/Palestine. Some recent scholarship, as we have shown above, has provided revisionist understandings of Jewish history, utilizing Postcolonial tools to show how Jews were practicing a local decolonization in Europe. I follow their example in chapter three, in which I demonstrate a long-standing German and Polish Marxist Jews confrontation with the term barbarism. In the last part of the book, however, I question the potential of European Jews to affect the level of systemic subversion that peripheral Jews have been able to achieve.

This text, however, also explores the experiences of other Jews. Drawing from an aforementioned critique of the reduction of Jewish history to a monolithic narrative, I present two cases that intend to escape the normative understanding of Jewish history reduced to

Europe. In chapter five, I propose that the most radical Jewish counter-narratives of barbarism emerge from the experience and writings of a non-European Jew. I explain, the counter-narrative of barbarism that Memmi elaborates in dialogue with his Global South networks. In chapter four, I show that even a European Jew, Lithuanian Levinas, can radically formulate a decolonial stand through the influence of a Latin American counter-narrative, that of Argentinean Dussel. My readings in these two chapters intend to problematize the Eurocentric location of Judaism. In the last part of the book, however, I problematize their proposals by showing that this re-classification ultimately undermined some of the most lucid formulations, even among theorists of the Global South.

The same question, however, can be formulated by scholars working within a more orthodox paradigm of Jewish studies. The problem for some of these voices would also be the inclusion of Jews among a collective of colonized. But their resistance will accord with a reading of anti-Semitism in general and the Holocaust in particular as a history and an event of unparallel dimensions, incomparable with other experiences. According to this trend, Jewish history is a chronicle of victimization and survival that only finish in the liberation of the State of Israel. Judeophobia represented another source of medieval anti-Judaism and evolved into a racial anti-Semitism in the modern era. Seen through theological lenses, Babylonians, Crusaders, Germans, Soviets, and Iranians were an undifferentiated group who adhered to an ideal typical construction of the Biblical Jewish enemy: Amalek. The modern racialization of the colonized, according to such an understanding, followed a very different logic than recent stratification. The suffering of the Global South notwithstanding, the Jews, according to this reading, hew to a more complex path than the Natives or Africans, who "more recently" made their first appearance on the historical stage. The racial construction of Jewishness represents, problematically, a contextual reaction to a pre-determined hatred for a special (or chosen) people in history and is unlike any other modern racialization.

I will explain in the second chapter, however, that a reading of the concept of barbarism defies this explanation. While there is a theological dimension to the persecution of modern Jewry, the anti-Semitism that led to the Holocaust started incipiently with the sixteenth century's persecution of colonized *marranos* and became increasingly racial. Again, without disregarding the suffering of pre-modern Jews, they were not barbarians. In the medieval era, under an Augustinian theological persuasion, the prototypical Jew was capable of correction via conversion. Starting in the sixteenth century and until the Holocaust, the Western narrative portrayed Jews as incorrigible barbarians and confused them with other collectives affected by colonial discourses. World-system theorists and especially Spanish-speaking decolonialists insist on this point. In the sixteenth century, a new world came into existence, which required a stratification of peoples with natural limitations. Modern anti-Semitism is part of the relations of domination that racialized Natives, Africans, and Muslims and is not a roughly linear and contiguous history of Jewish victimization. While this book contests this reading of privileged Jewish suffering and eternal anti-Semitism, I explore my own complicity with a history of Jewish victimhood toward the end of the book, acknowledging the difficult persuasiveness of this rhetoric.

We have explored the first problem as to whether Jews can be decolonial voices responding to hypothetical objections coming from Jewish and Postcolonial studies. I would like now to discern a second objection arising from some of the forerunners of the field. Some leading Jewish cultural theorists engage in post-Saidian Postcolonial studies in order to subvert the binary opposition of East versus West through studies of what Bhabha calls "hybridity."[25] One of the most lucid examples is the abovementioned Gilman. He argues that in contemporary discourses infused by multiculturalism, the prototypical Jew is rarely seen in the desperate situation *in-between* locations of knowledge. She or he is portrayed either as the prototypical, defenseless Oriental victim of oppression or as the best and most original embodiment of Western triumphant cosmopolitanism. In this way, Jews are viewed with an eternal timelessness, unaffected by either the space they inhabit or the currents of thought that challenge the Western discourse that also racialized them. Gilman, then, explores of the possibility of analyzing Jewish hybridity.[26] In this book, I follow Gilman's superb diagnosis but find an alternative path to a solution.

I will not deny that the application of the hybrid may not fully adapt to a variety of Jewish cases. While Bhabha's concept of hybridity does attempt to overcome a regnant racialist dualism, critics argue that the concept is vulnerable to several major limitations. First of all, given its difficulties acknowledging the asymmetry in the relationships of power between colonizer/colonized, one could easily question whether or not the celebration of the third space does not ultimately naturalize the unequal relationship between the two sides of the prototypical divide. Second, since the attempt is to challenge and efface this divide, it can finish disarticulating most liberationist discourses that attempt to confront the hegemonic discourse with a political alternative. Finally, the term is furthermore empirically limiting, as there exists a long-standing Jewish textual and historical tradition that does not accord with such an understanding of hybridity. I propose to replace the English-speaking term hybridity in favor of the term border thinking, as coined and used assiduously by the Spanish-speaking decolonial school. This concept not only overcomes the problems of hybridity but also illuminates the Jewish contribution among other colonized peoples.

The Spanish-speaking school of modernity/coloniality has a different starting point than post-Saidian Postcolonial theory. English-speaking discourses generally date the dawn of modernity to the eighteenth century, using one of the major revolutions (industrial in England and political in France and America) or the Napoleonic invasion of Egypt as the demarcating watershed event. Spanish-speaking theorists typically locate it at the turn of the sixteenth century, with the inauguration of Iberian, and later pan-European imperialism in the Americas. This school of thought designates imperial developments as initiating the first modernity, and major revolutionary upheavals as precipitating the second one. The first modernity starts with a process of capitalist primitive accumulation. It is the result of the expulsion of Muslims and Jews from the continent, the subjugation of the Native populations in the Americas, and the enslavement of Africans that Europe was able to find the resources that later would become critical to launching the Industrial Revolution and the second modernity. In other words, what became a colonial racialization of people funded the possibility of an economic revolution that gave a new bourgeois class the chance to demand individual freedoms. It is thus at the expense of exploitation, expropiation, and enslavement of, among others, barbarians, that Western liberties were achieved. It is not a coincidence, therefore, that in the sixteenth century groups that started to be considered barbarians and Jews, among others, became candidates for annihilation. It is even less of a contradiction, consequently, that champions of (European) liberties and rationalities, from the English Deists to the French *philosophes*, justified the narrative of barbarism.[27]

This new modern civilization created borders to circumscribe its epistemological and geographic boundaries. These borders were created not only in the formal colonies but also around the newly colonized areas post-(*Re*)*conquista*. An initial border is easily identifiable in the expulsion of Muslims and Jews from the Iberian Peninsula. The internal border, however, required a more challenging construction.

Jews were offered the possibility to stay in the kingdom provided that they converted. Nevertheless, as noted above, the Jewish converts or *marranos* were never accepted by the new society and found themselves under permanent persecution. The Inquisition and the Purity of Blood laws placed the *marrano* on the "borderland." The *marrano* lived under permanent fear in a space in which the borders did not apply. This historical account allows anti-Semitism to be inserted in the modern history of colonialism. The Jew was no longer socially defined by a theological perspective, whose redemption was contingent on conversion; the Jew was becoming naturally unable to overcome her barbarism. A destiny shared by other barbarians.[28]

The persecuted *marrano* residing on the borderland, Mignolo argues, is not a hybrid, the prototypical other of Postcolonial theory. The hybrid is a result of a permanently relativistic space of thinking beyond identity. The border thinker's identity has been externally constructed and imposed, leaving her to live in a protracted state of fear and insecurity. The *marrano* does not prevail over the dualism like a hybrid but reacts creatively to this imperially-imposed identity. The border thinker strips the power of identity creation from colonial knowledge. She/he builds an alternative worldview not by effacing these two intellectual systems, as in Bhabha's conception, but by acknowledging the difference and supporting the colonized side.[29]

The model of the *marrano* border thinker represents a persuasive alternative to the intercultural hybrid. The historical re-affirmation of this identity leads to a powerful process. The Inquisition, in order to reinforce its social control, imagined a conspiracy in which *conversos* surreptitiously adhered to Judaism. The reaction to the persecution that followed represents a borderland action undertaken by New Christians who understood that their new religious affiliation was inherently suspect (and their acceptance by society precarious at best and impossible at worst). They started to behave in precisely the manner in which the empire had predicted as a creative re-affirmation of their identity in times of persecution. This creative re-affirmation of Judaism in the borderland went well beyond the recently colonized south of the peninsula. In the formal colonial world, both in the Americas and later in Africa, Natives were accused of being Jewish. Reading inquisitorial documents against the grain proves that many positively re-affirmed their Jewish identity. As border thinkers they assumed an identity that may not have had a prior historical existence in order to counter imperial designs. Old Christians responded to this reaction by developing conspiracy theories about Jews leading rebellions in concert with Natives and Africans.[30]

In this instance there is a clear distinction between the hybrid and the border thinker. The former attempts to undermine colonial dualisms by dissolving identities; the latter creatively develops identities, even if those identities turn upside down the reified imperial constructions. The strategy that the border thinker employs might be glossed as "epistemic disobedience." In other words, the borderland allows the border thinker to create an-other reading of the situation in order to confront the empire and subvert fundamental tenets of its self-understanding.

This is not to suggest that this school of modernity/coloniality features Jews as central to its analyses. While the school insists that a stratification of non-Europeans begins in the sixteenth century, it especially highlights the generation of alternative epistemologies that emerged from the explicitly external borderlands. Some even insist in pointing out diverse, yet collaborative, analytical trajectories of racialization among Africans, Jews, Arabs, and Natives.[31] Even if I am heterodox by emphasizing commonalities over differences, I consider it imperative to analyze the interrelations among colonial experiences. I argue that distinctions among racializations should be noticed, but reducing the school's analysis of Judaism only to this point would be a superficial reading of its contribution. This is not only because images of barbaric Jews were well represented in Europe, the Americas, the Islamic world, Africa, and even the Far East. But it also due to the same reasons that Mignolo ends his analysis of the *marrano* connecting this "borderland" with Native thinking. He explains that in the twentieth century, the borderland that challenged the empire has come to constitute a locus of "desired epistemological privilege." The model he uses to describe this space is furnished by Guatemalan native Rigoberta Menchu, whom he credits as a "true" "Latin American border thinking."[32]

What then is the relation that the school identifies between Jewish and other borderlands? At this point Mignolo insists on retrieving Cesaire's conception of the Holocaust as the "crown" of colonialism. He adds that this iconic genocide "cannot be just explained by European history."[33] The process of barbarization that reaches its logical conclusion in African, Native, and Jewish annihilation is part of a same process that started in the sixteenth century and culminated in the twentieth. These are "outstanding cases of the 'naturalization' of bare/dispensable lives in a society in which reducing costs and increasing production and accumulation of wealth go hand in hand with politically saving communities from the 'danger' menacing."[34]

For Mignolo, the genocides of the Natives, Jews, and Africans, while analytically distinctive, are "logically linked to the colonial matrix of power."[35] These colonial discourses go well beyond the actual colonial experiencies. Drawing from Peruvian sociologist Anibal Quijano, Mignolo distinguishes between colonialism and coloniality. The former refers to the traditional political, social, and economical domination of one poltical entity over another, and the latter to the long-standing patterns of domination that emerged as a result of the stratifications employed during colonialism.[36] There is no doubt that Mignolo has a explicit preference for possibilities emanating from Native discourses as other members of the school do the same with the Africana diaspora. The inclusion of factors that exceed the temporal and spatial dynamics of political colonialism enables the school to recognize a multiplicity of Jewish experiences as interrelated and meaningful sources by which to understand the persistence of coloniality.

My intention here is to emphasize the inclusion of Jews in the network of populations affected by coloniality. It is not surprising that Jewish victims of the process appear once and again as dialogue partners of their alternative theorizing. Dussel, a key voice for the school, had already expressed how an encounter with Levinas "produced in my spirit a subversive overthrowing of all what I had learned until then."[37] He not only writes his iconic work, *A Philosophy of Liberation*, in conversation with Levinas's philosophy but he even goes further by co-authoring a book entitled *Emmanuel Levinas and Latin American Liberation*.[38]

Mignolo, for his part, complements Dussel. He explains that the "Jewish" (he explicitly remarks this identity) Frankfurt School helped to show "the limits of civilization and the rise of the barbarian" defining the later as, among others, "'Jewish,' 'Amerindian' and 'African.'" Furthermore, he explicitly defines the school as a type of "barbarian theorizing" and argues that the second generation of the institute, led by non-Jew Jürgen Habermas, abandoned the existential condition that made the Frankfurt School such an intellectual watershed.[39]

Both Dussel and Mignolo identify the epistemological potentialities of European Jewish thought. And in their path toward the construction of a decolonial thinking, they also acknowledge their geopolitical limitations, something European Jews share not only with other European thinkers but also with some Latin American proposals that preceded the school of modernity/coloniality.[40] I will soon follow this trajectory. I will not only re-read European Jewish intellectuals under the borderland lenses re-evaluating their epistemological potentialities and geo-political limitations. But also, influenced by current studies of

Jewish resistance, I explore how this school can illuminate the writings of non-European Jewish discourses as well.

In this way, and as a way of summary, the concept of the border thinker addresses the three significant problems associated with the concept of hybridity. In the first place, it fully acknowledges the asymmetry of power between both parties of the struggle. Second the acknowledgment of this "colonial difference" does not leave the border thinker caught desperately *in-between*. She has the potential to defy the construction imposed on her, at times even assuming and transforming the accusation itself. And finally, it illuminates the role of Jews as historically constituted part of this conceptual collective affected by colonial discourses and the patterns established by coloniality.

A Study on Conceptual Counter-Narratives

I propose to read Jewish reactions to the concept of barbarism through the framework of border epistemology (i.e., through the logic of decolonial epistemic disobedience). The concept of the border thinker enable us to acknowledge the asymmetry, to take a clear stand in the re-affirmation of identity, and finally to incorporate Jews as actors of this decolonial process. What remains to be analyzed, however, is what epistemic disobedience would look like in contemporary contexts. How might Jews confront imperial designs while simultaneously addressing local struggle? Just as the conception of border thinking will be the locus of enunciation for this subversion, so also the counter-narrative will be the practical strategy to confront imperial designs.

A counter-narrative, in the Jewish context, is a reversal of hegemonic conceptual narratives. It is an attempt to undermine the most powerful rhetorical resources of dominant thinking. Jews appropriate the concept of the enemy, but instead of reproducing its designs, turn the concept against itself. Just as some *marranos* and Natives self-identified as Jews when facing the Inquisition, some Jews consider themselves barbarians in the Postcolonial/post-Holocaust stage. The intellectual unfolding of a counter-narrative, therefore, is not the hybrid creation of an inter-space or a utopian unfolding a new reading of the world from parochial resources. The counter-narrative is the creative subversion of an oppressive construction. Counter-narratives are varied and diverse: some are formed underground while others take pride of place in the public sphere. Some are presented as consciously Jewish proposals while others do not explicitly refer to this ethnic/religious category. What makes them part of the same project is the fact that they are conceptual responses to an existential condition. In the context of post-Holocaust theory, the border counter-narrative is an alleged Jewish reaction to colonial anti-Semitism.[41]

This existential counter-narrative overcomes the disciplinary differences between history and philosophy. It is a conceptual confrontation that is written from an analysis of social conditions. As a result it is neither submerged in nor aloof from philosophical discussion, nor is it embroiled in a debate about the role of revisionist counter-histories. It overcomes both of these disciplinary limitations. While philosophical and historical methods can shed some light to the problem, I propose to follow an alternative intellectual trajectory. I will appeal to the interdisciplinary space afforded by a sociology of Jewish knowledge to study the social conditions that allowed for the emergence of a particular conceptual narrative. I am interested in how these conditions—especially the discourses that created a reality—allow this mode of thinking to arise. This study, therefore, is a work in the sociology of knowledge that analyzes the counter-narrative of barbarism that Jewish global thinkers elaborated in conversation with other barbarians.[42]

CHAPTER 2

The Narrative of Barbarism: Western Designs for a Globalized North

In the last quarter of the twentieth century South African author J. M. Coetzee wrote *Waiting for the Barbarians*. This novel, arguably the best-known book by the winner of the 2003 Nobel Prize in Literature, is an illuminating introduction to one of the most popular versions of the Western narrative of barbarism. The story takes place in a frontier city under the jurisdiction of a political entity known as "The Empire." The civilized inhabitants seem to have a comfortable life. Indeed, their only source of discomfort is a loose collective of nomads who live outside the immediate borders of civilization and who are designated as "the barbarians." Despite their relative inoffensive portrayal, a militaristic faction within the Empire begins fomenting hostility, proceeding to inform the population that the barbarians are preparing to invade and destroy civilization. Depicting the barbarians as anarchically seditious, sexually perverse, and brutishly uncivilized, the Empire engages in a preemptive strike, invading barbaric territory, and kidnapping, imprisoning, torturing, and even killing barbarians in a public spectacle.

The civilized crowd, awash in fears of counterstrikes and conspiratorial plots, soon fall prey to stereotyped and prejudicial understandings of the Natives and begin to sublimate their anxiety by fully assimilating the narrative of barbarism. They may be aware this justifies the civilizational mission at the border, but they are surely ignorant that it naturalizes a state of war that could ultimately challenge their own community. The inhabitants then re-affirm their sense of superiority and pride in their civilization at the expense of the barbarians. But a dissident voice, an empathetic "Magistrate," speaks his truth to power, protests the bellicose action of the Empire, and begins questioning its very legitimacy. Despite the fact that his actions reproduce central features of the narrative, this conscientious objector rapidly becomes a political target. He is denounced as seditious, imprisoned, tortured, and silenced; even worse for his credibility as an objector, he is portrayed as having barbaric loyalties. The invasion, predictably, never takes place. The barbarian, the reified imagining of the Empire, was never at the gates of civilization; the frontier city was never in actual danger. The end of the novel leaves the reader questioning what precisely underlies the civilization/barbarism dichotomy.[1]

Waiting for the Barbarians, written by a critical descendent of Afrikaners during the Apartheid era, provides a useful entrée into central features of one of the popular versions of the narrative of barbarism during the nineteenth and twentieth centuries. Building upon four or five hundred years of colonial discourses, this adaptation reproduces the longstanding racial stratifications we defined as central to coloniality. The narrative serves to unify a Western population who ennobles itself by constructing an enemy which it simultaneously if paradoxically fears and renders inferior to itself. In this narrative the barbarians are a reified collective exhibiting characteristics that incarnate the antithesis of civilization's desired self-image. They are accused of sexual, political, economic, and religious perversion. While civilization conceives of itself as the bearer of universal culture, the barbarian is understood as hostile to this cultural project, consistently breaching natural law, and seeking to regress history. Civilization receives a mission from God or history to engage in the most noble of enterprises and it is conferred the intellectual skills to realize these cultural goals. The barbarians not only are unable to match the civilized skills but also intend to destroy the creative capacity of the Empire. This narrative typically yields one of the following outcomes: the barbarians accept the natural right and self-evident superiority of civilization or face the threat of annihilation. In either eventuality, civilization invariably dominates the barbarians by a brute force ideologically supported by natural (divine, historical or scientific) self-righteous design.

One of the central characteristics of the narrative is the different degree of participation of each binary side. The barbarians usually suffer the consequences of the narrative, and their reactions are always subject of interpretation by civilization. But the design, execution, and many times even the humanist resistance to (or as we shall see modern collaboration with) the narrative are, a priori and just for now, dictated entirely by the enunciators. An account of this narrative, therefore, should start as a conceptual-historical account of unilateralism. In the next three chapters I will suggest, however, that the barbaric resistances emerge in parallel to the structures of domination. I will explore Jewish reactions against this narrative that racialized them among other populations affected by colonial discourses. Employing Benjamin's suggestion to "read against the grain," I will seek to bolster his assertion that all "documents of civilization" are actually "documents of barbarism."[2] In this chapter, however, I start by problematizing the hegemonic narrative that locates barbarism on/among the reified images of non-Westerners.

Contemporary readers influenced by genealogical thought, however, may question my reading as anachronistic. After all, I appear to be constructing a highly selective 2,500-year narrative informed by contemporary theoretical paradigms. For the last decades, a variety of scholarly trends have wisely cautioned writers against attempts to read the reservoirs of Greco-Roman thought as if they were naturalized Western history. My historical inquiry of the concept of barbarism intends to complement these trends. By explaining the distinct uses of the term barbarism throughout the reified history of the West, I will demonstrate that there is no logical sequential connection between Greece, Rome, and the contemporary West. This account of the different types of narratives, by contrast, seeks to illuminate how the West not only appropriated a Greco-Roman trope in the service of a global colonial project but also obscured the intellectual and material resources contributed by the alleged barbarians.[3]

For this reason my exploration has a two-fold objective. On the one hand, I reveal the modern re-appropriation of the narrative of barbarism, focusing in particular on how classical understandings have been re-articulated since the sixteenth century and ultimately led to the racialization of Jews and their insertion within a network of racial colonization. This does not naturalize Greco-Roman thought as Western history, but traces the resources employed by a modern project that thought of itself as organically descended from Greece and Rome. Taking into account genealogical cautions, I simultaneously explore a contextual discontinuity over time. This reading enables me to conclude that notwithstanding the effort made by modern intellectuals to connect their project to ancient models reified as Western, the deployment of the term barbarism had distinct objectives and generated very different political outcomes.

In order to reify its own history modern European powers re-appropriated some features of the Greco-Roman and medieval Christian models, but construed the larger narrative in different terms. With respect to the former it shares an operative suspicion of the natural limitations (sub-humanity, inferiority, and/or incorrigibility) of the barbarians, and vis-à-vis the latter it posits a unique and singular path toward redemption/liberation. Yet, it also innovated considerably. Prior to the modern era the alleged civilizations were predominantly provincial forces challenged by the strength of the alleged barbarians who were at times technologically, economically, or politically more powerful than the enunciators of the narrative. In the sixteenth century, however, modern European powers began a violent process of material accumulation that required the stratification of peoples in order to justify subjugation, expropriation, colonization, and/or enslavement. Modern Western discourses, however, obscured the ideological and material resources employed to achieve this development. European superiority was reified as a divine/natural gift and not as a product of the violent expropriation of barbarian resources. This process made the West the first truly global power, incorporating the provincial resources of its reified history into a universal framework.

It is during this modern/colonial period that the empire could ultimately veil its colonial project through recourse to a humanist rhetoric. On the one hand, the empire could offer a framework of development to disarm the barbarians of their communal resources and, on the other hand, challenge their access to civilization by insisting on their natural sub-humanity, inferiority and/or incorrigibility. This rendered the barbarians both epistemologically disarmed and racially fixed. As a result, the modern/colonial usage of the term could bear collaborative freight. One version of the narrative, for example, could deem the barbarians incorrigible. The colonizers would endow themselves with the right to exploit barbaric resources and exterminate any opposition in order to maintain the forward march of history. Another collaborative version of the narrative could insist on the barbarians' natural inferiority or limited corrigibility. The colonizer would profit from this barbaric fragility by forcing the abandonment of community resources while simultaneously regulating access to a civilized (or even human) status by insisting on barbaric limitations. Racialized by both versions, Jews become part of the over one hundred million people coerced and annihilated by discourses that supported collaborative versions of the narrative of barbarism.

Greco-Roman Ethno-Politics

When the term *barbaros/barbaroi* first appeared in Greek written records, it lacked two central connotations that modern discourses generally take for granted. First, the term is not originally Greek, but it is derived from the Babylonian *barbaru,* a word that described foreignness. Homer, recounting the Trojan wars in the eighth century BCE, used a Greek adaptation of the term to denote peoples who do not speak Greek. He referred to them as *barbarophoni* because the sound of their language, to Greek ears, was unintelligible (and sounded like an inarticulate "bar barb bar").[4] Second, the term did not presume a superiority of Greeks over barbarians. In the fifth century BCE Herodotus, the Greek father of history and anthropology, does not necessarily relate barbaric foreignness with inferiority. He uses the term indiscriminately to critique the Scythians tribes for cruelty and sexual depravity and the mythical Anthropophagi for their cannibalism, while also using it to declare his admiration for the architecture, theology, and political organization of the Egyptians and Ethiopians.[5]

A new socio-political situation, however, altered the meaning of the term toward the end of the fifth century BCE. During this period the Mediterranean witnessed the lengthy armed conflict known as the Greco-Persian Wars. Witnessing the escalating tension in their midst, Athenian discourses began popularizing the concept as an ethno-political tool. During this period the term became more capacious and was variously employed to denote a negative reification of political organizations, sexual behaviors, and cultural customs associated with foreigners and foreignness. Two iconic tragedians, Aeschylus and Euripides, serve as excellent social informants of this stage of the narrative. Aeschylus developed a clear dualism that would be re-appropriated during the European Renaissance and modern colonial Orientalism. The Greek world was depicted in terms of its dignity, simplicity, democracy, courage, collective generosity and thoroughgoing desire for peace. The Persian world, alternatively, was seen in terms of its avarice, despotism, cowardice, individual egotism, and propensity toward violence.[6] Euripides, who includes barbaric figures in many of his numerous plays, became a spokesman of Greek superiority. He compared the barbarians with animals and suggested that barbarism was contracted at birth. Given the supremacy of one culture over another, he asserted that "[t]he Greek should command barbarians" because the "barbarians are all slaves."[7]

Aristotle, whose construction of barbarism would be extensively re-appropriated in modern political philosophy, further explicated this difference. He unfolded a theory of natural slavery to justify the perception of Persian inferiority. According to Aristotle, barbarians lacked the ability to achieve the levels of rationality available to civilized pan-Hellenic citizens. The dichotomy between Persian and Greek customs illustrates the difference. The barbarian lived subjugated by despotism and the practice of brutish economic and religious customs. The Greek was a free man, living democratically and with dignity. The possession of rationality, shown not only in political but also in religious and sexual behavior, marked the natural right of dominion of the Greek over inferior human beings. The barbarian could use her physical strength to serve a superior society, while the Greek could use his intellectual capacities to aide in the development of culture. This natural right of dominion led Aristotle to describe the barbarians as "a community of natural slaves." In a formulation that will serve as the point of departure for modern narratives of barbarism, Artistotle justified his definition recalling Euripides: "Wherefore the poets say, it is meet that Hellenes should rule over barbarians."[8]

This new conceptual narrative was part of a contextual project. The dualism that was created between barbarism and civilization (tyranny against democracy, dignified customs against sexual perversity) permitted the generation of an anti-Persian ethno-political narrative. The outcome of this new narrative would be threefold. First, it was an exercise in self-definition to structure a community against an actual, external threat. The Greek cities, with a history of intercity fratricide, needed a unifying narrative to counter the Persian challenge. Second, it attempted to universalize a provincial model as representative of the projected community. Athens was able to conflate its particular, self-referential values (democracy, egalitarianism, intellectual labor, etc.) and linguistic definitions (including barbarism) with those of the newly emerging pan-Hellenic agglomeration of city-states. Third and last, it legitimized the superiority of this new imagined community. The war against the Persians, who had defeated the Greeks in several battles, was to be justified by the natural rule of dignified, free, (pan-)Hellenic men over the corrupt barbarians, understood as natural slaves. These outcomes express the core elements of the ethno-political reading that would allow them to be re-enacted throughout history.[9]

With its absorption/conquest of vast Hellenic territories, the Roman Empire thought itself as the heir to the ethno-political legacy of pan-Hellenic barbarism. It is not until modernity, however, that this legacy was fully discursively monopolized as exclusively Western Roman. Since its expansion, following the Punic wars in the third century BCE, the Greek term was freely applied to military and spiritual rivals including future Westerners (Celts, Visigoths, Germans, and Christians) and those who would remain barbarians (including Berber populations in North Africa). Cicero, the legal-political theorist of the first century BCE, explicitly reproduced the ethno-political use. He explained that the difference between civilization and barbarism should not be reduced to its original linguistic meaning. It is an irreducible dichotomy between cultures defining the opposite ends of a spectrum. Although the potential exists for the barbarian to adopt Roman law and rule, the two communities must remain historically irreconcilable.[10] The historian Livy, at the turn of the Christian era, further explained the permanence and irreducibility of the struggle. The Greeks, according to Livy, began a continuous stream of civilization that came to fruition in Rome. The civilized "wage and will wage eternal war" against "the barbarians . . . for they are the enemies perpetually by nature and not for reasons that change from day to day."[11] Barbarism thus slowly evolved into a more robust and complex Greco-Roman narrative.

In the first century of the Common Era, Christianity presented a challenge to this reading. Contrary to a progressive dialectical reading of history, Christianity was neither the first nor the last to question the narrative. Tacitus, to take one possible example, had already broached the possibility of barbaric virtue. The rise of Christianity presented one of the historical challenges to the ethno-political reading. The *ecclesia*'s universalist message severed traditional boundaries delimiting and circumscribing human action according to polis, nation, class, or tribe. In Pauline theology it was clear that binary fixed conceptions including free/slave, Greek/Jew, and even Roman/Barbarian were to be eliminated in the community of Christ. It is possible to trace a good number of Christian preachers in the third and fourth centuries supporting the inclusion of the barbarian in the *oecumene*. Scholars in both the East and the West of the empire (e.g., Bardesanes of Edessa and Paulinus of Nola) emphatically preached the dissolution of the ethno-political use of the term. Christianity, however, was not conquering Rome; Rome was subsuming Christianity in the state. Although a dissident current was gaining traction, the ethno-political narrative on barbarism remained hegemonic.[12]

During the fifth century CE, as fear of Rome's dissolution increased, even leading Christian figures reproduced the ethno-political reading. The bishops of Hippo and Milan, Augustine and Ambrose, as well as the

Christian poet Prudentius reproduced the binary legacy they inherited from the Greco-Roman world and not the unified vision of Christianity. Although Augustine, iconic figure of later medieval thought, understood the Fall of Rome as part of a providential plan, he often accused the invaders of cruel barbarism. He illustrated the irreducibility of the struggle by showing surprise and confusion when the barbarians, innately corrupt, engaged in acts of civility and mercy.[13] Ambrose was even more vehement; he admitted that Christianity was limited since not even faith could bridge the two irreconcilable entities. Prudentius, creating a new hybrid between Greco-Roman and Christian teachings, wrote: "As different is the Roman from the barbarian as man is different from the animal or the speaking person from the mute, and as they who follow the teachings of God differ from those who follow senseless cults and superstitions." [14] In times of exception, real or imagined, the narrative of barbarism continued to fulfill its ethno-political role. In Rome, as it was in Greece, the narrative represented the fruits of an exercise in self-definition on the part of a culture in contention with another. The result of the ethno-political narrative was to create a Manichean world in which the alleged asymmetry between two societies gave one the natural right to dominate the other.

From Medieval to Renascence Theo-Politics

The fall of Rome and the progressive conversion of barbarians led to a gradual decline of the ethno-political narrative. Between the fourth and twelfth centuries the narrative did not disappear but changed within the legacy of Western Christianity. It lost its ethno-political character and became a theo-political narrative. The ethno-political narrative would be eventually re-appropriated during the Renaissance. During the fifteenth century, the nascent Europe will proclaim itself as the only inheritor of the Greco-Roman world simultaneously negating Islamic contribution and barbarizing the Muslim Ottomans.

In the theo-political narrative of barbarism Romans and barbarians had increasingly merged and the conversion of the latter showed the possibility of leaving behind the accusation of barbarism. It is not a surprise, therefore, that those who were once described as lacking political or moral competence were encouraged to take public offices in the attempt of recovering Roman glory. Naturally, this possibility of leaving behind barbarism was conditional to the conversion to Western Christianity.[15] If we analyze history from the perspective of the reified history of the West, the new narrative did overcome the exclusivity of the ethno-political barbarism. At the same time, however, it reinforced the existence of only one path to salvation and the Christian moral imperative to bring others to this path. In modernity, when Western Christianity would shed its provincialism and became a global power, this would become a staple of the colonial narrative of barbarism.

During the medieval era, the pejorative concept of the term barbarian did not disappear, but rather merged with the Pagan and came to denote collectives who rejected the faith but generally had a potential to achieve correction and even redemption. The medieval permutation of the narrative was employed to classify a more variegated group of people. These included former barbarians-turned-heretics (i.e., the Arians) and the historical pre-Christian era of newly Christianized populations (i.e., the Franks). One of the exceptions was the accusation of the barbarism of monsters, especially at sea, that no surprisingly will be later related with newly colonized people. The term, however, was fundamentally used in intra-Christian accusations against those who presented alternative forms of normative Western Christianity. In the eighth century, for example, the Lombards attacked Rome. The pope, Hadrian I, called Charlemagne to his defense and blessed the work of the Franks, once called barbarians, by qualifying the attackers as "enemies of God" or, more explicitly, "barbarians."[16]

Although similar in many respects, the theo- and ethno-political narratives differ regarding the barbarians' potential for correction and ultimate redemption. Both ennoble a society and offer it a natural/divine/historical rule over the alleged barbarians. Furthermore, both justified local imperial enterprises. It is surprising, however, that neither Muslims nor Jews were typically seen as barbarians. The concept was already theo-political and the rivalry with both groups was extended since the first and seventh century. Large quantities of Jews lived in the midst of Western Christian societies until their expulsion from a number of territories at the dawn of early modernity, but the hegemonic Augustinian doctrines persisted. As we explored in the previous chapter, Augustine believed that Jews must remain Jews to witness the truth of Christianity and be converted at the eleventh hour of the elaborate eschatological drama. It is certainly true that some Jews were forcibly converted and, with the exception of certain cases in the premodern era, were generally integrated into Christian society. While they were not called barbarians, the eschatological reading of Judaism coupled forced conversions became indicative of the two most important features that the narrative reproduced: potential corrigibility and one distinct path to redemption. Nonetheless, given that Jews fulfilled a theoretically special and unique role in Christian narratives of the end times, they did not precisely fit the bill. The accusation of barbarism, therefore, was rarely applied to Jews.[17]

Although they had posed a real threat to Western Christian forces since the seventh century, Muslims were not generally seen as barbarians either. While it is possible to find sporadic accusations during the Crusades, this situation would change starting in Late Middle Ages, but the re-appropriation of the ethno-political reading of barbarism would not re-emerge until the Fall of Constantinople (1453). The Maghreb, inhabited by *Berber* Muslim populations, was re-named *Barbary* retrieving a Roman description further employed by Muslims, and the Tartars, a population in the Black Sea undergoing conversion to Islam, would be identified as barbarians. These narratives, however, did not have the dichotomic weight until the Renaissance.[18]

Before the middle of the fifteenth century Muslims had been an actual threat to the scattered Western Christian powers, occupying large regions in the Mediterranean (i.e., the Southern Iberian Peninsula and North Africa). The "Saracens," as Muslims were generally designated, were considered religious infidels, and accusations of barbarism were based on theology and not ethno-political considerations. In his seminal *Orientalism*, Said considered Dante Alighieri as an excellent social informant of the pre-Renaissance conception of Islam. In Dante's magisterial *La divina commedia* (early fourteenth century), Muhammad is portrayed as an impostor who is to be punished as a Christian schismatic. Most significantly, he is not conceived of as naturally inferior, or as a foil for the dignified Christian. Certain Muslim political leaders and intellectuals (e.g., Averroes and Saladin) were genealogically part of a venerable lineage of distinguished Greek and Biblical figures (ranging from Socrates to Abraham) who were depicted as dignified wise men who missed the truth of Christianity. While the identification of Islam with theo-political barbarism was emerging, before the Renaissance the ethno-political implications of barbarism had not yet been applied to the Saracen.[19]

The Fall of Constantinople, however, meant a growing modification in the employment of barbarism. As a strategy to shore up Western identity, Renaissance writers turned to the repository of Greco-Roman political theory, and not theology, to attack the Ottomans. This is not to say that Christian conceptions of a unique path to salvation were abandoned. They were rather reconceived in Greco-Roman vocabulary, creating a competing balance among typical aspects of the ethno- and theo-political narratives. This new development became one of the tragic ironies in the reified Western conception of barbarism. For centuries Greek thought was very well developed in Muslim philosophy and science. The analysis of Aristotelianism was preeminently a Muslim enterprise, and not a Christian one. It is impossible to understand Aquinas's retrieval of Aristotle without acknowledging the work of Al-Farabi, Ibn-Sina, and Ibn-Rushd. In the most generous historical reading of Western Christianity, Islam was co-heir to Greek thought. The Renaissance, however, left this intellectual debt unacknowledged and used the resources obtained from Muslim philosophy to ironically mobilize the Aristotelian conception of barbarism against the growing Muslim power.

The Renaissance employment of the narrative conceived of itself as closely following the Greco-Roman model. Athens constructed its Pan-Hellenic identity in contrast to the barbaric Persian. The same Renaissance humanists who coined the adjective "European" to describe their values built their definitions in opposition to the barbaric Turk. Lauro Quirini, for example, describes the Turks as "a barbaric uncultivated race, without established customs, or laws, living a careless, vagrant arbitrary life."[20] The "New Barbarian," in the narratives is an uncivilized group of sexually perverse, megalomaniac, lazy populations who engage in the mass killing of their enemies as well as their own people. Several humanists joined this evolving narrative of barbarism. Just as the old (Germanic) barbarians destroyed the first Rome in the fifth century, the new (Turkish) barbarians destroyed the second Rome, Byzantium. Some of these writers, such as Marsilio Ficino, actively resisted "losing the world of culture" for a second time. While the old intellectuals like Augustine had justified the barbarian invasion of the first Rome by appealing to a metaphysical plan, the new intellectuals intended to fight for the Second Rome. Ficino began writing "exhortations" to secular—not religious—powers to launch a complete "war" against the Turkish "barbarians."[21]

The Greco-Roman ethno-political reservoir enabled the Renaissance intellectuals to launch not only an early appeal to genetics but also a reformulation of the meaning of the Western Middle Ages. Alessandro Piccolomini, for example, reverted to the ancient Roman concept of the natural incommensurability of the Greeks and Barbarians. In a highly persuasive account he traced the ascendance of the Turks to the Scythians, one of the prototypically barbaric peoples for Herodotus and Euripides. In his view, the problem inhered in the eternal enmity between Western civilization and those communities of "barbarian stock."[22] The Turks were ontologically predisposed to sexual perversion, political despotism, and communal robbery. The medieval era's solution to Turkish depravity was the crusade. The theo-political language was not abandoned but innovated upon by Renaissance men. Francesco Petrarca, for example, agreed with Ficino that a new crusade was needed. The heroic models for the struggle, however, were neither popes Urban II or Gregory VIII, nor secular medieval monarchs such as King Richard of England or Louis IX (St. Louis) of France. The model of the crusader was Julius Caesar, the pre-Christian Roman ruler. The Renacentist not only reified the nascent European identity as the heir of Greco-Roman thought but also erased the intellectual debt barbarizing Muslims.[23]

Modern Colonial Barbarism

Though history lacks turning points, it is possible to trace processes that progressively inaugurate new eras. Renaissance humanists may have re-appropriated Greco-Roman political theory and barbarized the Ottomans, but they lacked the resources to dominate them. Beginning in the sixteenth century, European powers located the resources to launch a program of global dominance through the expropriation of resources and/or exploitation of labor of Amerindians, Jews, Muslims, and/or Africans. During this long process of material accumulation spanning the mercantilist and incipient capitalist eras, Europe would enjoy a comparative advantage vis-à-vis those designated as primitives, savages, or barbarians. As the Renaissance elided its intellectual debt, modernity obscured the material accumulation that preceded its own development. The resources that gave Europe its competitive advantage to launch scientific, economic, and political revolutions in the following centuries surfaced in this early period. The material advantage, however, was reified as a product of divine, natural, or historical design making those who opposed the development irrational barbarians.

Collaborative versions of the narrative of barbarism, then, played a central role in the establishment of the dynamics of domination that justified this process. They were employed to qualify alleged or actual opposition to European development and expansion from the sixteenth to the twentieth centuries. The colonial permutation of the narrative re-appropriated features from its reified history. On the one hand, it emphasized the theo-political existence of only one path to redemption and arrogated to itself the construction of this path. On the other hand, it re-appropriated the Greco-Roman description of the natural limitations (inferiority, limited or complete incorrigibility) of barbarians and regularly conceived them as sub-humans and/or powerful malicious threats to Western developments. From the beginning, the first of these impulses violently forced the barbarian to part with her communal resources in order to join a mono-linear path to salvation. But the operative strength of the second impulse left the barbarians at the mercy of a colonial system that profited from their fragility. Since these two narrative strands enjoyed different degrees of prominence that shifted based on geopolitical contexts, it is important not to overlook differences among racializations at any given time or space (we will soon explore distinctions between Occidentalist and Orientalist versions). It is nonetheless possible to discern commonalities among structures of domination vis-à-vis Natives, Africans, Arabs, and Jews in modernity.

The Natives of the Americas were among the first populations naturalized and barbarized as a collective in early modernity. Following the treaty of Tordesillas (1494) the emerging powers arrogated themselves ownership and spheres of influence in the Atlantic world. Blessed by the Pope, the conquest was supposed to extend Christian dominion over the newly discovered territories. Unsurprisingly the rights and interests of Native inhabitants were not represented in these treaties. It was they that would suffer the consequences. They would be qualified as barbarians and made candidates for annihilation. In the following centuries over eighty percent of the original population would perish as a consequence of the conquest.

Early in the process the proto-anthropological explanation of the newly discovered people was rooted in theological tradition. According to contextual biblical interpretation, the territories of the world were divided among Noah's sons. Japheth was associated with the nascent West, Shem with the Semitic world, and Ham with Africa. Unfortunately, Noah did not have a fourth son, so the discovery of new people presented a clear challenge to this tripartite framework. While many attempts were made to associate the new people with one of the three ideal types, those that identified the Amerindian Natives with the lost tribes of Israel were particularly prominent. This association with the descendants of Shem remained popular for the next four hundred years and was also applied by the European imperial powers to Africa and Asia. Subsequent classical studies linking indigenous populations linguistically and ritualistically to Semitic tradition helped to bolster and lend academic legitimacy to a scholarly construct, which helped European to deal with the unknown.[24]

In the Americas, however, the barbarization of the Natives complemented (and at times overshadowed) theological narratives. In the sixteenth century, King Charles V requested that the court of Valladolid determine the nature of the Natives. The court was not to enact judgment but rather to legitimate state policies. For the occasion, the court called one scholar, Juan Ginés de Sepúlveda, who had just translated and written a commentary on Aristotle's *Politics*. The role of the Spanish humanist was to integrate the Native in a re-appropriated Greco-Roman framework to justify the natural dominion of Christianity over barbaric populations, many of whom did not submit to subjugation peacefully.[25] Sepúlveda, contemporary interpreters argue, inaugurated one of the most perdurable trends in Western imperialist policies. That is, he justified the imperial subjugation and annihilation of entire populations as a necessary collateral damage in the process of liberationist expansion (i.e., "Christianization," "development," or "democratization").[26]

The Aristotelian Sepúlveda referred to the Natives as "barbarians" who "hardly have any trace of humanness."[27] Following a narrow selection of missionary accounts, he described them as sexually perverse, economically deficient, and politically despotic and seditious. The barbarians, according to the Humanist, lacked the basic ability to govern themselves and were unable to learn anything but rote, mechanical skills. This was conclusive proof of the natural asymmetry between Spaniards and Natives. The former was endowed with intelligence, discernment, and organized their life according to natural law and divine design. Though the latter possessed physical prowess, they existed in opposition to natural law due to their limited intellectual capacities. This alleged superiority of the Spaniard over the Native gave the former rights of dominion over the latter. In the words of Sepúlveda "given their barbarism, the latter should subject themselves to the natural laws and obey the imperial rule of the more civilized and educated."[28]

Sepúlveda already had proof that the reduction to servitude was going to generate resistance among the Natives. The twofold imperial objective was to save the Natives from their own barbaric behavior and secure Spanish safety on the continent. Sepúlveda asserted that only a forced subjugation and permanent surveillance would subdue the Natives and pre-empt the possibility that they would "plot uprisings against Spanish dominion."[29] There was no alternative to either Christianity or the colonial yoke. The forced subjugation of the barbarian was a necessary step to fulfil the divine mission. Consistent with a classical feature of the Occidentalist civilizational mission, Sepúlveda suggests that Native advancement is possible under the coercive tutelage of the empire. The barbarian, however, became more of a candidate for annihilation than assimilation. If the coerced barbarian acquiesced to colonial dominion, she/he would be integrated, but only as a "natural servant." As such, the barbarian would be denied all alterity and forced to endure extreme labor, including sexual servitude and permanent surveillance, in order to demonstrate she/he had not been "badly pacified" and thus achieve a heavily regulated and elusive civilized status.[30] If the barbarian resisted, she/he would be construed as an irrational obstacle and often exterminated. As a consequence, the humanist promise of the Native's corrigibility became a veiled colonial resource under the operative strength of the narrative. Hundreds of cultures were silenced and millions perished.

During the deliberations, Sepúlveda opposed Bartolomé de las Casas, the Bishop of Chiapas in contemporary Mexico, whose championing of the Natives earned him the honorific title of "defender of Indian tears." As a precursor of both Liberation Theology and the narrative of the noble savage, Las Casas bemoaned the genocidal practices justified by his rivals. His discourse, however, presupposed the narrative of barbarism. In one of his most celebrated texts he presupposes a typology of barbarism identifying the Turks, the contemporary personification of Islam, as "oppositional barbarians" (*barbarie contraria*) explaining that the barbaric Muslims were an incommensurable threat to Christian civilization.[31] It is true, however, that he attempted to expose Europe's brutality. But to contextualize the excesses of Spanish actions, he compares them not only with the "cruel Turk" but also with the "barbarian African."[32] It is not a surprise, therefore, that for most of his life he supported the trans-Atlantic Slave trade. He even suggested alleviating the weight of Native serfdom by transporting more enslaved Africans to the Americas. These descriptions and proposals made by no other than the champion of Native rights serve as a testament to how deeply the narrative permeated early modern discourses.

The narrative applied to Native populations of the Americas, as we have seen, also had an effect on Sub-Saharan Africans. Beginning in the fifteenth century, Portuguese explorers, predominantly financed by the crown, began exploring the African coasts. Africans, of course, were not as unfamiliar to European eyes as the indigenous inhabitants of the Americas. Since at least the eleventh century, black Africans resided in Muslim Spain. Beginning in the thirteenth century, a small minority of black servants could also be found in Italy. Though populations of Turks and Mongols were more numerous and prominent, this black population continued to grow in the Renaissance. The fourteenth century witnessed a two-fold deepening of Afro-European contact. On the one hand, commercial activities extended non-theologically based knowledge of Africans as Venetian and Genoese merchants engaged in trans-Saharan commerce. The merchants were particularly attracted by the region's wealth, which was especially in evidence during the West African King's pilgrimage to Mecca. On the other hand, the establishment of formal relations between the King of Ethiopia and the Papacy in Avignon permitted theological exploration. The pilgrimage of sub-Saharan Black Africans to Rome illustrates the extent to which the modern narrative was not yet ascendant. Africans were neither new nor dispossessed barbarians in premodern Europe.[33]

The modern narrative of barbaric Africa would not become hegemonic until the Enlightenment. But its origins can be located in the two centuries following the fifteenth-century explorations. These discourses enabled and justified the enslavement of Africans for backbreaking work on plantations, especially in the Americas. Gomes Eanes de Zaura, one of the most important chroniclers of the era, was deeply influenced by the Renaissance revitalization of the Greco-Roman imaginary. He conceived of the African exploration as a latter-day "Homeric quest" among strange and often times dangerous peoples. In contrast to the original version, however, the Africans were associated with the stereotypical traits of the barbarian: sexual perversion, cannibalism, and political sedition. A growing narrative about Africans selling their own wives and children into slavery led Europeans to justify their commercial interests and further subscribe to a belief in the innate barbarism of Africans. In the early seventeenth century, temporally coincident with the description of Natives and Ottomans as barbarians, European chroniclers began identifying Africans in the same way. John Pory, for example, an English administrator and adventurer, analyzed the religious, cannibalistic, and political behaviors of Africans before labeling some of these collectives as "barbarous."[34]

The flowering of the modern narrative of Black barbarism, however, did not take place until the Enlightenment when theological power was in decline and new liberal trends began to reproduce a new narrative of barbarism. In eighteenth-century France, Denis Diderot accused Africans of "cannibalism," while for Voltaire, black physiology "limits their power of reason." In England, David Hume described Black Africans as "naturally inferior to whites" and understood a "civilized nation" to be confined to European "white" populations.[35] In Germany Immanuel Kant went even further, claiming that African barbarism was not geographically circumscribed. Utilizing and creatively adapting climate theories, he argued that even liberated from the home continent, they would be unable to offer civilization any cultural achievement. For Kant, Africans were incapable of contributing to civilization or governing themselves. These attributes, already present in the rhetoric of Sepulveda, made them natural slaves. To paraphrase Kant, even if Africans could be trained by force, the best they could hope to achieve was servile status.[36]

In the nineteenth century, Georg W. Hegel offered an influential account of barbarism in his writings about Black Africans. Current scholarship argues that a younger Hegel may have been influenced by the slave-lead independence of Haiti when formulating his well-known master-slave dialectic that could lead to the abolition of slavery as an institution. The same sources argue that the forced decline of this experience, opposed by Euro-American powers who could not tolerate a successful slave-rebellion, made Hegel discard this early approach and align himself with a more stereotypical or "dumber" reading of Africans.[37] According to acclaimed Cameroonian philosopher Achille Mbembe, these later writings made Hegel's proposal "the archetype of what would become the colonial mode of speaking about Africa."[38]

Hegel referred to Subsaharan Africans as the "Negro hordes" who behave "with the most unthinking inhumanity and revolting barbarity."[39] Since Africans resided outside history, they made no contribution to universal development and were unable to attain consciousness of Being. By the sharpest possible contrast they live, as Sepúlveda described the Natives, in a permanent state of political, economic, and sexual perversion. While supporting his thesis, Hegel accuses Africans of cannibalism, unprecedented cruelty, and thoroughgoing sedition. His analysis of this natural perversion made Hegel point out central characteristics that were shared by Africans: the "lack of respect for human life" and the "intractability" of the "Negro character."[40]

Africans were to achieve participation in universal history only through contact with and submission to civilized Europe. Hegel insists that the needed path for this development is slavery. While he admits this is not the most charitable institution, Hegel justifies it by claiming that Africans have long grown accustomed to it. While intra-African slavery was "barbaric" because the difference between the master and slave was irrationally "arbitrary," the one practiced by Europeans was justified by their self-evident superiority and their privileged role in history. While some may protest this historical institution, Hegel recalled that in Athens, the reified cradle of Western culture, only the citizens were free.[41]

There are certainly differences among the variety of Occidentalist strategies. While Christian colonization emphasized the barbaric inferiority in space, the Enlightened version started to locate the inferiority in a temporal framework. But it is also possible to trace continuities. For Hegel and Sepúlveda before him, the narrative of barbarism is presented in the context of a civilized mission that insists in only one path toward liberation and could rhetorically offer a path of assimilation to a unique Western route (Christendom of Eurocentric history). The operational strength of the promised correction made the alleged inclusion genocidal, forcing the barbarian to endure extreme circumstances for a goal regulated or limited by the reproduction of the inferior nature of the colonized (i.e., natural servants for the Spaniard and natural slaves for the German). Hegel had already justified the annihilation of the Natives of the Americas explaining that they were destined to "perish" once the universal "spirit touched them."[42] He then further develops this line of thinking, explaining that the only possibility for Africans to be integrated to history is to be forced into a system of slavery. This system will make them disposable sources of labor operating under the permanent surveillance of their overlords. Over fifteen million Africans were enslaved and annihilated as a consequence of human development; with the passage of time, moreover, Africans became more rigidly racialized and the notion of their intractable nature more pronounced. Following the imperial distribution of Africa at the Conference of Berlin (1890) over thirty million Africans were annihilated by colonizers on the African continent alone.

The burgeoning of the African reading of barbarism in the eighteenth and nineteenth centuries did not occur in a vacuum; at this time the discourse of Orientalism in the Middle East and Occidentalism in the Americas developed and flourished simultaneously. The proto-Orientalism that created an image of the barbarian Ottoman Turk was employed between the fifteenth and eighteenth centuries, roughly spanning the Italian Renaissance/humanist revival and the Enlightenment French Revolution. In the nineteenth century, however, the Ottoman Empire began to decline and its colonial possessions thoroughly appropriated by European powers between the middle of the nineteenth century and the end of the First World War. In the nineteenth and twentieth centuries, a mature Orientalism would flourish, employing the modern colonial narrative of barbarism. But the rival this time, the Turkish Empire, did not constitute an actual political threat. The new barbarians became the Orientalized image of the Arab.

Beginning in the nineteenth century, as we have seen with respect to Africans, ideas of a scientific understanding of human inequality, or theories of race, would achieve discursive normativity. Given their predominantly non-Arabic origin, the Ottoman Turks did not precisely fit the bill. Especially significant in this context were discourses of Semitic backwardness permeating the Arab world from the Middle East to the Maghreb. The pioneering work in the discipline of Postcolonialism makes an important contribution to these particular historical-geographical circumstances. For the West, Said explains, the Arab, representing Islam, "comes to symbolize terror, devastation, the demonic, horde of hated barbarians."[43] The Orient appeared to be sub-human, despotic, and backward. The Orientalists, Said observes, pronounced the Arabs barbaric for their political, religious, economic, and sexual perversions.

Since our focus will be the Maghreb, Alexis de Toqueville is an excellent social informant regarding the barbarization of the Arabs. Classical Western sources define him as a "paladin" of liberalism and democracy. A priori the title is not unearned. He is known for opposing not only the incipient racial theories of the nineteenth century but also colonial violence. In his early writings he may even have used the term barbarism to criticize Europe itself. Yet, a closer look at his political activity and late writings may come as a surprise. Already in his early writings he had defined the Natives in the Americas as "barbarous," "uncivilized," and "repulsive."[44] But his central contribution came later in life when he became an expert on the Algerian Question in the French chamber of deputies. Since the 1830s France had occupied the territory and by the following decade established a colonial state that would survive until the 1960s. Tocqueville not only fervently supported colonization but also barbarized the Arabs by employing the modern colonial narrative.

The liberal intellectual explains that Algerian colonization was necessary both to ensure the role of France in the greater imperial competition and for the good of the region's inhabitants. He argues that it was indeed a land of promise, were it not for the fact that "one needs to farm with a gun in your hand." Toqueville explains that France cannot fear the challenge presented by these "little barbarous tribes" that irrationally opposed the advance of civilization.[45] In a quintessentially Orientalist manner he argued that the secret success of their colonizing enterprise resided in an intimate knowledge of the Arabs. After "studying" the Quran, he understands them to fundamentally constitute a fanatic people who break the political, religious, and sexual rules of civility. As a result, it was necessary to subjugate, expropriate, and, if necessary, eliminate opposition to the colonial advance. The annihilation of the barbarian represented a mere "unfortunate necessity" in the pursuit of universal human betterment and civilization.[46]

Toqueville, as Sepúlveda and Hegel had done before with Natives and Africans, insists that this was in the best interests of the Arabs themselves. The operative force of the narrative of barbarism was becoming, however, more and more clear. Toqueville emphasizes that given the fanatical Arab nature, the only way to limit irrational violence was with preemptive, redemptive violence. After visiting the Maghreb twice he became even more convinced of the innate distinction between Arabs and Europeans. Though he was not surprised that the settlers needed to protect themselves, he was outraged that even if a European like himself tried "to study" these "barbarous people," he needed to do so "with arms in hands."[47]

This experience led Toqueville to be cynical about barbaric corrigibility. He argued that only people who did not know the Arabs could entertain ideas of future conviviality or Arabic/Christian miscegenation. This paladin of liberalism unequivocally believed that mutual understanding and meaningful cross-cultural contact between Semites and Europeans could only occur in the "realm of fantasy."[48] This further underscores the point that the operative force of the narrative went beyond false humanistic promises. Toward the turn of the twentieth century and during times of increased scientific racism, colonial administrators would reproduce this dichotomy further explaining, for example, that the barbaric Oriental "acts, speaks, and thinks in a manner exactly the opposite of the European."[49]

After reading this account of the uses of barbarism throughout modernity, it is possible to argue that the closer one approaches the twentieth century, the more pronounced ideas of barbaric incorrigibility become. On the one hand, this reading has its merits. It is impossible to deny that in the nineteenth and twentieth centuries the cultural and later scientific understanding of race did reinforce the normative portrayal. For this reason, some accounts argue that during this period there was a formal separation between primitive and barbaric forces.[50] While the former emphasized the universal path of redemption, the latter were understood as existing in irrational opposition to civilization. Nonetheless, I resist understandings of radical discontinuity in the global project of modernity. A more comprehensive and compelling strategy would be to analyze the dramatic increase in the portrayal of the barbarian as incorrigible. While it is true that Christian, developmentalist, and democratic stratifications exhibit marked differences, the balance between a single path toward civilization and the operative natural limitation (sub-humanity, inferiority, and/or incorrigibility) of the barbarian was present from the sixteenth to the twentieth centuries.

Jewish trajectories are not foreign to this central feature of coloniality. The ensemble of Jewish experiences we considered in the last chapter are symptomatic of Jewish barbarization. From the sixteenth to the twentieth centuries, a large number of Jews were forced to adapt themselves to a unique Western path but were nonetheless ultimately considered incorrigible, and subsequently persecuted and/or annihilated. In the beginning of the period, Jews were forced to convert to Christianity, but their corrigibility was challenged by the purity of blood laws and persecuted under the Inquisition. Toward the end of the period, Jews were converted into citizens of the state. But the portrayal of their incorrigibility would lead to one of the most iconic genocides of the twentieth century. Evidence of Jewish barbarization is ubiquitous in this period and was once and again interconnected with other barbarians.

Jews among Barbarians

The modern barbarization of Muslims, Natives, and Africans has a common systemic root. Europeans discourses integrated the Jew into the mix. By exploring this reading I am not implying that barbarism is the only narrative that racialized Jews, that Jews were in each time and location equally colonized to other barbarians, or that Jewish experiences can be interpreted only as a reaction to their racialization. I am suggesting that throughout modernity imperial powers created networks of colonized described as barbarians and these networks, especially in our spatial framework, often included Jews.

In the eighteenth century, the accusation of Jewish barbarism can be found in two schools on the vanguard of liberal struggle: English Deism and French Enlightenment. As champions of secularism, the Deists reinforced the modern interpretation of Jewish perversity. One of the leading voices, Anthony Collins, wrote early in the eighteenth century that Jews were "an illiterate, barbarous, and ridiculous people." Ironically incorporating a Biblical reading to his explicit anti-clericalism, Collins pointed out that that not even God could "reason" with them and needed to use alternative "crafts" to communicate with these ignorant barbarians.[51] A few years later the Deist leader of the Tories and political philosopher Henry St. Jones, First Viscount of Bolingbroke, referred to Jews as "the proudest and most lying nation in the world," claiming "their ignorance and superstition, pride, injustice and barbarity" rendered them universally hated.[52]

Influenced by these readings, François-Marie Arouet—Voltaire—made even more inflammatory remarks, calling them ritual murderers, parasitic vagabonds, anarchical agitators, and sexually depraved. The anti-clerical fighter for equality, source for the French revolutionaries, compared them with other colonized peoples, especially in Africa and writes:

> You seem to me to be the maddest of the lot. The Kaffirs, the Hottentots, and the Negroes of Guinea are much more reasonable and more honest people than you... You have surpassed all nations in impertinent fables, in bad conduct and in barbarism. You deserve to be punished for this is your destiny.[53]

The champions of the Enlightenment thus considered Jews to be among the lowest class of barbarians. This situation may be perplexing for current readers. How is possible that defenders of religious toleration and the secular state characterized Jews in these terms? Scholars have debated this context for decades. Some call these writings accidents, while others explore the inherent anti-Semitism of the Enlightenment. Here I would like to suggest that it is not just the Enlightenment that is anti-Semitic. I agree with decolonialists that the edifice that constructed Jews since the sixteenth century has ultimately racialized them. In other words, the project of modernity from the Renaissance to Colonialism to Enlightenment to Fascism is responsible of the categorization of the portrayal of Jews as barbarians.[54] Many times they were dismissed as extreme barbarians leading subversions to defeat imperial designs; in others counted occasions this barbarism was presupposed as the Jewish starting-point when offered short-lived candidacies to assimilation in interchange for their collaboration in the execution of the imperial designs. Between the two poles, the narrative of Jewish barbarism became central in the construction of the modern narrative.[55]

The narrative confused Jews and Natives. In the sixteenth century, Natives were classified as barbarians in the New World; at the same time Jews were racialized with the Purity of Blood Laws emanating from the the metropolis. In this context, as we have already seen, Natives came to be identified as Jews. The research into the barbaric Native Jews first attempted to locate a common hidden language shared by both barbaric groups. Soon enough the research also included accusations of the shared perversion of sexual, religious, and political customs. It did not take long until writings emerged detailing the commonalities between Natives and Jews. In particular the accusations focus on cannibalism, sexual perversion, lust, and, most importantly, anarchical and seditious political behavior.[56]

The situation became explosive in the seventeenth century. Between 1635 and 1639, the Inquisitorial and colonial authorities allegedly discovered, à la Coetzee's "Third Bureau," a secret plot against the Empire. They termed it *La Conspiración Grande* (The Great Conspiracy) and accused Jews of plotting with Natives and Black slaves against Catholic Spanish colonization. Obviously the conspiracy did not exist, but as a surprising result of the accusations, some of the accused with no record of Jewish ancestry started to affirm a Jewish identity. There could be many reasons for this identification: perhaps they empathized with Jewish misfortune or perhaps it was a reaction to sermons that placed Jews as the predecessors of the Christians Spaniards. It may have been occasioned by the fact that practitioners of any alternative spirituality were accused of being Jewish or the fact that non-Christians were unable to avoid identification with their alternative spiritualities. But the Jews persecuted in the New World were not only *Marranos*. Those accused of being barbarians, among them not only Natives and Africans but also Spaniards who fell into disgrace, saw an opportunity to counter the narrative of barbarism by identifying themselves with Judaism.[57]

This opened, perhaps among the first times in modernity, a key association of Jews with one of the most salient characteristics of barbarism: political plotting and sedition. In the fourteenth century, European Jews had already been accused of poisoning the water to cause a pandemic. The Black Death, as the plague was known, annihilated approximately a quarter of the Central European population and extended to the Middle East. In the Americas of the seventeenth century, this behavior, this time leading a rebellion of barbarians, would be linked to the term barbarism. In the early twentieth century, multiple allegations of Jewish political sedition emerged throughout the Americas. In the South Cone, for example, a leading intellectual and future Argentinean Minister of Education, Gustavo Martínez Zuviría, wrote several anti-Semitic novels such as *El Kahal, Cuentos de Oro,* and *666 (The Community, Gold Stories, 666)*. In his writings, landmarks for Hispanic nationalists, Jews are portrayed as controlling the world financially by means of a central committee located in New York.[58] In the financial center of the US magnate Henry Ford would complement this example by writing *The International Jew: A World's Problem*. In the text he accused Jews of trying to control American life by infiltrating and dominating every aspect of culture including finance, media, entertainment, sports, and international relations.[59]

Illustrating the trans-Atlantic character of the problem, both authors of the Americas had a common source: a book written at the turn of the nineteenth century by a Russian spy who plagiarized a piece of French political satire. *The Protocols of the Wise of Zion* purports to reveal the ongoing plans of Jewish society to control the world using the tactics Martínez Zuviría and Ford later repeated. Jews were not only accused of being guided by "barbaric" Talmudic customs[60]; the author of the hoax, written just a decade before the triumph of the Bolshevik revolution, also explained that the Jewish plan to install Socialism was a "short stage" to nothing other than "barbarism."[61]

Jewish barbaric plots against European designs became an integral part of the modern narrative of barbarism. Both Natives and Blacks were accused of allying themselves with Jews in their conspiracies. Interestingly enough, the association between Jews and Blacks did not stop in early modernity: the supposed alliance continued thanks to the influence of the *Protocols*. In Germany, Adolph Hitler, who made explicit reference to the *Protocols*, retrieved the narrative of Jewish and Black political co-conspiracy. In his racist diatribe he recalled the post-World War I armistice of 1919. During this period the allies occupied the Rhine and sent troops to the area. Among them were African French soldiers, who were predominantly Senegalese. The right-wing press began to accuse these soldiers of "sexual immorality" (raping "pure Aryan" German women). Hitler adds to this accusation that the presence and perversion of the African soldiers was not fortuitous. The Jews, who had "stabbed Germany in the back" by betraying her in the First World War, had also convinced French authorities to install African soldiers in the Rhine. Jews were responsible, the leader of the Third Reich asserts, for bringing these "barbarians belonging to a race inspired by nature" who were unable to restrain their animal instincts from perverting German purity.[62]

From the dawn of modernity in the seventeenth century until the Holocaust in the twentieth century, the narrative of barbarism made Jews and Blacks political co-conspirators using political and sexual perversion to subvert coloniality's structures of domination. In the eighteenth and nineteenth centuries, the discourses of Jews and Blacks were constructed in parallel. This discourse was not only limited to the intellectual sphere but also became enshrined in law. While the French Assembly offered liberation and rights to all human beings in 1789, both Jews and Blacks were forced to wait to receive their rights five years later in 1794. A review of the rhetorical discussions about the incivility of Blacks and Jews shows that the discourses overlapped considerably. Both groups were accused of moral degradation, sexual perversity, cannibalism, and incorrigible character. While they were eventually emancipated, strong restrictions were imposed on both communities soon thereafter. Once Napoleon rose to power, he supported the re-establishment of slavery in the colonies and limited the professional activity and the possession of property by Jews in the metropolis. In the nineteenth and early twentieth centuries, the interrelation of narratives went beyond a possible "political alliance" and acquired a more pronounced racial dimension. As Gilman argues, "Being Black" and "Being Jewish" were "inexorably linked."[63] Two statesmen of the nineteenth-century German Empire and the twentieth-century Third Reich, Hermann Wagener and Alfred Rosenberg concurred on this equivalency. Wagener and Rosenberg, associates of Otto Von Bismark and Adolph Hitler, respectively, described Jews as "white Negroe[s]."[64] The influential British-German writer Houston Stewart Chamberlain went one step further, describing the Jewish race directly as being Black. He argues that at the time of Jewish exile in Alexandria they intermarried with Africans creating the lowest possible race. Treatises on the similarities between the physiognomy of Jews and Africans became a regular subject of study, and Jews increasingly came to be seen as a barbaric source of contamination vis-à-vis the project of creating a pure Aryan Europe.[65]

There are, however, two factors that problematize the conclusions just posited. The first is the record of Jewish collaboration with African racialization. This includes, but it is not limited to, the transatlantic slave trade.[66] The second is the existence of a multiplicity of Black African Jews that existed outside the networks of Jewish normativity centered in Europe or the extended Mediterranean.[67] Some scholars have tried to undermine these challenges. They point out, for example, that the first records were not at the center of the traffic of human life or that other Africans also collaborated with slave traders. With an unfortunately narrow historical perspective, others explain that large parts of the Afro-Jewish community resulted from the colonization of collectives that came to Judaism as a modern reaction to imperialism. Here I want to emphasize the existence of a European narrative of barbarism that qualifies Blacks and Jews as part of the same barbaric network. But it is important to clarify this is not the only interconnected history.

A third interrelation based in both historical accuracy and colonial fantasy was the correlation of Jews with the barbaric "Oriental" peoples, referred to throughout modernity as "Turks," "Arabs," or "Muslims." It is important to mention that the association of these groups did indeed have historical reality given the sizeable Jewish populations located in Muslim regions. These Jewries, mostly located in the region that for most of modernity occupied the Ottoman Empire, had been established communities since antiquity, having arrived between the sixth century BCE and the first century CE. It is impossible to reduce these communities to one monolithic amalgam. But for most of the European medieval age, Jews were recognized as *Ahl al-Kitāb* (people of the book) and favored with a legal protective status, *hl al-dimmah*. This does not imply that they lived in peace and enjoyed civil protections throughout the period. But these communities largely considered themselves and were considered to be Native groups and enjoyed extensive periods of cultural flourishing, especially in comparison to the protracted persecution Jews faced in Europe.

In early modernity, and in contradistinction to current understandings of timeless enmity between Jews and Muslims, these regions were loci of refugee congregation for different waves of Jews fleeing Europe to escape persecution. This includes, but is not limited to, Jews escaping the expulsion from Spain in 1492. This population suffered one of the earliest European modern interventions. In *al-Andalus* the cultural life of Jews and Muslims was intimately related. The growing Spanish empire helped to cement this connection with tragic consequences. Decades prior to the accusation of Jews leading a barbaric rebellion with Natives/Blacks in the Americas, converted Jews and Muslims (*Conversos* and *Moriscos*) were suspected of trying to undermine the strength of the kingdom by practicing their traditions in a clandestine fashion. They were not only restricted by Purity of Blood Laws, but they also suffered the persecution of the Inquisition.

Throughout most of the modern period, Jewish populations living under Arab and/or Muslim majorities considered themselves Native groups. This may *prima facie* appear counterintuitive. Toward the late nineteenth century, European powers began to dismember the Ottoman Empire and sometimes employed local Jews as proxies in their diplomatic and military endeavors. This was not an unusual policy applied to Jews, but it was a common practice used to divide Native populations. The division between Tutsies and Hutus in Rwanda is perhaps one of the best-known and tragic instances in the English-speaking academia. While in some areas the division became a de facto reality, in many others Jews reminded strongly connected to local Muslim populations. It is therefore no surprise that in the early stages of the Postcolonial state, it was possible to find Jews enrolled in decolonial movements and/or invited to participate in the new governance structures. Despite the colonial attempts to divide Jews and Arabs in the late nineteenth century, it was not until the establishment of the State of Israel that the division became fully naturalized.[68]

Yet, the European intervention in the relation between Jews and Muslims was not limited to the aforementioned communities, but also as a portrayal of European Jews as "Oriental people" throughout modernity. Said acknowledges early in his landmark work the intimate relationship between European anti-Semitism and Orientalism. Contemporary scholars in Jewish studies complements Said asserting that portrayal of Muslims has been "formed in extricable conjunction with Western conceptions of the Jewish people" and therefore "Orientalism has always been not only about Muslims but also about Jews."[69]

One of the first modern associations of European Jews with barbaric enemies arises in the Renascence. This is as soon as intellectuals fearful of Ottoman political power retrieved the ethno-political category of barbarism. When they were qualifying "the Turks" as barbaric, they were portraying Jews as Turks. This relation is particularly clear in the study of one of the most salient features of the period, its plastic art. Prior to the Renaissance, Jews were generally not represented as Muslims. They were depicted using "Jewish hats," principally, but not always, a yellow cone. During this period, however, Jews became associated to the dangerous barbarians by portraying them with Turkish Turbans instead. This was far from being an exclusive characteristic of the Italian Renascence. The invention of the printing press enabled it to become a feature of Western Christendom including cultural centers such as Flandes, France, Germany. Examples can be found until the very end of the eighteenth century. This common depicture went well beyond the Turkish period. When the Arab replaced the Turk in the barbaric role, Jewish portrayal also changed. Toward the nineteenth century Jews wore portrayed as wearing neither a Jewish hat nor a Turkish turban, they were depicted as Arabs wearing a kaffiyeh.[70]

This common plastic representation of Jews and Arabs had its broader correlate with the emergence of theories of Semitism. Following the classical description of the narrative, Europeans devised a dualist asymmetrical construction. The civilized European Indo-Arians portrayed themselves as possessing a natural dominion over the non-Western Semitic peoples, represented most commonly by both Jews and Arabs. During periods of intense Orientalism, key Western luminaries reproduced the same association of Renaissance intellectuals. Voltaire, Kant, Herder, and Hegel, to name a few examples we will consider below, categorized European Jews as having an "Oriental Spirit" or being "Asiatic refugees," "A Palestinian race," or "an Arab tribe."[71] Some European

Jews took advantage of this accusation in order to reclaim an Oriental pedigree that serve to undermine their racialized status. Between the nineteenth and twentieth centuries, European Jews including politicians such as Benjamin Disraeli, religious Reformers such as Abraham Geiger, and philosophers such as Martin Buber were part of the disruption of this narrative by proclaiming their pride in Jewish Orientalism and, on some occasions, directly including Jews among Arabs.[72]

While the Semitism discourse lost vitality in most liberal circles, reactionary elements enthusiastically appropriated it toward the end of the nineteenth century. Self-identified Anti-Semitic parties began to populate the political scene, particularly in central Europe, and depicted Jews with typical accusations of sedition and political barbarism. This was not a new accusation. Already in the seventeenth century Jews were accused of leading plots against the Spanish empire. In the eighteenth century, they were associated with the Freemasons, who drew significantly from "Oriental" symbolism in their attempt to undermine traditional Christian civilization.[73] Anti-Semitic conspiracies drew from the aforementioned French-Russian *Protocols*, the *International Jew* in the United States, gold in Argentina, and finally *My Struggle* in Germany. This trend would culminate in the concentration camps and would never free itself from its early barbaric Semitic association. As Auschwitz survivors narrate, there was place for the confusion of identities. A Jew, then considered the ultimate enemy of the Third Reich, could be stigmatized as a "Muselmann" before being annihilated.[74]

As we have explored in this chapter, the narrative of barbarism constructed modern Jews alongside other barbarians. This narrative witnessed the modern attempt of retrieving Greco-Roman tropes putting them in the service of a colonial project. As a result, by the end of this period, more than two hundred million people were annihilated by colonial designs legitimated by this narrative. Jews among other barbarians, however, began to revise this narrative. In the second part of the book I will engage in a further "against the grain" interpretation to understand not only the Jewish strategies used to confront this term, but also how, through the reaction to this narrative, Jews re-imagined themselves within an imagined community of barbarians.

CHAPTER 3

Negative Barbarism: Marxist Counter-Narrative in the Provincial North

In the aftermath of the Holocaust Isaac Deutscher wrote "The non-Jewish Jew," an essay that became a landmark of Jewish cultural studies within the English-speaking academy. The article features the provocative intersection of two biographical identities that a priori seem antithetical: rabbinical Judaism and European Marxism. On the one hand Deutscher was a prototypical traditionalist Jew. He grew up in an orthodox family, was educated in Talmudic houses of study, fled continental Europe to escape Nazism, and presented his essay for the first time in an institutional Jewish setting. On the other hand, he was a committed Marxist. He rejected a religious or national identification of Judaism, became a Trotskyist activist, wrote groundbreaking biographies of leaders of the Communist revolution, and committed his life to an international struggle against imperialisms and totalitarianisms. Defining his Jewishness in strident terms, Deutscher described himself as "a Jew by force of my unconditional solidarity with the persecuted and exterminated."[1]

In 1933, just months after the Nazi rise to power, and as both a Marxist and a Jew he encouraged a large common front against the threat of Fascism. Among his most renowned exhortations for this alliance, he wrote "The Danger of Barbarism over Europe" at the outbreak of the Second World War. In this article, which resulted in his expulsion from the party, he explained the need to increase the party's reach beyond the usual "popular" constituencies to "repel the offensive of Hitlerite barbarism."[2] The use of the term barbarism was not unintended. It was a long-standing Marxist counter-narrative largely developed and employed by Jews. This counter-narrative used barbarism in reverse to critique Western formations and, in the years leading up to the Second World War and its aftermath, made European Jews an epistemological alternative to the civilizational perpetrators of barbarism.

For Deutscher the vast number of radical Jews who joined the Marxist struggle and subverted the narrative of barbarism were not at odds with the tradition. On the contrary, the collective represented a historical core of Judaism. He begins the article with an interesting negotiation between Talmudic sources and radical thinking. He opens with a *midrash*, an allegoric interpretation of a textual source, that recounts the story of an orthodox sage, Rabbi Meir, and his teacher, the "heretic" Elisha ben-Abuya (referred to in rabbinical literature contemptuously as *Akher*—the other or the stranger). The story occurs during Shabbat when the mentor was riding a donkey and Rabbi Meir, aware of the prohibition against such activities on the sacred day, walked by his side. When they reached the limit that was permitted to walk during the holy day, the heretic told his student that it was time to part ways. While the student was advised to return to the Jewish community, the heretic continued "beyond the boundaries of Jewry."[3]

The product of an orthodox upbringing, Deutscher remembers asking as a child why Rabbi Meir, "the leading light of orthodoxy," became a disciple of "the heretic." What could a leader of rabbinical Judaism learn from a man whose name is condemned in Talmudic circles? Deutscher provocatively asserts that there is no contradiction. The radical Jew has a legitimate place within the very core of Jewish tradition. She belongs to a long line of revolutionary Jews who transgressed the boundaries of Judaism to defend the oppressed who resided beyond the group's communal limits. While these individuals may have found institutional Judaism too constraining and parochial, they nonetheless exported Jewish concerns to contexts far beyond and external to the tradition. They thus changed not only the way Jews relate to their surroundings, but the very surroundings themselves. "You may," Deutscher argues, "see Akher as the prototype of those great revolutionaries of modern thought," including Karl Marx, Rosa Luxemburg and Leon Trotsky.[4]

The Marxist Jews took the spirit of Jewish solidarity and "liberated" it within the dominant European societies that were racializing the collective of barbarians. Their quest was to liberate what Deutscher calls "the praxis of critical inquiry" in order to subvert oppressive mainstream discourses such as the narrative of barbarism.[5] In opposition to these discourses, this line of Marxist Jews elaborated a negative counter-narrative. They kept the negative valence of the term intact but accused Europe—meaning colonial Christianity for Marx, capitalism for Luxemburg, fascism for Deutscher and totalitarianism for Trotsky—and not Jews of barbarism. Marxist Jews continued this legacy during and after the Holocaust but with a qualitative difference. Three members of the Frankfurt School (Benjamin, Adorno, and Horkheimer) not only replicated the counter-narrative accusing the West (civilization and enlightenment) and exculpating Jews from barbarism, but they also retrieved Jewish textual maxims and re-purposed them as alternatives to the "barbaric" European civilization.

It is important to clarify, however, that Marxist Jews were neither the first nor the only to reverse the barbaric accusation. In Europe itself, and preceding Marx's and the Frankfurt's writings in the nineteenth and twentieth centuries, one could cite early modern dissidents who reversed the term such as Michel de Montaigne (a descendent of Marranos) in the sixteenth century to Denis Diderot in the eighteenth. During the twentieth century, furthermore, it was not uncommon to reflect on the barbarism of Europe. These intellectuals, however, did not necessarily employ the reversal of barbarism to simultaneously attack the West and exculpate Jews, nor did they present Jewish epistemological alternatives to a criminal Europe characterized as barbaric. It is not a surprise that this retrieval of Jewish epistemological alternatives took place during the narrative's high watermark in the 1940s. During the Holocaust, when a fraction of Jewish blood could result in the annihilation of an entire (Jewish) body, the potential for hybridism between European and Jewishness became impossible. In its place, border thinkers not only reproduced the negative counter-narrative of barbarism that blamed the West for its criminality, but also presented a conscious epistemological alternative by retrieving Jewish maxims in times of an abandoned presumption of Humanism.

This is not to say that Marxists Jews were successful in their quest. It is true that the counter-narrative became highly influential. The trend of thinking initiated in the second half of the nineteenth century has made its ways through time and space. After the Second World War it was employed and modified by public intellectuals struggling against/with Marxism such as Hannah Arendt and George Steiner in English-speaking locations.[6] In the last decades, and especially after 9/11, the narrative has found resonance in places like Buenos Aires where local Jewish voices employ it to reflect on twenty-first century Jewish geopolitics.[7] In between one and the other stage, dissident Latin American

Jewish intellectuals in Europe re-nourished the tradition re-inserting the problem of barbarism in eco-socialist proposals.[8]

This provocative influence notwithstanding, the negative counter-narrative is beset with geo-political shortcomings. The Holocaustic development of the trend naturalizes central European Judaism as normative Judaism and develops its framework overlooking conversations with other colonized peoples co-categorized as barbarians since early modernity. Furthermore, it minimizes the relevance of other racializations in order to elucidate modern dynamics. By ultimately focusing on the European Jewish experience, the Holocaustic versions of the narrative myopically construe Nazism as the product of the post-enlightenment and nation-state period and not as a product of colonial discourses and the patterns of domination established by coloniality. As a consequence they fail to perceive that the original civilizatory project was not predicated on a liberation that dialectically turned into barbarism. From the outset, rather, it was a process of barbarian subjugation and elimination that veiled its project with a liberationist discourse. This hermetic dialectical Eurocentrism renders them unable to appreciate the deep decolonial creativity emerging from the positive re-affirmation of the barbaric. There were, we will soon explore, contextual reasons that made it difficult to re-appropriate the term barbarism in the Germany of the 1940s. But the negative subversion of the narrative during the Holocaust offers only a restrictive critique of the ambitions of Western barbarism. This proposal, with all its limitations, became one of the most perdurable and influential subversions of the mainstream narrative ever to surface.

Jewish Barbarism in Central Europe

The counter-narrative of barbarism was a reaction to a project that intended to assimilate the difference to ultimately annihilate it. The difficult path of German-speaking Jews that ended in the Holocaust was preceded by a lengthy debate entitled "The Jewish Question." The controversy centered on whether or not local Jews could relinquish or transcend their barbarism and become part of a useful citizenry for a state in formation. The popularity of the topic had reached its peak at the outbreak of the Holocaust when over three thousand titles were in the extended German-speaking markets. While other European powers, such as Britain and France, directed their racialization outwards, Germany—which did not possess colonies until the end of the nineteenth century—focused inward. The Jewish Question, became a "symbolic substitute" and a "practical preparation" of and for German colonial expansion. Several enlightened intellectuals and policy-makers, at the beginning of the period, trusted that local Jews could achieve a normative Western status. By the end of the period, however, it was clear that any achievement would be undermined by the descriptions of Jews in particular and the patterns of domination established by the coloniality of power/knowledge in general.[9]

Those who opposed Jewish emancipation rejected the possible "encounter" between the only civilized path and Jewish barbarism. During the eighteenth century the topic enjoyed high visibility in the debate. Orientalist and Jewish polemicists, Johann Andreas Eisenmenger and C. W. Grattenauer, for example, condemned Talmudic texts for being "barbarous" and Jews for "infringing all universal moral principles."[10] Biblical scholar Johann David Michaelis further rejected the incorporation of Jews by comparing them with other barbarians. In an age of rising colonialism, he first condemned Jews as a "Southern race" and promoted deportation of European Jews to more suitable spaces for colonized subjects (island colonies).[11] This project would not end here. In the path toward the final solution in World War II, the Third Reich retrieved this plan and considered transferring Jews to Madagascar. Michaelis also employed Orientalist rhetoric to associate Arabs and European Jews. Both groups were portrayed as uncivilized Semitic groups that resided outside history and were impervious to the passage of time. Interestingly enough, the description of Jews was more apt than the one of the Arab vis-à-vis a more traditional description of barbarism. Arabs could be excused for living retrograde lives because they inhabited uncivilized lands. In Michaelis's perspective barbaric Jews, on the contrary, live in Europe and therefore consciously reject civilization.[12]

The accusation of Jewish barbarism, however, was not limited to those who opposed Jewish incorporation into society. Several liberal and revolutionary intellectuals who supported Jewish emancipation still reproduced the barbaric connection between Jews and colonized people, paying particularly close attention to the connection between Jews and Arabs. Toward the end of the century, statesman Christian Wilhem von Dohm supported the "improvement" of Jews and the extension of citizenship to them. But he referred to Jews as "Asian refugees" and emphasized the innate barbarism of Jewish texts and customs. Idealist philosophers followed the same path: Kant qualified Judaism as a "Palestinian race" and Herder described the Jewish spirit as "Oriental." While the teacher Kant considers Jews unable to reach maturity and achieve autonomy from their barbaric system of morality, the student Herder asserted that this morality is particular to the Asian world and not to Europe. Discourses that included the typical barbaric accusations frequently found expression among the leading lights of Idealism. Descriptions of Jewish cannibalism included, inter alia, human sacrifices in the service of capital, inability to escape reified fantasies, and plotting to subvert civilization by controlling the resources of host nations; these tropes attained normativity in the writings of Ludwig Feuerbach, Bruno Bauer, and Richard Wagner. While they did not join forces with reactionaries opposing emancipation, the most important idealists and revolutionaries of the eighteenth and nineteenth centuries seemed to have a clear end for Judaism in mind. Influential idealists such as Hegel and Kant were as iconic as leading forces of the era. Hegel calls Jews a "living fossil" and "ghost race" and Kant calls directly for "euthanizing" the barbaric race.[13]

While conservatives espoused a strong anti-Semitic perspective, it is important to note that the most influential qualifications of Jews as barbarians were articulated by the liberal and revolutionary-spectrum of German-speaking individuals. If we employ local lenses, this situation reveals a tension. On the one hand, progressive German forces reproduced the construction of Jews as the archetypes of opposition to the German ideal. They were described as lacking the typical characteristics ascribed to Germans (i.e., rational individual autonomy and freedom of conscience). Especially in a context in which the nation (*Volksnation*) was not seen as a free and elective contractual association of individuals but rather as a macro-lineage bearing a common ethnic ancestry, Jews were seen as a perennial theat. On the other hands, for the same collective of intellectuals, the duty to civilize Jews became an opportunity to demonstrate and conclusively prove that their liberal values were indeed universal. If even the barbaric Jew could achieve Germaness, every individual (or what they qualified as individuals) was potentiality able to achieve the ultimate goal of civilization.[14]

If we read the same situation, however, through the lenses of the globalized narrative of barbarism, the contradiction can be reinterpreted. If the assimilation was a veiled resource, mobilized to justify the elimination of difference, the luck of German Jews is not a product of the irrationality of the tension, but rather the rationality of the modern/colonial project. Jewish philosophers, from Moses Mendelssohn to Hermann Cohen, may have struggled to present the strength of Jewish sources as a basis for German/Western citizenship.[15] Yet, the narrative of barbarism would prove that this negotiation stood in opposition to an underlying aim of the project. While Jews were forced to accept the unique path to civilization, the operational strength of the narrative would keep feeding Jewish representation as lacking Germaness and as a threat to the constitution of the nation-state. In the sixty years separating unification and the Holocaust this description only gained traction. In the inter-war era, just before Hitler rose to power, blame for the country's defeat was placed largely on the shoulders of the Jews. In a popular and widely accepted theory of the time, Jews were portrayed as "stabbing Germany in the back" as part of their barbaric plot of world domination. In pre-Holocaust Germany, assimilated Jews were incorrigible barbarians who were allegedly trying to destroy culture and civilization.

European Decolonial Judaism

Early in the emancipation process a majority of Jews saw no option but accepting the promise of what would become an assimilationist trap. Some nominally converted to Protestantism as a necessity in this new society. The famous poet and master of cynicism Heinrich Heine justified his conversion famously arguing that it was a "ticket of admission to European culture."[16] Others even tried to dissociate themselves from any connection with non-assimilable Jews engaging in intra-communal discrimination against Eastern European Jews.[17] Between the early debates and the turn of the twentieth century, German-speaking Jews embarked on a project of collective action in the pursuit of social advancement. The change in Jewish demographics was striking. Toward the last quarter of the nineteenth century, seventy percent of Prussian Jews lived in small villages; after only fifty years, eighty-five percent were living in large cities. Jewish urbanization was not limited to Prussia. In large Austro-Hungarian cities, such as Budapest, Jews comprised twenty-five percent of its two-hundred thousand inhabitants. This rapid increase was clearly evident in the regional demographic shift, but it was particularly significant in intellectual settings. While before the 1850s the presence of Jewish students in Prussian universities was very limited, toward the turn of the century they were one thousand percent over-represented in the student population. Many Jews radically changed their lives to achieve the emancipation on offer toward the end of the nineteenth century. The ultimate patters of domination, however, made this process of assimilation destined to fail.[18]

Toward the turn of the twentieth century the situation became more clear. The term anti-Semitism was coined at this time and anti-Semitic parties started to populate the German-speaking political arena. While most Jews would not renounce their abiding identification with German culture (*Kultur*), the discourse of integration came under attack. Cohen, the aforementioned Neo-Kantian leader of the school of Marburg, serves as a good barometer for these trends. For years he has advocated for a German-Jewish symbiosis and explained how a Kantian religion of reason had its ideal origins within Jewish scriptural sources. But he ultimately had to acknowledge the strong anti-Semitism persistent within the larger culture and concluded that "the trust" between German Christians and Jews "was broken."[19] Hegelian scholar Mortiz Goldstein expressed the same feeling very clearly: "We Jews are administrating the spiritual property of a nation." But the growing racism that limited structural changes "denies our right and our ability to do so."[20] Many Jews seemed very willing to pay their dues and assimilate to the alleged one path of development. The strength of the narrative of barbarism and their innate comprehension of their supposed racial incorrigibility would render this aspiration unattainable.

A large number of Jews, some consciously and others not, reacted to the resulting tensions of the German narrative that colonized Jews within central Europe. As noted above, the debates over Jewish emancipation reproduced patterns of colonialiaty and became a symbolic substitution and a practical preparation for German expansion. Simultaneous with these developments, Jews began to create a hybrid space by developing, many time unconsciously, a "sub-culture" that helped them navigate the transition between the ghetto and the presumably secular society. After eventually acknowledging the many impediments in this process, some started rebelling against the same society that had confined them to and rendered them intelligible within the narrative of barbarism. Several innovative cultural historians date these resistances to the middle nineteenth century and term this process the "revolt of the colonized."[21] Some Jews subverted European epistemology, using an existential European Jewish condition as their point of departure. Re-envisioning their barbarism was not a choice but a decolonial reaction to their intra-European colonization.

The local Jews who experienced and confronted a "cultural shock" between what was formally promised and what was actually delivered became known as "troublemakers." Another leading sociologist, arguably, defines local Jews as the "avant-garde" of the post-war "decolonized people."[22] As radical but also heretical Jews, they added themselves to the collectives of the colonized who were confronting the narrative of barbarism. These Jews were ideally positioned to become border thinkers. They had access to the intellectual tools of European society but understood the inherent systemic contradictions inscribed within their barbaric bodies. From this position of intellectual sophistication but social marginalization, they explored, comprehended, and theorized the contradiction that put their lives on a path that would culminate with the Holocaust. The formulation of a negative counter-narrative of barbarism can be understood, therefore, as a decolonial path formulated by border thinkers in order to challenge their racialization.

Preparing the Negative Counter-Narrative

Two heretical Jews, Karl Marx and Rosa Luxemburg, prepared the field for the irruption of the negative counter-narrative of barbarism during the Holocaust. They both elaborated these incipient first steps of the negative counter-narrative in debate with contemporary socialist alternatives. The first of these confrontations was Marx's disagreement with utopian socialism. In the nineteenth century, utopian socialists followed other European theorists and constructed evolutionary taxonomies that largely reproduced the Western narrative of barbarism and an illuminist reading of history. In this context the conception of spatial difference (with Jews portrayed as "Orientals") had temporal ramifications as the stage of barbarism was usually placed on the evolutionary trajectory following primitivism and preceding capitalism or socialism. While it could be argued that this was an attempt of European social theory to pave the way for the development of the non-Westerner, it was usually employed to justify not only the regnant social order, but also the immutable characteristics of racialized collectives frozen in time.

Charles Fourier was one of these social theorists and had a significant influence on Marx. He elaborated a model of seven evolutionary stages with barbarism right in the middle. The barbaric stage is described with political (despotism and conquest), sexual (oppression), and anthropological-economical (slavery) features. His understanding of Europe, however, provides a means to evaluate the narrative. On the one hand, like most of his contemporaries, he asserts that Europe is in a civilizing stage and explains that the use of the resources of colonialism is both reason and indicator of this economic advance. Employing a common theme in utopian socialism, Fourier argues that Europe fails in moral terms. The cruel face of colonialism made Europe regress toward (but not necessarily reach) barbarism: "[O]ur ships circumnavigate the globe only to initiate Barbarians and Savages into our vices, our excesses, and our crimes...causing Civilization to retrograde toward barbarism."[23] Fourier may admit that this colonialism is necessary to achieve a socialist utopia, but he questions the European ability to achieve the next stage in the evolutionary sequence if colonialism continues to cause it to regress.

While Fourier does exhibit a general, abstract sympathy for the suffering of the barbarians, not all populations contextually portrayed as barbarians receive a high degree of empathy. Fourier, for example, is not very sympathetic to "Mosaism" and declares it to be as dangerous as Islam. Both "races" belong to a pre-civilizing stage and are defined by characteristics resembling barbarism and patriarchalism. In particular, he rejects the integration of the "Jewish race" into European societies. Despite his presumed Humanism, he reflects that the incorporation of the Jewish "horde" with its "vicious principles" would "ruin the body politics." He solves the problem in the same way as many extreme anti-Semites who rejected emancipation. Well before any Western Zionist attachment to this discourse, Fourier proposes to relocate Jews to where they belong—Palestine. Despite Fourier's empathy for the suffering barbarians and his critique of European cruelty, Jews were still confined by their incorrigible barbarism.[24]

The incipient formulation of the counter-narrative, going beyond Fourier, can be found in the founder of scientific socialism. Marx was born in a Jewish household in 1818. A descendent of two prestigious rabbinical heritages from Western and Eastern Europe, his father, a lawyer, converted to Lutheranism as his *ticket of admission to European culture* one year before his son was born. It was not a free choice; in the early nineteenth century Jews were banned from practicing law in Prussia. His family, however, never fully embraced Christianity. While his father always pronounced his doubts about religion, his mother, who converted several years later, kept periodical ties with her extended eastern European rabbinical family.

Marx was deeply influenced by left-Hegelian debates and would develop one of the most influential of modern theoretical frameworks—dialectical materialism. Scholars have long discussed the Jewish context of his writings, the meaning of his attacks against Christianity in its religious and secular forms, the prophetic spirit of his work, and the interesting perspectives he elaborates in his central text discussing the reality of Judaism in the nineteenth century (*Zur Judenfrage*). In this section we do not aspire to identify Marx as a conscious Jewish writer, let alone a border thinker. It is not only that there are innumerable factors, including sociological and psychological, that make such an interpretation challenging. It is also that his dialectical materialism leaves little alternative spaces to the one allegedly "universal" path of Western development. We will rather read Marx using Deutscher's model of the heretical master. This will enable us to understand that Marx, aware of the philosophical shortcomings of Christian political theory and the capitalist system, made a perdurable contribution that enabled his followers to subsequently elaborate a Jewish negative counter-narrative of the term barbarism during the Holocaust.[25]

Early in his writings, Marx follows Fourier's reading of barbarism. Co-written with Friedrich Engels, the propagandistic work, *Manifest der kommunistischen Partei (The Communist Manifesto)* (1848), follows the utopian socialist critique of the new bourgeois society that, transforming the previous feudal stage (barbarism for Fourier), had "established new classes, new conditions of oppression... [and] simplified class antagonism... into two great hostile camps."[26] Fourier interpreted colonialism as the force that made the bourgeois society grow. More explicitly, it was the colonial extension of Europe in the Global South and the East that increased the exchange of commodities and catalyzed commerce and industry.[27] Up to this point, Marx and Engels follow Fourier's conception of barbarism as a stage in social evolution that finds its aggressive end in the colonial enterprise: "the bourgeoisie, by the rapid improvement of all instruments of production, by the immensely facilitated means of communication, draws all, even the most barbarian, nations into civilization."[28]

In the next twenty-five years, however, Marx makes an original contribution. He engages in this task by reflecting on the consequences of colonial conquests. Independent of the non-Jewish Engels, Marx challenges the illuminist reading of history to explain how European civilization became barbaric. In the first place, he explains how a political conqueror can be culturally conquered. In his journalistic writings about colonialism in India he notes that: "Arabs, Turks, Tartars, Moguls, who had successively overrun India, soon became Hinduized, the *barbarian* conqueror being, by an eternal law of history, conquered themselves by the superior civilization of their subjects."[29] Second, in his mature work, *Das Kapital* (*Capital*), he explains that those who can be culturally conquered are not only those with supposedly superior culture. The actions of Christian Europe over those whom they had called barbarians renders civilization, and not the peripheral people, barbaric:

> The discovery of gold and silver in America, the extirpation, enslavement and entombment in mines of aboriginal population, the beginning of the conquest and looting of the East Indies, the turning of Africa into a warren for the commercial hunting of black-skins, signalized the rosy dawn of the era of capitalist production. These idyllic proceedings are the chief phenomena of the primitive accumulation... the different moment of primitive accumulation distribute themselves now, more or less, in a chronological order, particularly over Spain, Portugal, Holland, France and England... [this is] brute force, e.g. the colonial system... Force is the midwife of every old society pregnant with a new one... of the Christian colonial system, M. Howitt, a man who makes a specialty of Christianity, says: "the barbarities and desperate outrages of the so-called Christian race throughout every region of the world, and upon every people they have been able to subdue, are not to be paralleled by those of any other race, however fierce, however untaught, and however reckless of mercy of shame, in any age of earth.[30]

Marx, of course, is not the first to reverse the term accusing the Christian West and not the colonized of barbarism. As noted above, there exist ample Spanish and French precedents of such a reversal and Marx, in this work, directly quotes a British Quaker historian when formulating his own. What is relevant is that his critique of political economy enables him to incorporate a challenge to the narrative of barbarism within one of the most important revolutionary European trends—socialism. Within this debate, Marx's counter-narrative goes one step beyond Fourier. The utopian socialist considered civilization cruel (moving toward but not yet barbaric) and the colonized barbarians as victims. Marx considers civilization as barbaric, and the colonized, at least in these writings, seem to be exculpated of barbarism.

The process is not yet complete; Marx still limits the barbarity of colonial/capitalist Christianity to its actions in "the periphery." The founder of scientific socialism, however, will also bring the accusation of barbarism to civilization in the center of Europe. To complete this picture we should turn to a belatedly discovered text, the *Ökonomische-philosophische Manuskripte* (*Economic and Philosophical Manuscripts*). In this text Marx protests against "the crude modes (and instruments) of human labor" that reproduced old Roman techniques of exploitation (such as the treadmill) in the continent.[31] Only three years later he returns to the same example in the text on *Labor and Wages*. In this essay he calls

Europe itself barbaric with respect to its treatment of people inside and not necessarily outside Europe. Commenting on the exploitation of the treadmill Marx writes that "Barbarism reappears, but created in the lap of civilization itself and belonging to it; hence leprous barbarism, barbarism as leprosy of civilization."[32] By then Marx had abandoned the accusation of peripheral people as barbaric and explains how the actions of civilization in both the colony and the metropolis make it barbaric. It is in this context of intra-European colonialism that he finally deems Europe (i.e., Christianity, civilization, capitalism) barbaric.

For Marx barbarism is a characteristic of the West and not of the victims it exploits both inside and outside of Europe. The only way to escape this barbarism is revolution on a global scale from the metropolis to the colonies. He argues that "the profound hypocrisy and barbarism of bourgeois civilization is unveiled before our eyes, turning from its home, where it assumes respectable forms, to the colonies, where it goes naked." For Marx the "bourgeois period of history" was not in vain. Still trapped by Eurocentrism, Marx points out that capitalism created a "material basis for a new world." This world will follow a "great social revolution." In the words of Rosa Luxemburg, it would be the choice of Socialism over Barbarism.[33]

Marx goes beyond utopian socialism. He represents a turning point in what will be a European Jewish counter-narrative of barbarism by portraying the center as barbaric for its action in the periphery. As the term barbarism changed, Jews, a people colonized in the metropolis (a Eurocentric reading of Judaism was presupposed), do not remain barbarians in Marx's portrayal either. Recall that for Fourier Jews are seen as retrograde people whose financial role does not allow them to engage in actual capitalist advancement. He describes Jews with one of the most important characteristics of barbarism: non-European parasitism.

Marx's position regarding Judaism has received lengthy attention by scholars, especially his reflections in the aforementioned *On the Jewish Question*. The text was a response to Bruno Bauer, an atheist theologian who was an older member of the Left-Wing Hegelians. Scholars usually emphasize one of two seemingly contradictory common interpretations. On the one hand, Marx seems to have written the text struggling with a Jewish context he was explicitly trying to disavow. His work, influenced by Jewish Utopian Socialist Moses Hess, was viewed with suspicion by non-Jews. In addition, he wrote the text at the time of his marriage to the daughter of a noble Protestant minister. On the other hand, the text, especially the second part, was understood as a landmark of Jewish self-hatred. In this section Marx explains that the God of the Jew is money and that the modern development of European society made it became Jewish. He argues that the Christianity that "arose from Judaism" will ultimately be "dissolved in Judaism."[34]

A careful reading of the first part, however, reveals a tension in Marx's work, and this is what Jewish intellectuals interested in the problem of barbarism will emphasize. Bauer presupposes a clear religious hierarchy in asking Jews to convert to Christianity as the only path to citizenship. Marx, however, rejects this hierarchy showing that the problem is not necessary Judaism, but religion as such. Marx explains that the liberation promised by the state, this "political emancipation," is limited. If the question about religious belonging arises, it is because the state is not truly secular, but rather a reification of Christianity. This is a state that "evangelizes" to incorporate an action that is not unfamiliar to Jews. In other words, assimilation and its subsequent hybridity is a trap.[35]

Here we find an implicit message to Jews (central European Jews) in Marx's words. If a state allows the religious discussion, Jews should pay attention because this is not complete liberation. Marx, as a son of a Jewish convert discussing the Jewish Question, can accept neither Bauer's evangelical request for conversion nor the full acceptance of Jews within the state. He discourages Jews from accepting the limited emancipation and advocates a real "human emancipation," one that cannot be granted by a state that is a religious reification. Only one year earlier, Marx declared this religion an "illusory happiness," "an inverted consciousness of the world," and the "opium of the people."[36] Now he declares that religion is the basis of a Christian evangelical state and Jews should not participate in this limited liberation. Toward the end of his life, as we have seen elsewhere, Marx would explicitly call this reified religion that evangelizes in the metropolis and the colonies barbaric.[37]

Marx represents a clear turn in the conception of barbarism and the place of the Jew with respect to Fourier's proposal. On the one hand, the Christian utopian socialist accuses the West of cruelty because of its actions over barbaric peoples. On the other hand, the Jewish scientific socialist understands that this cruelty, practiced in both the metropolis and the colonies, is what makes Christian Europe (and not the colonized peoples) retrograde and barbaric. For Fourier, the Jew is a commercial parasite who should not be granted emancipation. Marx, however, despite seemingly following Fourier in accusing modernity of being Jewish, shows the false pretension of the secularity of the state and advises Jews not to pursue a limited emancipation. Naturally there exist tensions in Marx's *oeuvre*. It is not only he universalizes central European Judaism and Western development as global Judaism and development. The central problem is that Marx is far from being a conscious Jewish writer and even less a straightforward barbaric thinker or decolonial intellectual. His contribution, however, is to start a lengthy trend within heretical Judaism that would categorize the center and not the periphery in Europe and the globe as barbaric.

In the next stage of the development of our concept within the Marxist Jewish tradition, the problem of barbarism as a description of the West will rise to prominence. Understanding the significance of barbarism in Marx's texts requires careful consideration. Rosa Luxemburg thoroughly excavated his texts and brought the discussion to critical attention. Luxemburg was born in 1871 to a Jewish family in a Poland under Russian control. After years of strong Marxist activism in Germany, she was murdered in Berlin in the aftermath of the (very heavily Jewish) Spartacist uprising in 1919.

Luxemburg is well known for her polemics against the late nineteenth- and early twentieth-century modifications of socialist doctrine informing the Russian Soviet revolution and the reformist social-democracy of Germany. Luxemburg opposed the professional revolutionary vanguard of the former, and she rejected the abandonment of the armed struggle by the latter. It is in the context of the German polemic that she made a lasting contribution to Western Marxism: the dichotomy of "Socialism and Barbarism." Luxemburg not only rediscovered the power of the counter-narrative of barbarism fifty years after its creation; she also found a place for Jews among the victims of capitalist barbarism.[38]

As explained above, Marx started to revise his conception of barbarism through a reconceptualization of his (illuminist) philosophy of history. Following this example, Luxemburg, in her article "Die Krise der Sozialdemokratie" ("The Crisis in the Social-Democracy") criticizes the role of the party in revising the conception of history espoused by the Social Democrats. According to the Social Democrats, there is a determinate and inflexible path of history culminating with the final socialist stage. They chose reform instead of revolution because they understood the path to be dialectically determined. In distinction to this deterministic reading of historical materialism, Luxemburg explains that "socialism will not fall as manna from heaven." Luxemburg believes the party has the responsibility to awaken consciousness. She urges the social democratic leadership to engage in the "long chain of powerful struggles" which will help the proletariat "become instead of a powerless victim of history, its conscious guide."[39] In other words, as Luxemburg contends, what will engender socialism is not reformist passivity in anticipation of class conflict, but rather the awakening of class-consciousness that accelerates class struggle.

For Luxemburg the lack of "progress" toward socialism was not merely an issue of the conservation of the status quo. If the Socialists were unable to raise class-consciousness and create the contextual conditions for the revolution, the world would fall into barbarism. Constraining alternatives within Western development, we should admit, she explains there are only two paths; Luxemburg writes, "capitalist society faces a dilemma: either an advance to socialism or a reversion to barbarism." Placing herself within a Marxist intellectual trajectory, she asks, "What does a 'reversion to barbarism' mean at the present stage of European Civilization?" Barbarism entailed the regressive destruction of culture that we find in imperial Europe: "at this moment, once glance around us will show what reversion to barbarism is bourgeoisie society... the triumph of imperialism leads to the destruction of culture... if the period of world wars which has just begun is allow[ed] to take its course to its logical end."[40]

Socialist forces, therefore, should make a decision. They can wait for socialism as if history is deterministic and become accomplices in the regression to barbarism. In other words they can choose to be responsible for the "the triumph of imperialism and the destruction of all culture." Alternately they can acknowledge the need to raise consciousness and create the conditions for the revolution through armed struggle. As she contends, the leaders ought to aspire to "the victory of socialism, that is, the conscious struggle of the international proletariat." Two years later, and shortly before being murdered by the right-wing "barbaric" forces that would shortly reappear in the Holocaust era, she became even more strident vis-à-vis the choice between Socialism and Barbarism. As such, she made it clear that "the future of culture and humanity depends on whether the proletariat throws the sword of revolutionary struggle."[41]

With Marx we witness a prevalent discourse that achieves normativity in Luxemburg's writings. Both make clear that barbarism is not a colonized peripheral ontology, and both understand it as a regressive path of Europe (i.e., Colonialism, Christianity, Capitalism) herself. As she establishes her position regarding barbarism, Luxemburg does the same with Judaism. Citing Marx's work, *Class Struggle in France*, she writes, "[t]he present generation is like the Jews who are led by

Moses through the wilderness. Not only must it conquer a new world; it must go under to make way for those who are equal to a new world." Surprisingly for some she declares, "We are truly like the Jews whom Moses led through the desert...we are not lost."[42] Again citing Marx, the historical Jews become the revolutionary, anti-barbaric model for Luxemburg. Unfortunately, she does not use the same model with respect to her contemporary Jews, at least in Europe. In a letter written at the same time as her aforementioned text, Luxemburg protests to a Jewish friend who was advocating solidarity with suffering Jews: "Why do you come with your particular Jewish sorrows? I feel equally close to the wretched victims of the rubber plantations in Putumayo, or the Negroes in Africa." She concludes asserting she has "no separate corner in my heart for the ghetto: I feel at home in the entire world wherever there are clouds and birds and human tears."[43]

Luxemburg makes two contributions to the incipient counternarrative on barbarism. In the first place, she follows Marx in understanding the inherently regressive barbarism of capitalist imperialism. At the same time, she goes beyond the founding father, making the alternative between barbarism and socialism the central aspect of her proposal. In the same text, and now naturally connected, the Jew appears as a model for liberation (so conceived by reference to an obscure quote by Marx). This can be read as the adoption of a Hegelian model that limits the entire Jewish contribution to antiquity. Nevertheless, it also can be read as the model to engage a socialist history based on Jewish sacred history. This final reading is complemented by the quote referenced above regarding solidarity with European Jewish suffering. Even though it is usually understood as Luxemburg's complete disassociation from Judaism, this is not the case when seen through the lens of the development of the concept of barbarism by non-Jewish Jews. Luxemburg understands the sorrows of the ghetto as an integral part of the human tears of colonized groups trapped in the narrative logic of barbarism. She similarly generalizes the experience of European Jews as the global Jewish experience.

In the development of negative barbarism, Jews went from representing barbaric parasitism for Fourier to becoming aspiring assimilationists for Marx to being another victim of Western barbarism for Luxemburg. Jews are not seen within barbaric civilization, but rather they are among the sufferers who, though not necessarily integral parts of the proletariat, are wretched victims of capitalist barbarism. While historical Jews could be considered emblematic of emancipation, contemporary "ghettoized" European Jews are now understood as among the oppressed who had the potential to become the "conscious guide" to liberation. Of course this liberation would still be predicated upon a (unique) Western path toward development. This is one of the specific problems the negative counter-narrative would challenge during the Holocaust.

The Negative Counter-Narrative

The Marxist Counter-Narrative finds its most articulate exponents in the collective (sometimes collaborative, sometimes conflictive) known as the Frankfurt School during the Holocaust. The latter is a nickname elaborated by circumstantial rivals for intellectuals belonging or related to the Institute for Social Research at Goethe University in Frankfurt. Founded in the 1920s, this was the first Marxist institute attached to a German university. The first generation directed the Institute between the 1930s to the 1960s, including periods of exile in Switzerland and America during the Second World War. Virtually all the members of the Institute were Marxist Jews who formulated a revitalized Western Marxist theory by exploring mass culture, the renewal of ideological reformulations of political economy, and the social mechanisms of inclusion/exclusion operative in post-liberal societies. The school, during times in which a fraction of Jewish blood would result in extermination the whole Jewish body in a gas chamber, retrieved Jewish scripture to fully develop the negative counter-narrative of barbarism.[44]

Walter Benjamin was born into a culturally assimilated bourgeois Jewish family in 1892. In 1940, he allegedly committed suicide fleeing from Nazi persecution on the French-Spanish border. During his lifetime Benjamin was admired by a very limited group of friends who were aware of his work, among them Bertolt Brecht, Gershom Scholem, and Hannah Arendt, but his path to fame—becoming a sort of postmodern celebrity in American academia—was posthumous. His work is located at the "crossroads," borrowing Lowy's formulation, of multiple trends and disciplines. He was a literary critic who renewed the study of Marxist aesthetics, but he was also a mystical writer who went beyond materialist analysis of class struggle. He was a neo-Romantic who passionately developed an alternative philosophy of history but also a sarcastic poet that offered some of the most articulate understandings of the limitations of universal consciousness powers. Overall, and perhaps more important for us, Benjamin offered a deep renewal of the Jewish counter-narrative of barbarism. He not only blamed the West and exculpated European Jews. As a border thinker, knowledgeable of both the barbarism of the West and the wealth of his tradition, he retrieved Jewish Messianic texts in order to challenge one of the most ingrained features of coloniality in general and the narrative of barbarism in particular, its teleological reading of history.

The text I introduce here is probably Benjamin's most overly cited work in the English-speaking academy. It is, however, rarely appreciated in its context and seldom viewed as a continuation of Luxemburg's counter-narrative. It is usually understood as a diffuse post-modern call for any ambivalent intellectual, and not as part of an evolving Jewish Marxist counter-narrative during the Holocaust. The text is found in thesis number seven of the essay entitled *Über den Begriff der Geschichte* and translated as "The Concept of History" or "Theses in the Philosophy of History." Following Luxemburg, Benjamin presents the problem of civilizational barbarism in the revision of his Marxist philosophy of history. While the incisive Luxemburg accuses Social Democrats of expecting "manna from heaven" because of their certainty of the socialist triumph, the sarcastic Benjamin criticizes the pretension of the "puppet called 'historical materialism'" that wins a priori each battle as if the game was pre-determined in favor of the Socialists.[45]

Benjamin makes the connection explicit by associating this critique with the ideas of the "Spartacist Group," co-founded by Luxemburg, which "have been objectionable to Social Democrats."[46] Benjamin's introduction of barbarism, however, goes beyond this critique of social-democratic triumphal inertia. He rejects all historicist approaches (not just the Marxist perspective) since they inevitably "sympathize with the victors." A teleological reading of history makes "all [the] rulers... the heirs of those who conquered before them." In his anti-historicist approach, Benjamin formulates a powerful critique in his notion of dialectical materialism. He muses that the "empathy with the victor invariably benefits the rulers." Benjamin argues that Marxists are well-acquainted with the meaning of these words: "whoever has emerged victorious participates to this day in the triumphal procession in which the present rulers step over those who are lying prostrate."[47]

Marx had already demonstrated the connection between Christian civilization and cruel barbarism. Luxemburg asserted that if barbarism arises with its retrograde culture, this automatically represents the destruction of any liberationist culture. Benjamin, writing at the end of the Second World War, takes the existence of a barbaric civilizational culture for granted. Following this reading of history, Benjamin understands that according to what he calls traditional practice or historicism, "the spoils are carried along in the procession...of the conquerors...They are called cultural treasures." Benjamin asserts that these cultural treasures are not simply products of the "great minds" that had formally authored them. They are also and especially in debt "to the anonymous toil of their contemporaries." In other words, what is considered civilization has only been built upon the blood of the anonymous vanquished.[48] It is in this context, and in a brilliant negative expression of the Marxist Jewish counter-narrative of barbarism, he declares:

> [T]here is no document of civilization which is not at the same time a document of *barbarism*. And just as such a document is not free of barbarism, barbarism taints also the manner in which it was transmitted from one owner to another. A historical materialist therefore dissociates himself from it as far as possible. He regards it as his task to brush history against the grain.[49]

In this portion of the text, Benjamin offers two conceptions that would prove to be deeply influential in post-war intellectual debates. First, the documents of civilization could not be composed without the cruelty of barbaric civilization. Second, if one seeks an alternative, the critic will need to read history against the grain. By doing so, and thereby discovering the forgotten sources of the vanquished that are not understood as documents, Benjamin finds a place for Judaism. These two elements, the barbarism of the center that forgets the vanquished who help construct its monuments and the need to discover the sources of the vanquished, will be shared by Levinas in our next chapter. Marx conceptualized Jews as both prototypes of modernity and also as modernity's victims. Luxemburg understood Jews as both victims (among other victims) and as representatives of a historically situated model for liberation. With these traditions in mind, Benjamin follows his proposal to read history against the grain as he formulates his understanding of Judaism.

Benjamin concludes his essay by retrieving negated Jewish experiences and knowledges. Against the procession of documents of civilization/barbarism, there is an alternative heritage that the vanquished pose: "like every generation that preceded us, we have been endowed with a weak Messianic power to which the past has a claim." Jews, according to Benjamin, "were prohibited from investigating the future. The Torah prayers instruct them in remembrance however."[50] While some classical rabbinical scholars may discuss the meaning behind the retrieval of messianic Judaism, Benjamin's presentation offers a restriction to the Christian teleological reading in history, a reading that may have been presupposed and reproduced by Marx and Luxemburg. Messianism, in contrast to the illuminist versions, does not intend to create a Messianic future of "homogenous, empty time." Benjamin writes that there is no preparation for the future since "every second of time was the strait gate through which the Messiah might enter."[51] Jewish Messianism, in the words of the border thinker, becomes a restrictive alternative to the Christian teleological mission. Redemption will not be achieved by the action of warfare but by the expectation of the unexpected that is beyond human teleological designs.

Benjamin, conscious of both sides of the reified colonial divide, decides to draw from the maxims of one of the vanquished and to thus present an alternative rationality that confronts Western barbarism. This option defies the hegemonic reading of history as a triumphal march that required, as we explored in the last chapter, the sublimation of all the dispossessed the West considered barbaric. Benjamin, during the Holocaust, is not only describing civilization as barbaric and incorporating Jews among the vanquished. He is also consciously making use of Jewish texts to demonstrate the futility of the conceptual framework that justified the annihilation of the alleged barbarians. In moments of complete polarity, when a simple fraction of Jewish blood condemned the whole body to total annihilation, Benjamin takes an alternative and more nuanced route. Discovering that the hybrid symbiosis was impossible, the border thinker retrieves the negative counter-narrative and modifies it anew. He not only, as Marx, identified Western civilization as barbaric and, like Luxemburg, incorporated Jews as one vanquished among the colonized. He also deploys Jewish Messianic texts as a defiance to the teleological reading of his history reproduced by coloniality and offers a restrictive alternative to a barbarism that in its forward march has categorized these sources as barbaric.[52]

Less than five years after Benjamin's suicide, the two luminaries of the Frankfurt school, Max Horkheirmer and Theodor Adorno, director and leading researcher of the institute respectively, completed the association of Jews with the opposition to barbarism. The former was a social scientist from an industrial family; the latter was a cultural critic and son of a mixed marriage. They led the Institute from the 1930s until the 1960s, including periods of exile in Switzerland and

America as well as the return to Germany in 1949. Their independent work includes a renewal of Marxist epistemology, the rise of a Freudian Marxism, the critique of cultural industry, the study of authoritarianism, and, perhaps more importantly, the elaboration of the method of negative dialectics. Their co-authored work, *Dialektik der Aufklärung* (Dialectic of Enlightenment), can easily be read as the most influential of their common work and their greatest contribution to the negative counter-narrative of the term barbarism.[53]

If in Benjamin's work Judaism is seen as the alternative to the barbarism of civilization, in Horkheimer' and Adorno's texts the central European Jewish experience is the prism through which it is possible to reflect on the "advance" to this civilizational barbarism. *Dialectic of Enlightenment: Philosophical Fragments*, was written "from America" where the critical theorists were in exile during the Holocaust and "the book is shaped by the social conditions in which it was written."[54] This text marks a turning point for the Frankfurt School in general and the two authors in particular.

The role of barbarism in the argument is central from the very early pages of the work. The critical theorists attempt to explain why during the Holocaust humanity was not entering a "truly human state" (i.e., either democracy or socialism), but was rather "sinking into a new kind of barbarism." While the first chapter of the work ("Begriff Der Aufklarung"/"The Concept of the Enlightenment") aims to uncover the conditions of this new barbarism, the fifth section (entitled "Elemente des Antisemitismus"/"Elements of Anti-Semitism") "engages with the reversion of enlightened civilization to barbarism in reality." In other words, while the first chapter traces the development of scientific and social thought, and how it betrayed the project of liberation and sank into barbarism, the fourth explains, through the Jewish case, how this "barbaric irrationalism" took place in history. The records of Jewish history became, as previously in the other versions of the negative counter-narrative, the framework through which the new barbarism was denounced.[55]

According to Horkheimer and Adorno, modernity promised liberation. As developed in the aforementioned first essay of the work, "the Enlightenment's program" a priori represented "the disenchantment of the world."[56] The project's aim was to acquire the necessary knowledge to avoid dependence on external forces to and finally establish one master of nature: the human being. This quest for knowledge, however, was also one for possession, "which is power" and "knows no limits." In the attempt to gain control over all nature and soon enough all human beings, the enlightenment reduces everything to a formula and excludes what is not calculable or assimilatable. In other words, it "amputates the incommensurable," that which cannot be reduced to unity.[57]

In Horkheimer and Adorno's words barbaric modernity attempts to possess all that cannot be assimilated to this basic unit. The difference is initially considered with "suspicion." When it proves impossible to incorporate, it is "exterminated." The same ideological process that leads to mathematical formulation, therefore, is ideologically linked to the mechanization of death, the Holocaust.[58] The myth of modernity—the promise of permanent progress and the equality of people—is based on this structure of forced assimilation and ultimate extermination of foreign elements. Paradoxically, the attempt to disenchant the world became not only a new enchantment but also a "fraud." This fraud leaves the "rational organization in the hands of the utterly enlightened," the civilized capitalist, "as they steer society toward *barbarism*."[59]

Horkheimer and Adorno explore fascism, their contextual threat, within a rationalization that permits the repression and the regression to barbarism. They follow and extend an orthodox Marxist interpretation: fascism as the logical extension of the barbarities of the Marxian Christian race, Luxemburgian capitalist liberalism, and Benjaminian civilization. Adorno and Horkheimer write:

> Enlightenment throughout the liberalistic period has always sympathized with social coercion...The horde a term which doubtless is to be found in the Hitler Youth Organization, is not a relapse into the old barbarism but the triumph of repressive egalité, the degeneration of the equality of rights into the wrong inflicted by equals. The fake myth of fascism reveals itself...blind to its victims...that has been the trajectory of European civilization.[60]

Once again, recalling Marx, the European Christian and National Socialist civilization is seen as committing barbaric outrages that are an integral part of its development. It is not a regression but an illuministic advancement to barbarism. The Jews are mentioned once and again throughout the diverse essays but they are central in the fifth (*"Elements of Anti-Semitism: Limits of the Enlightenment"*).[61] In the essay, Horkheimer and Adorno follow their analysis of National Socialist ideology to explore the limits of the barbaric European civilization. As with Marx, the (central-European) Jew in this context becomes the witness and suffering subject of the Enlightenment's limits. The authors' analysis applies not only to the context of the Holocaust, but also to the American dualist, racial society that the US government would reinforce soon after the war by incorporating Jews into the white and Western society. Fully aware of this context, the critical theorists write:

> Race today is the self-assertion of the bourgeoisie individual, integrated into the barbaric collective. The harmonious society to which the liberal Jews declared their allegiance has finally granted to them in the form of a national community. They believed that only anti-Semitism disfigured this order, which in reality cannot exist without disfiguring human beings. The persecution of the Jews, like any persecution, cannot be separated from that order.[62]

The European internal racialization, however, is weighted differently according to its context. Jews and only Jews (well, only European Jews) become the test case for the racialization that enables the systemic reification. Horkheimer and Adorno contend that according to fascism, "the blacks must be kept in their place, but the Jews wiped from the face of earth...in the image of the Jew which the racial nationalist holds up before the world they express their own essence." In other words, it is "in the face of the Jews," and only in the European Jewish face, that "the harmony of the nation is established."[63] Far from being a novel idea, however, Horkheimer and Adorno are simply following the trajectory of Marxist theory to its logical extension. While Marx recommended Jews not to pursue an inauthentic liberation, Luxemburg located Jews among other sufferers, and Benjamin considered Jews an alternative among the vanquished, Horkheimer and Adorno understand the fate of the Jews as a litmus test by which to gauge and crucially assess the limitations of the enlightened project. At this point the negative counter-narrative has been successful in inverting the term, attaching it to the West, and finally considering Jews the victims and not the perpetrators of barbarism.

Up to this point, modernity is understood as barbaric with Jews as its central victims. The border thinkers, however, also follow Benjamin by re-purposing negative Jewish texts as an alternative to the criminality of the West. It is unsurprising that the same Jews who have been exiled by the forces of mythical reification turn to the persecuted tradition as a way to confront their annihilation. Marx had already denounced the modern state as a barbaric reification of Christianity; these two scholars now explain that Western regimes, from the French revolution to the Third Reich, were simply social reifications that self-righteously follow a superior call from God (God-reason, God-nature, or God-*Volk*) to justify their programs of conquest and extermination. This plan, according to Horkheimer and Adorno, is a barbaric "illusion"—it is a reification that attempts to pass "falsity as God, the finite as the infinite, the lie in truth."[64]

Jews, by contrast, are the central victims of this barbaric system. They are not, however, simply passive victims. Having been oppressed by this reification, they possess the resources to confront this "illusion." According to the Horkheimer and Adorno, Jews tried to destroy the myth by postulating the "prohibition on uttering the name of God." In other words, by rejecting the possibility of justifying criminal atrocities on behalf of God, they undermine the reified self-righteousness of European Christianity. The salvation for the West lies in the effective "extermination" of the difference justifying this quest with the superior call. For Jews, however, "salvation lies in the rejection of any faith" that reifies a call and justifies its crimes answering to its own false claims.[65] It is no coincidence that all Marxist Jews, from Marx to Horkheimer/Adorno via Luxemburg and Benjamin, make of this rejection of barbaric reification their central critique. The difference, however, is that the Holocaustic counter-narrative engages with this task by retrieving Jewish maxims that act as a restriction to Western barbaric designs.

The Frankfurt school became successful in fully developing a strategy of subversion practiced by Jewish Western Marxism. This counter-narrative retains the valence of the term and while predicating it of Western formations, exculpates Jews of barbarism. In the last stages of the counter-narrative, Jews even appear as alternatives to Western triumphalism(s). This negative counter-narrative, however, contains the problems we have enumerated throughout the chapter.

There is one central limitation I would like to identify at the conclusion of this chapter. During the Holocaust the school seems to go beyond the ratification of a unique path to development as described in earlier versions. The school nonetheless conflates the experience of European Judaism with normative Judaism and the European Jewish experience as the quintessential, canonical genocide. This particular orientation leads the school to construe the project of enlightenment as a project of liberation that tragically turned into barbarism. They thus overlook the fact that the process was not the logical entailment of a post-eighteenth century dialectical development. It was, on the contrary, a long-standing process which had attempted to actually subjugate and eliminate the barbarians since early modernity. This hermetic Eurocentrism and broad isolation from a dialogue with other voices restricts the perspective of the Frankfurters and makes their sociological perception limited. They do recover an alternative Jewish perspective, but can be seen just as a restriction to the Western model and not as a potential creative reclamation of the term barbarism.

It is important, however, to qualify this critique for two reasons. In the first place, we must acknowledge that a retrieval of the term barbarism in 1940s Germany would have been difficult. National Socialism proactively sought to recover pre-Christian traditions and there are alleged stories of movement leaders retrieving the term (although those versions are usually considered as frauds).[66] In the second place, the Frankfurters, loyal to the counter-narrative, quickly recognized the suffering of other collectives beyond the Jewish case. It is clear there were sensitive to other racializations and, following the previous steps of the narrative, exhibited a deep solidarity with them.

The problem is not that the term was not retrieved nor the ignorance of the suffering of racialized groups. The problem is that the privilege accorded the canonical genocide leads them to overlook the origins of the process and fully comprehend its ultimate dynamics. The solution they develop, a negative restriction to Western discourses, assumes the dialectical nature of the historical development. For this reason, it is no surprise they opt for a negative restrictive appraisal instead of a positive alternative to the West. But if the process is read before the formation of the nation-state, the dialectical reading of history is perforce challenged. The process was from the very outset a genocidial project that was many times represented in a humanist persuasion. Before continuing this critique, it is first necessary to explore the reasons that lead the other two projects to positively re-appropriate the term barbarism and analyze whether they are able surpass the limitations of the negative counter-narrative. Only then will we have the opportunity, at the book's conclusion, to analyze not only the possibility and limitation of the negative counter-narrative but also its provocative retrieval in the twenty-first century Global South.

CHAPTER 4

Transitional Barbarism: Levinas's Counter-Narrative and the Global South

Post-war Paris was a popular locus of congregation for intellectuals affected by the wounds of coloniality. During the period of political decolonization, border thinkers across the barbaric networks engaged in lengthy debates and subverted the discourses that racialized their communities. Jews were not foreign to these discussions. Lithuanian Emmanuel Levinas, arguably one of the most important Jewish philosophers of the twentieth century, made a seminal contribution to the debate. Despite the distance he routinely took from the existentialist Marxism that was permeating society, he adopted a conventional negative counter-narrative in his early writings. That is, the Eastern European social theorist inverted the traditional use of barbarism, preserving the negative valence of the term. He thus blamed the West for the atrocities committed against the alleged barbarians, exculpated Jews from these accusations entirely, and mobilized Jewish thought as an alternative. His late career, however, marks a significant turning point as he came to strongly support a second alternative, a positive counter-narrative of barbarism.[1]

This transition between the positive and negative counter-narratives was not unanticipated. It was the result of his profound encounter and engagement with the social theory emerging from the Global South. Levinas was not new to developments within the fluidly delineated colonized regions. For decades he was the director of an institution that was in charge of inculcating universal French values in the next generation of Jewish Maghrebi intellectuals. It is possible to locate incipient traces of a re-evaluation of the colonial implications of this universality during this early period. His personal sea change, however, took place after he left his post, assumed a formal university position, and entered into conversation with another decolonial discourse, Latin American Liberation Philosophy. Following encounters in the early 1970s, Levinas was challenged by a group of South American intellectuals. He then expanded his critique of the West, mobilized the positive conception of barbarism from his new conversation partners, and recognized that the future of humanity resided in the barbaric margins of the West. He rubricated his turn by employing Talmudic texts to explain the need to form a large community of barbarians. This new community would be instrumental in challenging criminal imperial formations represented symbolically by Rome and contextualized as Europe and the United States.

As we shall examine below, his readings contain problematic tensions and contradictions. One of them will be of particular interest for our work. I am referring to the manner in which he chooses to integrate Jews to this barbaric decolonial community. Throughout his career, including this last stage, Levinas sustained a consistently positive position vis-à-vis the state of Israel. For Levinas, the Jewish state in the Middle East represented an opportunity to practice the social law that Jews had been cultivating for centuries. Following this understanding of the role of the Jewish state, he insisted that the integration of Jews within this barbaric collective should be accomplished via this particular political entity. This plan of integration, formulated just a year before a first Intifada overwhelmingly supported by Global South networks, would prove difficult. It is not simply that other colonized peoples would regard this enterprise as suspicious at best and nakedly imperialistic at worst, but it is also—as we shall see later in this book—that the State of Israel, with all its internal complexity, repeatedly reproduced a traditional narrative of barbarism. As a consequence, there existed a tension in Levinas's proposal between his support for a decolonial project and the manner in which he opted for the integration of Jews within the project.

This tension is more readily understood when we consider the personal transformation he underwent in his early work. His pre-1970s writings, especially his denunciation of Western crimes, were highly influential among intellectuals of the Global South. This may come as a surprise to many given that, as critics have pointed out, his particular critique smacked of Eurocentrism and racism. During this period Levinas had explicitly modeled history on a Western framework and understood the European Jewish people to constitute the paradigmatic instance of historical victimization. He complemented this reading by describing Third World inhabitants as threatening masses that were unable to furnish any meaningful contribution to humanity. In his late work, however, Levinas significantly modified these stances. He began to recognize the potentiality of a multiplicity of colonial voices outside the West and placed his hope for the future of humanity in them. He went as far as including the Jewish people in a decolonial community that both struggled against criminal imperial formations and which created human dispossession and misery itself. This observation raises an important question. Is his decolonial integration of Jews through Israel a trace of his early Eurocentrism or does it represent his inability to acknowledge the changing role of Jewish political powers during the second half of the twentieth century?

The exploration of Levinas's project, his transition and its limitations, illuminates much more than Levinasian philosophy. Given his ascendance in Jewish thought, Levinas represents a privileged social informant of Post-Holocaust Judaism. He is a seminal Jewish philosopher who, influenced by Global South thinking, re-evaluated the place of Judaism across the globe and, as a border thinker, repositioned Judaism in a barbaric decolonial community. Levinas's change enables readers to reflect on the possibilities of a decolonial project that blurs geographical boundaries and emerges from a mixed Northern location in dialogue with the Global South. It can similarly help to explain the limitations of this enterprise. It raises questions about the potentiality of European intellectuals to understand both the provincial dead ends of their proposals and the changing racial nature of Jewish politics.

Local Narrative

The encounter of Levinas and other border thinkers with the narrative of barbarism arises from a multiplicity of histories of racialization and dispossession. In metropolitan France, the narrative of Jewish barbarism has been a recurrent fixture for nearly three centuries, roughly spanning the French Revolution and the French May. This is not to say that the history of Jews in metropolitan France or the colonies in the Maghreb can only be read through the history of barbaric victimization. But what makes this narrative distinctive is that in every century, Parisian society was divided over this debate. This is one of the local frames of references that the intellectuals would re-interpret enabling a simultaneous reflection on both Post-Holocaust and

Postcolonial legacies. Levinas, like many other intellectuals affected by the patterns of domination of the coloniality of power/knowledge, will respond to this local history with resources furnished by networks within colonized locations.

The narrative of Jewish barbarism in this context can be traced to pre-1789 developments. In the years immediately preceding the French Revolution, enlightened intellectuals allegedly paved the way for a radical epistemological challenge to the theological and political values associated with the *Ancien Régime*. An ardent champion of individual freedom, equality, and the separation of Church and State, François-Marie Arouet, better known by his *nomme de plume* Voltaire, was an exemplary figure within the French revolutionary vanguard. In the spirit of the new Humanism he even wrote an acclaimed essay advocating religious tolerance in 1755. He expressed his views on Jews in an entry of his 1764 *Dictionnaire philosophique* (Philosophical Dictionary) that is rarely translated in English editions of the book. The views he articulates in this entry reveal the extent to which he subscribed to a very modern/colonial narrative of barbarism.

Voltaire accused Jews of virtually all the evils commonly associated with the trope of barbarism. These stereotypes included Jews as cold-blooded murderers, systematic and surreptitious thieves of the wealth of nations, anarchical agitators against legitimate authority, sexually depraved and parasitic vagabonds. Voltaire is incredulous that this people managed to survive historical oblivion and justifies all of the persecution Jews suffered from antiquity to modernity. While he suggests that a modern rational individual should not "burn them," as the "medieval man" had done before, he succinctly summarizes his distaste in the following terms: "In short we find in them only an ignorant and barbarous people, who have long united the most sordid avarice with the most detestable superstition and the most invincible hatred for every by whom they are tolerated and enriched."[2]

Voltaire's narrative on Jewish barbarism was as influential as his struggle for individual rights. The late eighteenth, nineteenth, and twentieth centuries witnessed adaptations of his famous indictment. In each period the narrative of Jewish barbarism represented a source of social division within French society. The question always centered on the extent to which Jews could leave behind their alleged barbarism. With high public visibility in the debate among public intellectuals, the Jewish question became a key litmus test of the fraternal universality espoused in French Humanist discourse during the height of its colonial period.[3]

While in the late eighteenth century the National Assembly presumably granted early citizenship to all human beings under the Declaration of the Rights of Man and Citizen, controversy over the conferral of personhood and civil rights to minority populations persisted. While some revolutionary factions understood this extension of rights to naturally include Jews (or Subsaharan Afrians), others stridently opposed this interpretation. The rhetorical posture of the latter often reproduced Voltairian and other anti-Semitic discourses which conflated Jews with barbarians. Jews were accordingly portrayed as uprooted "vagabonds" who, if accepted into society, would only foment discord and "butcher" others in their unrelenting pursuit of wealth. It took four months of very heated debate to reach a decision. A moderate compromise articulated the words that later iterations of liberal French discourse would mobilize to describe the relationship between France and its minorities: "The Jews should be denied everything as a nation." As a community, the Jewish people would still be considered barbaric. But if Jews were to leave the communal resources, they were promised to be granted individually "everything as citizens."[4]

In the late nineteenth century, however, these "fundamental" rights were denied at the individual level as well. Various constituencies crystallized around the defining legal case of the turn of the century. Alfred Dreyfus, an assimilated Jewish officer in the French army, was accused of treason, found guilty, and subsequently demoted, and imprisoned in a colonial location. Despite the fact that investigations found he was innocent, half of French society fervently supported his imprisonment and the continuation of legal action during the twenty years the affair played out in the public arena. Voltaire's definition of Jewish barbarism resonated throughout this case. The Jew, now stripped from communal resources, was popularly conceived as a "deceiver," interested in his or her own monetary gain, and "betraying" the nations that generously integrated him or her. The leaders of the anti-Dreyfusard party, led by Edouard Drumont and Charles Maurras, portrayed Dreyfus and Jews as incorrigible barbarians consciously plotting to destroy the French state. The intellectual defense of Dreyfus was preeminently presented by the poet and journalist Émile Zola. In his famous manifesto *J'accuse* he demanded the president of France to review the case making clear that Dreyfus was not condemned for his actions. He was a sacrificial "victim" of a persuasive and pervasive "obsession" of the society for the "dirty Jew" who was allegedly polluting the social fabric and threatening the purity of the nation.[5]

In the second half of the twentieth century, France was once again divided over discussions of Jewish barbarism. This time it was a political event that immediately precipitated the controversy. In late 1960s students and workers united to oppose the forces of systemic oppression. They declared a general strike and marched in opposition to the whole representative system, including the Gaullist government, the radical opposition (PCF, *Parti communiste français*) and the central Union (CGT – *Confédération générale du travail*). More than two-thirds of the French working force supported the strike. Among the leaders of the revolt, a young student whose parents were Jewish German refugees, Daniel Cohn-Bendit, rose to fame. The anarchist known as *Danny le Rouge (Danny the Red)*, became a symbol of the struggle, especially when he was denied entrance to France after a brief propagandistic trip out of the country.

The division between pro-revolutionaries and anti-revolutionaries soon helped to re-stimulate discussion about Jewish incorregibility. The anti-revolutionaries reanimated the caricature of Jews as anarchic agitators who betray the common good of a civilized society that generously tried to integrate them. Under the slogan "Cohn-Bendit à Dachau!" ("Cohn-Bendit to the concentration camp of Dachau!") this political faction delineated the barbaric ancestry of the revolt and advocated the completion of the Holocaust to complete the universal de-judification of society. In response, the revolutionary forces coined the slogan "Nous sommes tous des Juifs allemands" ("We are all German Jews") dividing French society once again over the Jewish question. This time, however, the liberal motto was expanded in its consideration of Jews as a community of sufferers and not only as individual people. Paradoxically this identification would start acknowledging the integration of Jews, this time not only European Jews, into civilization.[6]

Post-war Counter-Narrative

Jewish barbarism was a key source of division in modern French history. The final articulation and acceptance of a Jewish corporate identity was paralleled by a radical demographic change within this community. While Paris was known for hosting Jewish refugees before the Second World War, most historically established French Jewries were annihilated by either French collaborators or German occupiers. By the 1960s, Jews who had either fled their territories of origin or were children of those who fled constituted two-thirds of the entire Jewish population within France. This new Jewry was composed not only of Central and Eastern European Jews who escaped Nazism and the Soviet orbit but also of a sizeable population with origins in Muslim and Arab regions. The largest immigrant group fled the new decolonized countries of the Maghreb, while a minority originally hailed from Egypt and the Middle East.[7]

This generation inherited both the accusations of barbarism and the Marxist counter-narrative we explored in the previous chapter. This narrative reversed the accusation of barbarism deeming Western imperial formations as barbaric and exculpating Jews in the process. Within this context, barbarism retained its negative valence, and was simply applied to entities or discursive formations such as colonial Christianity (Karl Marx), capitalism (Rosa Luxemburg), civilization (Walter Benjamin), or the enlightenment (the tandem Theodor Adorno and Max Horkheimer). These readings were anything but foreign to this new young generation.

An analysis of the 1968 protest movement bears witness to the significant participation of Jews operating within a Marxist political framework. A cursory glance at the leadership of the revolutionary groups provides a clear idea of the engagement of this generation with radical politics. One of the most respected and active revolutionary organizations was the *Trotskyist Ligue Communiste Revolutionnarie* (LCR). Its leadership (politburo) was comprised of twelve members, eleven of whom were of Eastern Jews of stateless origin and one Maghrebi Jew. One of the most radical organizations, the *La Gauche Proletarianne* (GP) was led by two Jews, one stateless European and one Egyptian Jew. The phenomenon of Jewish overrepresentation within these radical movements has been analyzed elsewhere.[8] Of importance here is simply the fact that this young generation of Jews, whether from Eastern Europe or colonies in Muslim countries, engaged very actively with Marxism.

As integral part of their Jewish-Marxist tradition of systemic struggle, these revolutionary movements also mobilized the negative counter-narrative of barbarism. The voices emerging from this movement showed increasing concern about the "anti-Semitism" that arose from Fascism during the Second World War and Gaullist French period. This is why one activist declared that "For [him] the famous phrase of Rosa Luxemburg 'Socialism and Barbarism' is a reality in our times..." The activist goes on to explain that anti-Semitism as a form of racism was going to "disappear" after a choice was made "to favor socialism" over the barbarism of capitalism and imperialism. Socialism was understood as a means by which to formulate a counter-narrative of barbarism.[9]

A variety of sources connected the pre-war German and post-war French Jewish revolutionaries. Paris, for example, became a center of re-reading traditional Marxist theory. The influential journal entitled *Socialisme ou Barbarie* was published from early in the post-war era until the middle of the 1960s, while the Jewish anthropologist Lévi-Strauss —still in his structuralist stage—declared to UNESCO that "the first barbarian is the man who believes in barbarism."[10] Overall, what is clear is that both the Marxist legacy and counter-narrative of barbarism was still very much alive in this period of radical effervescence that critically contemplated questions pertaining to class and identity struggles.[11]

Emmanuel Levinas

Living most of his life in post-war France, Emmanuel Levinas exemplified the new local Jewry, immersed in both the narrative and counter-narrative of barbarism. On the one hand, he was like so many Eastern European Jews who had lost the world of their childhood along with most of their families in the Holocaust. Born in Kaunas, Lithuania, he later settled in France, where he obtained citizenship, and fought for the French army during the Second World War. He was imprisoned in a POW camp where he was separated from his comrades as a Jew while his birth family was being murdered in Lithuania and his wife and daughter were in hiding in Paris. After the war he became one of the most prominent representatives of a cultural phenomenon known as "Vilna in the Seine."[12] This refers to a reconstituted Eastern European Jewish community that was thoroughly permeated with radical potentials. It simultaneously subscribed to the Enlightenment values that consider Judaism barbaric and the deep knowledge associated with Talmudic sources.

In another capacity Levinas was charged with the education of the successive waves of Maghrebi Jews descending on Paris for pedagogical training. After the Holocaust Levinas considered the recovery of Jewish vitality a particular "mission" and understood North African Jewish communities as affording a particularly promising cultural opportunity by which to embark on such an enterprise. For more than twenty years after the end of the war he was the director of the *École Normale Israélite Oriental* (ENIO) of the *Alliance Israélite Universelle*. The school's mission statement was to train the leaders of the future North African Jewish communities in universalist French values. He witnessed the period of decolonization and accounts of his life report his own changes through the contradictory feeling this process engendered among his students. His re-envisioning espistemological efforts to train future leaders for the North African communities were soon recognized. Descriptions of Levinas as "one of their own" by Parisian Maghrebis abound in his biographical narrations.[13] Levinas was, therefore, was able to situate himself at the intersection between the two communal worlds that comprised post-war French Jewry: Eastern European survivors of the Holocaust and Maghrebis engaging in the process of exploration of the meaning of intellectual and political decolonization. Not surprisingly the committee that established *L'Institut d'études lévinassiennes* (The Institute of Levinasian Studies) was integrated exclusively by Jews with biographical ascendance in North Africa and Eastern Europe (yet, as we shall see later, the racial re-classifications of Jews did not make this enterprise as promising as it sounds).[14]

While Levinas did not belong to the 1968 revolutionary generation (he was over sixty at that point), he ultimately became an inspiration for many of them. Describing his youth in Eastern Europe, he claimed that he "didn't remain indifferent to the temptations of the Leninist revolution, to the new world which was about to come."[15] In this way it is not surprising to see that he reproduces what was originally (albeit not exclusively) a Marxist counter-narrative of the term barbarism.[16] He nonetheless went beyond Marxism. He criticized the Marxist enterprise as totalitarian, compared the concepts of Marxist and Jewish revolutions, and related anecdotes in which he expresses frustration with the Marxism espoused by his students. In addition, he goes beyond the narrative of barbarism because he gestures toward something else discursively and substantively at stake in the discussion.

At the center of Levinasian thought, however, were issues distinct from those of Marxist Jews from Central Europe. As a border thinker his engagement with Enlightenment values did not a priori reject peoples and discourses that were largely considered barbaric by modernity. While Marxists either rejected Judaism *tout court* or accepted some select elements thereof, Levinas was able to engage with an alternative corpus that positively regarded the sources discarded by the West. For some commentators Levinas became one of the heirs of the vanished worlds of both Eastern Europe and the Maghreb. The capacity to see through the multiple lenses of extant communities that represented the remnants of annihilated worlds allowed him to experience the many possibilities that alternative or marginal locations of knowledge could afford. While he was deeply committed to re-envision the educational structure that was traditionally a medium of Humanist colonialism, his identification with North African Judaism should be taken with extreme caution. This stage of his thought remains largely understudied. What can be suggested, however, is that this early experience may have helped Levinas to go beyond his Eastern European background and ultimately create a transition beyond the negative Eurocentric counter-narrative of barbarism.

Eurocentrism and Negative Barbarism

The description of Levinas as occupying a global progressive space may not be a surprise for those acquainted with his philosophy. It is not uncommon to see academic introductions to his thought describing him as a champion of racialized voices. As such it is not unpredicted to see how some interpreters construe Levinas's programs as a coherent project and attempt to apply his ethics to a wide-array of global problems. Levinas, at first blush, occupies a rare subject position. He is a philosopher from Europe who, because of his Eastern background working with Magrhebi students, has the potential to transcend the Eurocentrism we explored in our previous chapter.[17]

A cursory glance at his philosophy supports such a contention. At its core, Levinas's project centers on a scathing critique of the consequences of Western egocentrism and narcissism. He finds a common thread in the proclamation of "a humanist ideal" that is reproduced in the philosophy of history spanning "Parmenides to Heidegger." This humanist ideal is achieved by "ignoring the vanquished, the victims, and the persecuted, as if they were not significant." Levinas argues that the epistemology underlying this strain of Western thought is ontology, or "thinking of Being." Levinas accuses the West of focusing on the desires of the narcissistic Self, while ignoring the consequences that conquerors' triumph could have for the other. It logically follows that alterity cannot be tolerated and must be eradicated. Such eradication can be accomplished by either attempting to kill the other in the other (i.e., assimilation), or when this process fails, by killing the other directly (i.e., genocide).

Levinas offers several examples to explain this situation in the context of Jewish life. In the European context, Jews were forced to assimilate and when their barbaric character subsequently rendered their full integration impossible, they were exterminated. Levinas therefore rejects ontology as the first philosophy and replaces it with ethics, defined as an interpersonal orientation in thinking involving a Self and an Other. The attack against Selfhood may appear to conflict with the dialectical materialism of Marxism. Both philosophies, however, try to understand the potentiality of the voice of the oppressed: the proletariat for Marxism and "the other" for Levinas. As a result it is not surprising that Levinas's readings on barbarism do not a priori differ from the Marxist perspective. For Marxists the Empire/Europe/Enlightenment is barbaric. Levinas, who identifies the same subjects with Self or Being, agrees and adds that the "civilization that accepts Being—with the tragic despair it contains and the crimes it justifies—merits the name 'barbarian.'"[18]

Levinas's ethical project sounds promising. It represents a perspectival shift in the history of philosophy—theretofore a history of Being—to the history of the vanquished (or, the history of the other). At the same time one wonders whether the reproduction of the old counter-narrative on barbarism is an indication of his inability to dispense with the idealist structures of European thought. Several critics have pointed out that Levinas not only fails to abandon Eurocentric lenses but also falls into a reproduction that even Marxists were successful at avoiding. Some of these commentators have pointed out that Levinas does defend alterity, but he reduces it to the intra-European other (the European Jews) and ignores the wounds of coloniality and the suffering of the non-European difference. Some go one step further demonstrating that Global South thinkers influenced by Levinas also tend to fall short of their potentialities because of this oversight. Furthermore, radical critics have questioned the relationship between this centralization in the Jewish case and the post-1945 role of Jews in the global arena. In other words, they question whether Levinas's elevation of the Jewish experience as the paradigmatic case of suffering represents a veiled Western "theological justification" on behalf of the "colonial" state of Israel.[19]

While Levinas's philosophy has the potential to overcome Eurocentric readings, critics have plenty of textual evidence to help sustain accusations of provincialism and prejudice. During the interwar period, for instance, Levinas defended the integrity of (a very early) "Jewish-Christian civilization" against intra-European "barbarism."[20] In the early 1960s, he contended that one of the major problems facing modern Jewish thought was the need to account for the "underdeveloped Afro-Asiatic masses" that threatened Western Judeo-Christian "Sacred History."[21] In an interview he rejected the application of his ethics to the Palestinian case. He reduced philo-anthropological analysis to the encounter between Athens and Jerusalem: "Humanity consists of the Bible and the Greeks... All the rest—all the exotic—is dance."[22]

At first blush Levinasian philosophy appears like a helpful perspective from which to confront Western sources. For he challenges the reduction of history to the European design, emphasizes the existence of alternative sources to egocentric thinking, and finally, but no less importantly, accuses the West of being barbaric. Alternatively, he also retains a conventional understanding of Europe, explaining that the Global South/East does not enter into history until the 1960s, thereby reducing the definition of humanity to an intra-European framework. Levinas thus clearly reproduces a traditional Eurocentrism. While he levels a strong critique against the monopoly of European history, he in turn monopolizes the conception of otherness by limiting it to the intra-European case of the Jew. When reflecting on the power of alterity to change history, he responds that "the history of Israel" is the only source for alternative thinking. It "invites us to create a new anthropology, a new history" and to bring the end "of Western triumphalism."[23]

It is thus unsurprising that his understanding of barbarism, while still retaining the negative valence of the term, reproduces this Eurocentric provincialism by fixing paradigmatic otherness onto Judaism. This problem can be seen throughout his corpus of texts. For example, he reflects on the context of a twentieth century full of "barbaric names" including the atrocities of "Hitlerism, Stalinism, Hiroshima, and the genocides of Auschwitz and the Gulag and Cambodia." Among all of these atrocities the Jewish case is foregrounded: "the Holocaust of the Jewish people under the reign of Hitler seems to me the paradigm of gratuitous suffering."[24] A few years later he describes this situation even more dramatically: "Among the millions of Human beings who encountered misery and death" because of the barbaric atrocities of the empire, "the Jews alone experienced a total dereliction."[25] The reproduction of this negative conception of barbarism is an indication that Levinas is still operating within the confines of Eurocentrism.

Decoloniality and Positive Barbarism

All the texts quoted above, however, were written before the 1970s. Levinas's position vis-à-vis barbarism radically changes in the 1970s and 1980s. This will help Levinas begin to abandon his European parochialism and think beyond traditional continental confines. Before this period Levinas limited the term barbarism to Europe and distanced himself from the Afro-Asiatic masses supposedly devoid of history. After the 1970s he accuses Europe as a whole of being criminal and starts thinking differently about barbarism. He relocates Jewish thought among those masses previously considered bereft of history and labels the latter barbaric (with the term now valuated in a positive way). This change can be traced in two general stages. In the 1970s he expresses an epistemological openness to barbarism while in the 1980s he further expands this openness into a geo-political decolonialism. Let us explore Levinas's twin trajectory below.

In 1974, Levinas published *Autrement qu'être, ou au-delà de l'essence*. According to most Anglophone scholarship on the topic, this book primarily addresses criticisms of Jacques Derrida and his general French intellectual milieu.[6] A closer look at the last pages of the text, however, reveals a different constellation of concerns. Levinas contends that the only possibility of engaging with ethics is "to introduce some *barbarisms* in the language of philosophy." In a text with strong semiological constructions one might wonder if he is not just talking about playful linguistic turns. But Levinas further clarifies his intentions. He thinks that ontology fails to express what is "beyond essence," the other. The "barbarous expression" of what is "otherwise than being," emerges from the "margins" of European "triumphal history."[26]

In these paragraphs Levinas distinguishes between Europe and its barbaric margins. On the one hand, European history is defined as the record of "conquest and jealous defense" of the center of power and thought. It is a testament to the epistemological egoism and aggressiveness of a Self who is unable to acknowledge her responsibility for what is beyond herself. In the past Levinas might have called this the negative barbarian, but in this text Levinas is very clear not to use this term for Europe. The barbaric terrain is where Levinas finds the space to think "beyond essence." It is "in the margins" that "the trace of events" of Western history carries "another signification." According to Levinas, that signification is created by the suffering of "the victims of the triumphs" who are located (and can think) "beyond essence."[27]

In this text he does not reduce the civilizational alternative to Judaism as he did previously. This text is different for two reasons. First, as a border thinker he changes the valence of barbarism: it is not an accusation against the empire but a positive revalorization of imperial alternatives located in the margins of the West. Second, he clearly uses the plural signifying the multiplicity of voices that are found in the margins of the West. If he were talking about Judaism alone, there would be no need to invert the term barbarism or to render it in the plural. This represents an epistemological openness to multiple alternatives beyond being. In the discussion below we will explain in more detail how he arrived at this multiplicity of positive barbarisms. For now it is important to note that the term has significantly changed and that he is beginning to include Jews among the voices located at the margins of the West.

This openness to barbaric epistemologies crystallizes ten years later in Levinas's geo-political Talmudic lectures. In *Les nations et la présence d'Israël,* he applies the new epistemological barbarism to decolonial geo-politics. The lecture, an interpretation of *Pesahim 118b* written in 1986, distinguishes between two communities struggling for geo-political survival. The first community is represented by Rome, the egocentric "criminal empire."[28] The second community consists of the barbaric forces at the margins of the West: the Jews (Israel), the close adversary (Egypt), and the far away other (Ethiopia), by which Levinas—problematically—symbolizes the entirety of the Third World.[29] The ethical community of those displaced by history confronts a common enemy: an empire that amasses wealth merely for the sake of accumulation while it condemns other peoples to starvation. Levinas quotes the Talmudic text directly: "There are three hundred and sixty-five streets in the great city of Rome; in each one there are three hundred and sixty-five towers; in each tower, there are three hundred sixty-five storeys; and in each storey there is enough to feed the whole world."[30] This is, in Levinas's words, an "economy of the wealth of pure accumulation."[31]

Levinas does not restrict the criminal ethos of egotistic empires to the ancient world. According to him, the empires of Greco-Roman antiquity have been re-edited in the modern imperial powers. He variously identifies these political formations as the European "fraternal West" and the United States. In other words, he sees a continuous stream of economic accumulation from ancient Rome to the "American" empire, which he identifies as nothing short of the "rabbinic doctor's futuristic nightmare."[32] He sees no reason to accept the existence of this egotistic community, and follows the rabbis praying for an end to "a collectivity destined to violence by the kind of society that is fond of war."[33] He is less interested in reform than in the defeat, destruction, and dispersion of this community grounded in "bloody history" and "racial, social, and economic injustice"[34]—whether it be Rome, the European West, or the United States.

Levinas goes further in lamenting the empires' inability to reorient their ethos, even if they were to desire to become part of the new community of others. He questions any kind of assimilation of the powerful to the new community. As he writes earlier, somewhere between his initial epistemological openness and the later geo-political decolonialism, "this pure assimilation" is not more than "a facile virtue of the West, [a] hypocritical pretext of the colonizers."[35] In such statements, Levinas—who has always been viewed as a Eurocentric philosopher—seems to place Judaism within a radical geo-political decolonial space.

Levinas's contemporary appeal to a common community is contained in his source materials. He particularly follows one of the most authoritative medieval interpretive sages, Rabbi Shlomo Itzchaki ("Rashi"), who wrote his own interpretation in the north of France in the eleventh century. Levinas makes this retrieval explicit: "Rashi reminds us that there is a rabbinic tradition that understands Egypt and Ethiopia as being included in the community of Israel."[36] The medieval interpretation, I suggested elsewhere, was likely re-imagining potential allies for Judaism in a context of desperation during the crusades.[37] For Levinas himself, this retrieval achieves multiple ends. In the first place, it serves to legitimate a longstanding Jewish confrontation with Western powers. Secondly, it de-naturalizes the relationship between Judaism and Western civilization. In the third place, it recognizes the existence of alternative entities beyond Europe who are themselves Jewish allies. Yet (and I now anticipate one of the problems with his counter-narrative), he subsumes other struggles and experiences within a Jewish experience. Retrieving his frame of reference from the Talmudic texts, he calls this ensemble of experiences and peoples the community of Israel. Eager critics of Levinas may point out he is reproducing the same accusation he made to the West (the impossibility of recognizing the other beyond its reduction to the same). They can correctly suggest that Levinas is reproducing stratifications existent since early modernity. But he breaks with the unique Western path by recognizing the duality and opting, still problematically, to incorporate the others in the history of otherness wounded by coloniality and not the history of the "criminal" and "imperial" sameness.[38]

Levinas's revaluation of barbarism caused him to radically change his politics. When he was employing the negative counter-narrative of the term barbarism, Levinas dismissed other non-European possibilities. As he comes to exhibit an openness to multiple barbarisms, Levinas expands the scope of history beyond Europe to encompass a common community including Jews and other marginalized peoples.[39] While Jews are problematically represented by "Israel," this change in the conception of barbarism, this new openness to multiplicity, is indicative of a promising geo-political rethinking on his part. Two central questions emerge from this reading. The first is why he changes from the negative counter-narrative to a counter-narrative embracing multiple positive barbarisms. Otherwise stated, what are the historical and intellectual reasons this partisan of Eurocentrism came to support a decolonial geo-politics? The second question is directly related to the term barbarism. While the turn in his thought does seem to be related to the concept of barbarism he does not use the term in the interpretation of his Talmudic reading. I argue that both questions can be answered when we read Levinas's historical encounter with Third World thinkers in general and Argentinean-Mexican philosopher Enrique Dussel in particular.

The Barbaric Encounter

As mentioned above, Levinas's detractors have criticized the limiting Eurocentric model he used to analyze otherness. His articulation and application of this model coincides with the use of a negative counter-narrative of the term barbarism. But I contend here that this view overlooks the decolonial barbaric openness that Levinas comes to exhibit in the 1970s and 1980s. The first question posed above centered on the reasons why Levinas changed the geo-political framework of Jewish thought during the last twenty years of his life. Why should a Eurocentric partisan of the Western Judeo-Christian tradition re-evaluate the use of barbarism and consequently place Jews among colonized forces? I contend that this openness cannot be explained without an exploration of Levinas's overlooked historical encounters with Third World intellectuals. These conversations took place in the 1970s during a simultaneous period of Post-Holocaust and Postcolonial reflection.

Let me elaborate this often overlooked historical-conceptual encounter. In early 1970s Paris and Louvain, Levinas crossed paths with a young and "sympathetic" group of Latin American intellectuals, among whom was Dussel. Both scholars remember their initial conversation with great interest. Levinas describes Dussel as "doing geopolitics," and articulates that "there is a very interesting attempt in South America to return to the spirit of the people." He declares how "happy or even proud" he feels when hearing "the echoes of my work in this group." Levinas describes this "as a fundamental approval" for his project. This approval is understood in terms of the historical-conceptual relationship between Jews and Southerners: "It means that other people have also seen the 'same thing.'"[40] Dussel also remembers the initial meetings, describing how he was in charge of gathering together "a group of

Latin American students to talk to Levinas in 1971 in Paris and in 1972 in Louvain."[41] Subsequently, Dussel writes that his reading and encounter with Levinas "produced in my sprit a subversive overthrowing of all that I had learned until then."[42] A few years later, he would title his new book *Emmanuel Lévinas y la Liberación Latinoamericana*.[43]

Evidence of Levinas's and Dussel's mutual influence can be traced to 1973, only a year after they met. As Dussel writes, "The real overcoming of the [ontological and dialectical] tradition... is found in the philosophy of Levinas. Our overcoming will consist in re-thinking the discourse from Latin America." His project came into being from what he described as "a personal dialogue I maintained with the philosopher [Levinas] in Paris and Louvain... What I expressed in a European university at the beginning of 1972 is precisely a '*barbaric philosophy*.'"[44] A year later, Levinas himself published *Autrement qu'être*. In its final pages, perhaps to emphasize the late incorporation of the term, Levinas writes the words already quoted: the only way to engage with ethics is to "introduce some *barbarism*s in the language of philosophy." He also encourages revising the meaning of history through the vision of the barbaric margins of the West.[45]

Levinas's epistemological openness to decolonialism arises from his encounter with Third World scholars. Why does that encounter find its epicenter in the term barbarism? As we explained in the first chapter of this book, this is a common narrative Jews shared with other colonized. In modernity the narrative of barbarism was a tool of the coloniality of knowledge that trapped barbaric peoples inside and outside Europe. Eventually, those stigmatized confronted the term. In the previous chapter, we saw how Jews of Marxist persuasion confronted the trope constructing a counter-narrative that considered the empire barbaric. They left the negativity of the term intact but reversed the accusation, describing the imperial capitalism of Christian Europe as the barbaric system. In time, however, post-Marxist Third World decolonialists not only appropriated the term but also inverted its meaning, and began to create a community of barbarians invested in resisting political and epistemological colonization. We explore this topic in more detail next chapter. But for now we can say that Afro-Caribbeans such as Aime Cesaire, Latino Americans such as Rodolfo Kusch and Leopoldo Zea, and Maghrebis such as Albert Memmi left behind socialist alternatives to engage in decolonial politics and inverted the concept of barbarianism, investing it with positive associations.

Following the lead of his new interlocutors, this explicit resistance to empire would be the next step for Levinas: a switch from epistemological to geo-political decolonialism. In their encounters, the Third World decolonialist Dussel, aware of Levinas's earlier Jewish-centrism, asks the Jewish Talmudic interpreter to define the limits of his conception of otherness. For example, years before Levinas had observed that "among the millions of human beings who encountered misery and death, the Jews alone experienced a total dereliction."[46] In response, Dussel mounted the following objection: "What about the fifteen million Indians slaughtered during the conquest of America, and the thirteen million Africans who were made slaves?...Aren't they the 'other' you are speaking about? What about all of us who are not Semitic?"[47] Levinas answered Dussel's question very clearly. But this time the question was not framed in theoretical terms but rather in the practical responsibilities of the Europe Levinas defended in the suffering of non-Jews.

Levinas's response would be couched in geo-political terms, which he had theretofore described as Dussel's field of expertise. Levinas references the anti-colonial community from *Pesahim 118b*. In his interpretations of this text, as we have already seen, Levinas understands the community of Israel and other barbaric peoples as constituting a common front. He outlines his hope that the suffering and starving would give way to a "regenerated humanity." This is only possible through an alliance of Third World people that is able to face the egotistic "wild beast of Rome"—also known as "the fraternal West" or "America." Levinas's response to Dussel is that there is room for all the "others"—that is, the new decolonial community, both "Semitic" and "non-Semitic"—within a decolonial front. As Dussel requested, Levinas expresses his solidarity with both the Semitic—the Arab and the Jew—and the non-Semitic—the Black representing the whole Third World. However, by reducing the non-Semitic to the Black, Levinas problematically uses Ethiopia as a symbol of the entire Third World. As a result, he fails to recognize the diversity among these voices, including the specific case of the "Indians" of the Americas, a historically marginalized people of great concern to Dussel.[48]

The encounter between Levinas and Dussel made the Jewish Talmudic interpreter alter his previous reading in two ways. First, the negative counter-narrative of the term barbarism is replaced by a positive use, describing knowledge that is outside the West. Second, this openness to alternative thinking leads him to recover a Talmudic text in which Jews are part of a wider community that confronts imperial designs. This is a radical change from the Levinas who had supported a Jewish-Christian

European alliance, was afraid of the Afro-Asiatic masses, and reduced anthropological ideal types to Athens and Jerusalem. Levinas's construction, however, has multiple tensions. Here, as we have done in the previous chapter, I will limit myself to enunciate one central limitation. I will further explain and analyze the implications of the problem once I have finished detailing the counter-narratives in chapter six. In 1986, Levinas attempted to integrate Jews within a larger ensemble of barbarians through a political entity he calls Israel. In other words, he seems to identify the Jewish path in a state that was seen with significant mistrust by the colonized. Furthermore, one year after his Talmudic lecture, this state faced the first Intifada, a movement of resistance overwhelmingly supported by Global South decolonial constituencies. A simple solution to the problem would be to suggest that the Israel Levinas is referring to an "ideal type" not related to the actual State of Israel which had been established almost forty years before. This attempt to solve the problem, however, overlooks Levinas's own understanding of both the Jewish state and the politics of his Talmudic texts.

In the first place, if we were to accept this solution we would need to dissociate Levinas from the State of Israel. The Lithuanian philosopher, however, has been a longtime advocate of the Jewish state and had explicitly written several texts supporting the Jewish enterprise in the Middle East. In some instances his support was framed in an idealized version of Jews fulfilling a mission in the realm of holy history and in others it was a historical reading reproducing what renowned Israeli critic and historiographer terms the "foundational myths" of secular political Zionism.[49] Perhaps Levinas's most clear formulation can found in a short text entitled "Etat d'Israël et religion d'Israël" ("The State of Israel and the Religion of Israel"). In this particular early essay, Levinas recognized the "idolatry of the state" in modern political thought. But he argued that the State of Israel did not fall within this framework. Levinas states that, given the special role of Jews in history, Israel constituted an alternative social formation and a creative space in which Jews could put in practice the "social law" that they had been cultivating for centuries in exile.[50] The Jewish state, in Levinas's argument, represented an opportunity to fulfill a long-term project that went beyond the traditional role of the nation-state. This conception of the state of Israel is fully compatible with the one in his late work. In both proposals, the State of Israel represents a liberation from national interests by an appeal to an alternative (glossed in the late work as "barbaric") that will manumit the oppressed from the aggressive and limited nature of Western political formations.

There is a second reason that his supposed dissociation between Israel and the State of Israel is weak. Levinas is generally conscious of the political implications of his texts. There are several instances, such as his Talmudic interpretations, in which he follows his analysis with a clear political posture vis-à-vis contemporaneous politics. French debates, the Holocaust, and the Middle Eastern conflict are some of his most recurrent themes. There are, however, other occasions in which he explicitly requests not to be interpreted in the context of contemporary events. One of these examples is his Talmudic interpretation of *Yoma 10a* entitled *"Qui joue le dernier"* ("Who Play Last?") that was published just after the Iranian revolution of 1979. Here he requests his audience not to interpret the ideal types (Rome and Persia) as the United States and Iran. This request, however, is not related to his objection to be interpreted politically. He just admits that he wrote the text before the events and, in a humble turn, he tries to explain that his writings may be ethical/political reflections but they are not "oracles."[51]

When he interprets *Pesahim 118b*, however, Levinas himself has absolutely no problem contemporizing the text because he was making a political intervention. The original Talmudic text referred to the empire as Rome. Levinas explicitly makes a political move by associating this political formation with Europe and the United States. These two formations are obviously not in the original text. And naturally they are not in the classical medieval interpretations either. The contemporization of the political models is purely Levinas's work. As a consequence, it is difficult not to understand the Israel Levinas presents as a conduit for Jewish decolonialism as also so contextualized. Israel overlaps with the other ideal types. It is a contemporary community that represents, first, global Jewry, and second, the totality of decolonized world, including Egypt and Ethiopia. It is without any doubt a very problematic move for the reasons we explored above (the assimilation of otherness this time to otherness instead of sameness). This interpretation, however, makes Levinas's proposal coherent at the intra- and inter-textual levels. It follows the contemporization of ideal types of this same text and the role described for Israel as a Messianic model beyond the idolatry of the modern state in other texts.

Levinas's construction is successful in making a transition, but still needs to confront the fact that the proposal was contextually quite problematic. The question that remains to be answered concerns the reason underlying his insistence on incorporating the Jewish people through the State of Israel within the community of barbarians. One option would be to suggest that this is a trace of his Eurocentrism. His permanent interest to build an alternative to the West, first the Hebrew, later the barbarian, that includes Jews, challenges a simplistic reading that only take into account this factor. A second, and perhaps complementary, option would be to explore the extent to which the reason behind his incorporation was the impossibility of acknowledging the change in Jewish politics. Levinas may have an ideal version of what Israel should have been. This idealism, however, is undermined by the fact that the Jewish state, as we will see soon, identified itself with civilization and not barbarism and, consequently, ended up reproducing the same traditional narrative he was confronting. Perhaps, and now I anticipate the argument of chapter six, Levinas's Eurocentrism made him unable to recognize the changing nature of Jewish politics in the second half of the twentieth century. This is exactly the step that Magrhebian Memmi was able to recognize.

CHAPTER 5

Positive Barbarism: Memmi's Counter-Narrative in a Southern Network

Amid the tumultuous years of decolonization in North Africa, Albert Memmi wrote the *Pillar of Salt*. The book is a semi-autobiographical novel texturing the life of a Tunisian Jew during French colonial rule, the Axis occupation during the Second World War, and the incipient Postcolonial struggle in the Maghreb. Soon after its publication, the book became a landmark in North African Jewish writing. Besides the perdurable insights it offers about local Jewry, the book is a powerful testament to the deep-seated decolonial struggles of Global South Jews. In this novel Memmi represents his semi-biographical character as a border thinker. He does recognize the complexity of his identity as, in his own words, "a Jew in an anti-Semitic world," "a native in a colonial country," and an "African in a world dominated by Europe." Acknowledging the common root of the narrative that thrice objectified him, he proudly declares himself an "incurable barbarian."[1]

This third counter-narrative of barbarism, the positive version, significantly differs from two we have thus far examined. The first emerged from a monologue within European Jewry and the second as a dialogue between an Eastern European Jew and Global South theory. This third option arises from the networks of Global South Judaism. Immediately following the Second World War, over thirty percent of global Jewry resided in the Third World (not even including the British mandate in Palestine). Following the massive departure of Jews from the Middle East, the Maghreb became home to the largest Jewish population until a new exodus pushed the balance to Latin America. Local communities from this region dated from the early centuries of the Common Era. Far from being static, their constitution and complex changed after various conquests and with the arrival of Jewish refugees fleeing Christian persecution in Europe. The Maghreb, or the Barbary Coast as the region was known to some European discourses, was home to Jewish populations who largely understood themselves as natives to the region. For most of the modern period European imperialist discourses largely portrayed Jews as non-Westerners and many times as barbarians. In the century preceding decolonization, and as a result of the oscillating colonial policy, some Jewish populations were used as pawns in French colonial maneuvers that offered them a political path to assimilation. The French powers were aided by Western Jewish organizations eager to show Jewish adaptability to Westernization. Yet, only a fraction of Jews and mostly concentrated in Algeria achieved the desired goal. Even the minority that able to pass the racial re-classification test saw their redemptive possibility aborted when they were discriminated and annihilated in interment and concentration camps during the Vichy and German occupation. While some Jews feared decolonial struggles, the leadership of the Tunisian and Moroccan liberationist movements largely embraced their Jewish inhabitants. Some Jews actively participated in the struggle. Memmi was one among them.

Memmi's decolonial proposal will not be read as a Jewish dialogue with the Global South. It will be understood as a Southern Jewish counter-narrative. The elaboration of positive barbarism, from which Memmi draws his inspiration, had been developed as an integral part of decolonial epistemological resistances. As a self-declared African he welcomes the political applications that Africana intellectuals were developing. If the counter-narratives of chapters three and four created monologues or dialogues struggling with European frameworks of thought (Left-Hegelianism for Marxism, Phenomenology or Neo-Kantianism for Levinas), one of the most provocative counter-narratives emerges from an Africana influence. When Jews were being portrayed as agents of imperialism, Memmi finds within the Global South the resources to reinscribe Jews into the barbaric struggle.

In this chapter, then, we will explore the positive counter-narrative of barbarism by analyzing both its antecedents in Africana thought and the actual Jewish Magrhebi formulation. Introducing Memmi's proposal by evaluating the formulation of Cesaire and Senghor will help achieve two objectives. In the first place, it will unveil the Southern network presupposed in Memmi's writing, illuminating the decolonial nature of his proposal. The counter-narrative was developed by border thinkers who did not confront the narrative as hybrids. On the contrary, they re-affirmed the colonial experience as the source of a critical consciousness able to confront the patterns of domination established by both colonial discourses and the coloniality of power/knowledge. They developed a double critique by confronting Humanist assimilation and native returns to mythical pasts for a project that can establish an alternative relationship among communities. Second, they also elucidate Memmi's internal struggle in order to dislocate the presumed European location of Judaism. This is the space in which Memmi challenges simultaneously Western, Jewish, and even decolonial thought by elaborating another location to understand the colonized nature of the Jewish experience.

Memmi's project became provocative and innovative, but is abandoned near the end of the period. Like Levinas's project, the Tunisian's early work is premised on the integration of Jews within the barbaric collective through the national solution to the Jewish problem (i.e., the creation of the State of Israel). Furthermore, he defines Zionism as a movement of national liberation comparable to the others he witnessed in the Maghreb, Africa, and the rest of the world. Such a framework entails the same tension of Levinas's positive stage. The decolonialist Memmi, however, is able to acknowledge the changing politics of late twentieth- and twenty-first century Judaism. After the 1980s, he explicitly recognizes the geo-political change. Confronted head-on with this tension he abandons the barbaric project and re-imagines a more orthodox Humanism he had been previously dismissed as yet another colonial discourse. While this demonstrates a level of frank sincerity and intellectual suppleness, Memmi's abandonment of the counter-narrative will render his positive contribution uncompelling to his heirs in the post-9/11 Global South.

Decolonial Networks, Epistemological Fronts

Political opposition to colonization is simultaneous with the rise of colonization itself. As soon as Europeans attempted to rule, enslave, and expropriate resources from natives, movements of resistance arose against imperial designs. Some of these rebellions left an enduring legacy of struggle that was re-enacted between the 1940s and 1980s. Departing from an Atlantic perspective, for example, in the sixteenth and eighteenth centuries, Tupac Amaru and Tupac Amaru II led rebellions against the Spanish colonial socio-political structure. While both ultimately failed in the battlefield, they left a memory that deeply influenced South American struggles against American neo-colonialism in the 1970s. In the late eighteenth century slaves led by Toussaint Louverture rebelled in Haiti and created a republic inspired by the French revolution. The state, however, became unviable after colonial powers—who theoretically embraced such revolutions—opposed this slave-lead rebellion. The experience, nevertheless, became a keystone for transatlantic Francophone national liberation movements in the Caribbean and Africa in the 1940–1950s. In the early nineteenth century, Shaka led a Zulu Kingdom that neither Dutch nor English could uproot. His powerful image, interpreted as a "Black-Christ" figure, was championed by those engaged in similar struggles in and beyond the continent. The iconic imagery became a provocative call to arms during the South-African anti-apartheid struggles of the 1980s.[2]

In the late eighteenth and early nineteenth centuries, however, Creole populations initiated an alternative process known as political emancipation. The offspring of colonialists took advantage of the distance and/or relative weakness of the imperial centers in an attempt to attain political independence. In the preponderance of cases, however, such efforts insisted in the basic tenants of the narrative of barbarism (one path of development and displacement of local populations). In the late eighteenth century American colonialists resisted British attempts to strength her control over commerce and taxation. The settlers formulated a distinctive American identity and declared independence of the colonial power, inaugurating the United States of America. In the early nineteenth century, Spanish vice-royalties followed a similar trajectory. The descendent of European settlers took advantage of a kingdom debilitated from the Napoleonic wars, and declared independence. They emancipated most of South and Central America between the 1810s and 1820s. In South Africa the Boer settlers faced the British Empire. At the end of the first war they provisionally secured independence from imperial rule. What Americans, Latin Americans, and Boers shared, with counted exceptions, was their disdain for the resistance of native populations. Sometimes they were ignored, while other times they were repressed, or converted into canon folder. National emancipation, especially in the nineteenth century, predominantly reproduced the basic tenants of the narrative.[3]

Despite permanent resistance of both colonized and settler struggles, European rule continued to expand throughout the world. After the First World War, the West ruled over half of the globe. If we include the settler colonies under formal independent rule, over two-thirds of the globe found itself under the aegis of a Western imperial power. This was a slow process that started in the sixteenth century with Catholic popes blessing Spanish and Portuguese dominion across the Atlantic and reached its fullest expression with the League of Nations handing over protectorates to the triumphant forces of the First World War in the early twentieth century. During this half millennium, colonial European forces dismembered the Ottoman Empire by taking over the Maghreb and the Middle East in the late nineteenth and early twentieth centuries as well as dividing Africa in the earlier part of the period. Following the Second World War, however, the situation changed. Europe was economically depressed, the metropolis had been debilitated by intra-European confrontations, and the incipient Cold War challenged the primacy of Western and Central European dominion. The colonies and protectorates launched the era of global political decolonization.[4]

In the English-speaking world the Indian struggle led by Mahatma Gandhi was iconic. This "jewel" of British imperialism had passed from Dutch, Danish, French, and Portuguese rule, only to achieve independence in 1947, two years after the end of the Second World War. The South-Asian sub-continent, however, was not alone. India was soon joined by a growing collective of colonized communities and liberation movements. Situated strategically between African and Middle Eastern politics, Egypt was divesting herself of residual colonial ties, and taking the lead in anti-imperial discourses. In the Americas Cuba liberated herself from American hegemony and in the process became a revolutionary experiment worthy of imitation throughout the new empire. In Europe, Yugoslavia broke ties with the Soviet Union and was forced to re-evaluate geographies in an otherwise Southern project. In the Maghreb and South Asia, the enduring struggle of Algerian and Indo-Chinese decolonialists were striking at the heart of French imperialism. Between the late 1940s and early 1960s a new Global South movement was emerging and the region was challenging the very foundation of the imperial project.[5]

These myriad struggles were not isolated. In the following years leading forces of the movements created a collective that took different names (non-aligned, Tricontinentalism), and will here be referred to as Third-Worldism, an alliance among Latin America and the Caribbean, Africa, and Asia. While European Marxism may have influenced their background, the movement explored the lengthy resistances against coloniality and radically revised dialectical materialism. Orthodox Marxism had understood that the socialist revolution would be launched in advanced industrial societies when (simplifying the logic explained in chapter three) the mode of production, bourgeoisie capitalism, clashed with the forces of production, the socialist proletariat. Vladimir Lenin and Mao Tse-tung had already explored modifications of this doctrine. The leader of the Russian revolution argued that imperialism was a superior form of capitalism, profiting from colonies outside the industrial metropolis, and that a socialist revolution was not limited to nonindustrial societies. The head of the Chinese revolution added that in nonindustrial societies a perforce non-industrial class, such as the peasants (described once as "sack[s] of potatoes" by Marx), could very well become the universal guide.[6]

Among the lessons Third-Worldism would assimilate from these modification was that the understanding was extending its reproduction through profiting from the colonies and that a revolution in colonized societies lead by nonindustrialized forces was indeed a possibility. Various intellectuals thus re-evaluated Marxism in geo-political terms and renamed the anti-colonial struggle through recourse to Marxist categories. Throughout the globe, colonial countries incarnated the bourgeois agenda. The colonized countries or movements of liberation represented the proletariat—now not necessarily industrial—as capable of leading the international revolution. By reconceiving the classical materialist dialectics within a geo-political dualism (i.e., "bourgeoisie nations" vs. "proletarian nations"), Third-Worldism incorporated the national problem into the more traditional dialectical materialist framework. The movement still maintained the orthodox pre-Stalinist aspiration of world revolution. But the path toward this revolution was going to be mutual assistance of the local national struggles that could prepare the ground for an interrelated global project.[7]

The struggle, therefore, was not only limited to political confrontation with imperialism but also involved a needed theoretical and epistemological decolonization of social theory. The wounds of coloniality led decolonizers to confront the Marxist difficulty to understand national causes and what could define the proletarian nations (i.e., religion or race). Decolonialism required a fundamental reconceptualization of systems of thinking and not just of empirical politics. European thought, even the most radical strands thereof, were still unable to account for the experience of the proletariat nations. Epistemological confrontation with imperialism and coloniality, we should recall, was far from a geo-political *novum*. Postcolonial historiography has explored a large number of cases in which reading against the grain of history allowed us to understand the cultural challenges colonized populations have instrumented since the early colonization century. In the twentieth century, epistemological decolonization, however, increased in momentum for two central reasons. The first one is that, thanks to modern communications, epistemological resistances were able to permeate borders and held forge larger communities of colonized peoples. In addition, access to Western education on the part of colonized populations meant the possibility of confronting colonization with the same cultural tools that were used to subjugate them in the first place (i.e., philosophy, poetry, literature, and so on).[8]

One of the most successful examples of these new bonds of solidarity was the global African thought that would eventually evolve into pan-Africanism and Africana thinking. Already in the 1920s and 1930s, the descendants of slaves residing in New York launched a cultural movement that would come to be known as the "Harlem Renaissance." The movement opposed the derogatory language of African barbarism, and embarked on a program of politically-engaged artistic production which helped pave the way for the civil rights movements in the 1950s. Deeply influenced by the Harlem movement, African and Afro-Caribbean students in Paris launched the *Négritude* collective. The movement would take a new literary pride in being black and its leaders became some of the most incisive anti-imperialist theoreticians and subsequently, political leaders of the decolonial movement. The simultaneous critique of racialization and re-affirmation of identity is what would enable the Negritude movement, and in turn Memmi, to elaborate a positive counter-narrative of barbarism.[9]

Negritude, Barbarism, Jewishness

As a prelude to discuss the Jewish counter-narrative of barbarism, I will explore its immediate antecedent, the positive alternative elaborated by the Negritude movement between the 1920s and 1950s. This exploration will not only unveil Memmi's proposal within a Global South network but also show the tensions Memmi needed to re-evaluate in order to dislocate an alleged European location of Jewish experiences that was largely reproduced in decolonial discourses.

The negritude movement was an unintended consequence of French model of colonization. Throughout its history, French imperial discourse was adamant in its conviction that France's role in the colonies was not, at least primarily, politically or economically motivated. Under the aegis of the *Mission civilisatrice*, they supported more than any other project the interrelation between the co-option of the indigenous elites and the reproduction of the regnant imperial narrative of barbarism. Consistent with their imperial mission statement, they established a robust education system in the colonies and, especially in the interwar period, trained colonized elites in premier Parisian schools. The students, however, faced intense racism and understood the depth of the barbaric narrative in the metropolis itself. Yet, in emphasizing the universality of French knowledge, promoting the French language, and bringing the elites to the metropole the colonial system set grounds its own subversion. Interwar Paris became a locus of radicalized and dissatisfied colonial congregation—despite their diverse provenance, France's imperial subjects could now share their experiences of racialization in the same language, and by means of the same cultural references.[10] The reclamation of their negated exteriority, however, would ultimately challenge any dialectical reading of history.

It was in the turning of the 1930s that three Africana students met in Paris: Aime Cesaire, Leon Damas, and Leopold Senghore from Martinique, Guiana, and Senegal, respectively. They were affected not only by their experiences of colonization at home and racism in the metropolis but also by the growing cultural antagonism to colonization in Paris. In the early 1930s, these three students founded the journal *L'Etudiant noir*. The publication became not only a forum of Africana protest against colonialism but it also represented a place for a border re-affirmation of effaced values (histories, literatures, cultures) usually categorized as barbaric. The three leading members supported the movement by editing the journal, publishing independent works and compiling anthologies of Africans authors. The basis of solidarity among the members of the movement was the positive appropriation of a black identity that superseded any regional limits. In other words, they were able to go beyond the myriad factors dividing Blacks throughout the Atlantic world, and reflect on the common existential conditions that enslavement and colonization engendered in Africa and its diaspora. Inspired by Africana thinking well beyond the French-speaking environment—including, for example, the aforementioned English-speaking Harlem renaissance—they repudiated the primitiveness the colonizer had predicated of Africans, but will eventually reclaim their barbarism. These border thinkers validated Africana culture (instead of French education), as a legitimate source for cultural and political resistance.[11]

In so doing, the movement became an enabler of later political Third-Worldism. The latter, we recall, radically modified Marxism in order to support local struggles in a context of solidarity among the proletarian nations and constituencies of the world. Already in the interwar period, the movement understood the local struggles of

Africans or African-descendants as a means of forging an overarching pan-African solidarity that would constitute a new Humanism of the vanquished (soon to be barbarians). The conception of Negritude and later political pan-Africanism was not only influenced by movements outside the Francophone world—it also influenced subsequent movements which blurring linguistic boundaries. Radical anti-apartheid struggles in South Africa, especially as represented by Stephen Biko in the 1960s and 1970s, witness the imprint of the recovery of Blackness. Negritude would influence Africans around the world, and the reclaiming of barbarism would have similarly global resonance. As we shall see below Magrhebi Jew Memmi, for example, was one of the decolonialists influenced by the movement.

Aime Cesaire would represent a pivotal actor in this process. He was a Martinican intellectual born in the second decade of the twentieth century who passed away in the first decade of the twenty-first century. In the 1930s, he was the first Black admitted to the prestigious *École normale supérieure* and co-founded the *Negritude* collective. In the 1940s, he engaged in political activity, becoming Communist mayor of *Fort de France* and deputy to the French parliament for *Martinique*. In opposition to the Soviet occupation of Eastern Europe (and French Communist politics) the following decade, he renounced the party because of the limitations Marxism had in acknowledging coloniality and addressing the political and social complexities in the classical class reductionism of dialectical materialism. After coining the term Negritude in the 1930s, he became a prolific poet and social theorist. A distillation of his early thought can be extrapolated from three of his texts written between 1939 and 1955: the critical manifesto of Negritude (*Chaier d'un retour au pays natal*), his reclamation of barbarism (a poem entitled *Barbare*) and finally the elevation of this barbarism to an anti-colonial project that struggled with the geo-politics of Jewish experiences (*Discours sur le colonialisme*).[12]

Cesaire's long poem *Notebook of a Return to a Native Land* became a seminal work of the Negritude collective. The book was initially printed in 1939, but it was the 1947 re-publication the influential version. Cesaire compiled the book from diverse pieces written during a visit to the Balkans and through an imaginative exercise or returning to his homeland after a decade's absence. Cesaire had already written an article entitled "*Negreries*" in an early issue of *L'Etudiant noir*. In this poem he further extended his simultaneous critique of Western epistemology and re-affirmation of the barbarized black identity. In this piece he simultaneous is able to provincialize an "overrated Europe" and re-interprets the wealth of "the smell," "the magic," "the music," "the prodigious ancestry," "the prophesy," and "the dance" of the "bad" and "revolting nigger."[13]

The poem is a non-linear narrative of expectations and realities of a re-encounter with his old homeland as well as with African epistemology itself. It starts before the hybrid returnee physically comes back to his hometown. It narrates the pre-empty impressions which lurk behind an imposed European veil. The old town looks "flat," "perverted," "stagnant," and "muted." Imperial discourses gloss such circumstances as, of course, barbaric. The cultural and economic sources of civilization allowed the returnee to perceive the general injustice as well as the complicity of Western powers with the "des-humanization" of the natives. It is clear that he feels disdain and pathos for the current situation of his people. But the critique is not necessarily against their nature but against the structural conditions that rendered them barbaric in the first place. These sources, permeated by an illuminist conception of civilization, prevent him from understanding any positive characteristic of the natives. Indeed, he launches a critique against a nativist stance, which seeks to return to a "golden age" of this "putrefied" community. This project is a "futile" romantization of a barbaric reality.[14]

But the prodigal son returns, the European veil starts falling, and the ambiguous lenses of mimicry begin to allow a border perspective to emerge. The people that the poet had seen as lacking temporal consciousness or historical perspective, actually possess a collective memory of struggle. The aforementioned Haitian revolution repressed by Euro-American revolutionaries became an iconic remembrance of the potentiality of revolt.[15] Slowly the returnee begins to perceive the value of alternative sources of knowledge: "poetic reason," "communal speech" and, ironically employed, "irrational" thinking. He rejects European knowledge, deriving from the "tower and the Cathedral," which has served to repress and stigmatize alternative rationalities. Instead he discovers there is another knowledge autochthonous to his community—something that derives from the "root" in the "soil" and "sky" of the communal patrimony.[16]

This is not, he insists, a naïve nativist return to an idealized past. It is not a celebration of mythical Africa. The alternative knowledge is alive and inheres within the "captive"—it takes its vitality from, and continues to be transformed by their reality. He soon rediscovers the resources that the alleged barbarian has used to resist her status as colonized: the smells, the dance, the music, and the gastronomy of his people. He understands that they are sources that allow the poet's brothers/sisters to live and think otherwise. Furthermore, "resentment" for the deprivation of these riches on the part of white people represents the source and reservoir for rebellion. Similar to the poet's rejection of the "nativists" stance based on an ahistorical nostalgia, he launches a similar critique against those considered to be "good niggers" by the colonialists. The "bad niggers" represent the collective of culturally revolutionaries beckoned by Cesaire to dance. The corporeal eruption is what promises the possibility of liberation.[17]

Following Cesaire, however, the pan-African collective is not sufficient to overcome the dehumanization of subjugated peoples. The critique of Western epistemology soon allows him to realize that they do not represent the totality of the wretched of the earth. In the *Notebooks*, Cesaire points out (unfortunately inflected by patriarchal language contextually prevalent) that "a Black" is de-humanized next to "a Jewman[,]" "a Kaffir-man[,]" "a Hindu-man-from-Calcutta[,]" and "a Harlem-man."[18] Cesaire starts to develop an existentially-inflected Humanism of the vanquished that will soon be glossed as barbaric. The revolt will not be limited to Africans, but will encompass other diasporic communities within South Africa, the Americas, and elsewhere. He also specifically identifies Jews in this context. The inclusion of Jews among the traditional colonized should not come as a surprise. Between the two publications of the Notebooks the world had witnessed the Holocaust and the dawn of Postcolonial struggles. Indeed, the iconic intellectual patron of post-war decolonization, Jean-Paul Sartre, had popularized the (European) Jew and the Black as relational models of otherness.[19] In this spirit Cesaire conceives of a collective of barbarians beyond pan-Africanism that largely includes oppressed Jewry.

He will return to the parallel of the Jewish and colonized experience in his *Discourse sur le Colonialisme*. While the Notebooks particularly emphasize the re-affirmation of identity, the *Discourse* powerfully extends the critique of imperialism. In the text, Cesaire offers a critique of rational colonialism and explains once again the de-humanization of "the Arabs of Algeria, the 'coolies of India'...the "niggers" of Africa" and, once again, "the Jews" who are being thrown to the "bonfires" (thereby circumscribing, once again, Jewish misfortune within a European frame of reference). He further alerts Europeans that they should not be "surprised" by the eventuality of the Holocaust. Jews suffer on the continent what colonized had suffered elsewhere for centuries. Curiously, in a text written to alert the Western world of its criminality, he returns to a traditional negative counter-narrative of the term barbarism. Deeply influenced by Marxist Jewish writers—he repeatedly mentions the need to return to the early Marx and complete him—Cesaire explains how the de-humanization of Arabs, Africans, Indians, and Jews causes Western society to relapse into "barbarism."[20]

In his poetic text written for his dehumanized community, however, he would use barbarism differently. In this new text he goes beyond the African re-affirmation of identity and, based in his critique of Western epistemology, creates a barbaric community of the colonized. In 1948, one year after the second edition of Notebooks, Cesaire published a collection of poems, *Soleil cop-coupe*. The text included one poem entitled *Barbare*. In the Notebooks, we recall, he re-claimed the word "Negro" and gave it a positive valence. The Negro was no longer a petrified, atemporal, atomized character. She/He now formed part of a revolutionary collective with a rich history of socialized communities. *Barbare* follows the same structure identically. Cesaire acknowledges, after writing the poem, that it was Europe who elaborated the "idea of barbarism."[21] The colonized's engagement with a pejorative term and the inversion/re-inscription of its meaning represents "the true operative power of negation," which undermines the Western denial of the colonized value and worth. In other words, positive barbarism represents a refusal to accept the devaluation of the cultural and economic richness of colonized culture.

As he had done before with Negritude, Cesaire underscores the "beauty" of barbaric "faces" and "languages," making the multiplicity of the new project clear. As with Levinas, the new collective of barbarians had a clear mandate. This did not emerge from textual sources, but rather from a voice emerging from "the veins of earth." It is the "cry of unheard revolts" of those murdered during the resistance who "curse" the Western designs. The sound of their cries pierces the "walls" of the "ears" of the barbarian and incites them to action. The barbarian is thenceforth responsible for confronting the racialization, enslavement, occupation, and annihilation that was justified with the colonial narrative.[22]

The multiplicity of the new front is further emphasized in the text. While describing the re-affirmation of Negritude, Cesaire mobilized imagery of African fauna which gave expression to the existential phenomenology of Blacks in Africa and the diaspora. He did similarly with the barbarian. But rather than making use of fauna indigenous to the African continent, he depicts fauna (allegoric or actual) native to the Americas/Caribbean, Africa, and Asia. These decisions accentuate the global consciousness of the new barbaric project. The problem, however, is that Jews have been described mostly as Europeans and (inverted) zoological allegories seem to bypass them entirely. Cesaire's Jew, indistinguishable from the European Jew, assumes an ambiguous status. While there is a full acknowledgment that the sources of her oppression proceed from colonial strategies and were generally welcomed by the new community, the new barbaric construction seems to leave "the Jew" bereft of larger symbolic significance. Ten years later Cesaire complements himself. While he confirms the intimate relationship between the Holocaust and colonization, he explains that civilization is scandalized with Hitler only because his victims were European.[23]

Cesaire, then, offers a positive counter-narrative that engages the particular struggle with global consciousness. Conforming to the classical definition of border thinker, he mobilizes an alternative rationality that leads him to both critique Western systemic designs and re-affirm an alternative identity. Soon enough, however, he acknowledges that this project of critique and identity construction is necessary but insufficient. There exists a systemic racialization, actualized through the narrative of barbarism, that transcends the problem of Africa and her diaspora. He is able to bypass this particularity, by situating this problem within a more traditional barbaric front which appears to reproduce the Third-Worldist imagery. The portrayal of the Jew, however, bristles with tension. On the one hand, he fully recognizes the common root of the racializations of Jews and the colonized. It is no surprise that his student, Fanon, identifies anti-Semitism with Black racism and refers to "the Jew" as his "brother in misery."[24] On the other hand, the intra-European portrayal limits Jewish access to the new symbolic community. Fanon, just a few pages earlier in the same text, calls the Jew a "white man" and describes Jewish persecutions in Europe as "little family quarrels."[25] An Arab/Berber Jew from Africa, Albert Memmi, would be in charge of disrupting the European location of Judaism and explicitly considering the incorporation of the Jew into the new positive counter-narrative of barbarism.

Albert Memmi and Maghrebian Jewry

Cesaire, in his positive counter-narrative of barbarism, identifies the relational histories of "the Arab," "the African," and "the Jew," despite the fact that the European portrayal of Jews may have left them outside of the barbaric community. Memmi, an Arab Jew from Africa, however, retrieved, revised, and complemented the proposal by exploring the inclusion of global Jewry, not just European, within the new barbaric space. Memmi was born on the border of the poor Jewish *hara* (quarter) of Tunis in 1920. Like Cesaire, he took advantage of the educational opportunities extended to colonized elites in Paris, but after encountering the racial limitations in the metropolis he returned to Tunisia to join the struggle of decolonization. While he took an active part in the revolt, he quickly became disillusioned with the place the revolution left for Jews and returned to Paris. His contribution, however, was still officially recognized when he was awarded the Order of the Tunisian Republic years after independence. Memmi's national and cultural writings, the formal reason for this honor, were deeply influenced by the social location of his discourse. As he expressed in his first novel, he writes from the standpoint of "a native in a colonial country, a Jew in an anti-Semitic universe [and,] an African in a world dominated by Europe."[26]

Memmi belongs to a community that settled in the Maghreb during the first centuries of the Common Era. Before the seventh century Jews intermingled with diverse local groups, known generically as Berbers. Following the Muslim conquest Jews were recognized as *Ahl al-Kitāb* and favored with a legal protective status, *hl al-dimmah*. This does not imply that the Jewish communities were free of all conflict. The historical records indicate that there were periods of peaceful coexistence as well as moments of communal violence during this time. It is commonly agreed, however, that despite the legal differentiation, pre-modern Jews in North Africa enjoyed a superior quality of life than their counterparts in Christian Europe.

Indeed, the area became a locus of Jewish immigration, from populations fleeing early modern persecutions. At the turn of the sixteenth and seventeenth centuries waves of Iberian and Italian Jews, escaping expulsion, or economic/social oppression in Europe, joined the berberized Jewries. Now under Ottoman rule, the local Jewries largely considered themselves a native group. This situation would start changing after the French invasion in late nineteenth century, but in Tunisia—as in the largest Magrhebi Jewry in Morocco—remained the case until the establishment of the State of Israel and the Suez Crisis of 1956. In the 1970s, however, Memmi would still hold this long-term conception dearly. In a letter directed to Libyan leader Muammar Gaddafi, Memmi insisted that his portrayal of Jews as alien to the region was highly inaccurate. In a statement that simultaneously speaks to the length of Jewish relation to the Maghreb as well as the nature of this integration, Memmi writes: "our ancestors, Judaized Berbers were older [residents of the Maghreb] than yours."[27]

The region remained predominantly under Muslim rule for over twelve centuries. In the first decades of the nineteenth century, however, the Ottoman Empire began its protracted decline and European

Christians powers, most notably France, colonized the area. For the pre-vious centuries Europeans had confused the term Berber and barbarian; naming the area "Barbary" conferred Memmi's counter-narrative with regional and global significance. While most Jews did consider them-selves autochthonous to the region, France, aided by Western Jewish organizations, followed a classical strategy of dividing the native popu-lation. Jews became, Memmi would write in the guise of the colonizer, "eternal candidates for assimilation."[28]

This was not the case of all the Maghreb, but rather a policy par-ticularly developed in Algeria where local Jewry became associated with the settlers (*pied noirs*) and acquired collective citizenship in 1870. Non-Algerian Jews, however, represented over three-quarters of the population in the Maghreb. While an elite could have aspirations of assimilation, the majority of the Jews—like most of the native popu-lations—lived in the chronic poverty and suffered multiple layers of discrimination associated with colonial occupation. In both his novels and his work in social theory he acknowledges this situation not only at the biographical but also at the conceptual level when he talks about his "triple racialization" (as a Jew, Arab, and African). Legally speaking, Moroccan Jews retained their old legal status and only a small fraction of Tunisian Jews was able to achieve French citizenship before inde-pendence. Notwithstanding French policy, these communities shared a common fate in the Second World War. During the Vichy puppet regime or direct invasion, Magrhebi Jews suffered discrimination, internment camps, and sometimes deportation to death camps in Europe.[29]

The decolonial movements, especially in Morocco and Tunisia much less in Algeria, trusted in the time-honored bonds linking native Jews with the region. Leading figures of the nationalist movements in the soon-to-be Postcolonial states showed early intentions to include Jews in the movement. President-to-be Habib Bourguiba became an icon among Jewish masses, and King-to-be Muhammad V became a strong advocate of an Arab-Berber-Jewish national solidarity. The intention became a reality when their ruling organizations included Jews in gov-ernment posts (either cabinet and/or parliament) once the nation states achieved decolonization.[30] The two nation-states, however, achieved independence in 1956, just months before the Suez crisis. During the conflict, Israel, England, and France, faced Egypt and Palestinians. As a result, Muslim Third-Wordlist populations became largely identified with the Arab side and the situation of Jews became instable. This was not, however, an ancestral confrontation. In previous years, especially during the Second World War, colonial forces had tried to encourage

Arab violence against Jews but large pogroms were exceptional. After independence, however, the situation became more volatile. It was then that the longstanding native status of Jews suffered a major drawback and they started fleeing the region.[31]

Prior to this date, however, a good number of Jews insisted on their long-term bond with the region and joined the decolonial struggles. Memmi himself returned to Tunisia, helping to launch a radical newspaper (*Afrique Jeune* or African Youth), and became an active part of the movement. He insisted, however, that he was not an exception. While the total number of Jews, Memmi argues, may not be striking the "percentage was not so very much lower than for the great bulk of the non-Jewish Tunisians."[32] It is during the forthcoming passage of Jews from barbarism to civilization that he will declare himself an incurable barbarian. He will do it by combining legacies that confront French imperialism, Negritude, and Maghrebi Judaism, simultaneously subverting European and European Jewish narratives.

Positive Barbarism in Network

Memmi's *Pillar of Salt* exhibits provocative overlap with other texts of his decolonial network, such as Cesaire's *Return*. The two texts were written when the authors were preparing to depart Paris for their homelands. Both were finalized and became known once the authors had returned and were engaged in local politics in colonial spaces. One of the particularities is that in each text there is a turning point in the perception of barbarism. Cesaire, as we have read, first observes the barbaric nature of his people from behind a colonial veil. Subsequently, however, he engages in an epistemological break with the colonial mentality. As a border thinker he appreciates the characteristics of his community of origin and, in time, positively re-appropriates barbarism to describe them. Memmi seems to start were Cesaire had left off. In the first part he enunciates a clearly positive counter-narrative of barbarism. Soon thereafter, however, while still affirming Jewish belonging to this network, he becomes disappointed with the exclusion of the Jew in the Magrheb and re-evaluates the location of the barbaric.

This difference deserves further elaboration. In the first part of the novel, presumably written in Paris, the idealist young Tunisian Jew of working-class background is tempted by the French system. He takes advantage of the educational opportunities extended him and excels in the practice of "universal" culture. Toward the end of his childhood, as he reflected on the colonized dimension of his identity, he underwent a sea change similar to Cesaire. Comparing the cultural values of Europe and Africa, he declares himself, with partisanship, an incurable barbarian. The second part of the book, presumably finalized in Tunisia, questions the possibility of this identification in the Maghreb. In his teenage years, the character is invited to join a liberationist front of decolonizers as a Jew. He promptly realized that the same people the movement tried to liberate had engaged in armed attack of the Jewish quarter. As an adult he witnessed the Axis invasion of Tunisia. His barbaric comrades, however, allegedly collaborated instead of defending the persecuted Jews. These two events disappoint the character. He realized that the solution for the barbaric Jew was not in the Maghreb and ultimately fled to another Global South location, Argentina.[33]

While the character of the semi-autobiographical novel does not always overlap with the life of the author, Memmi describes his life in Paris and Tunisia in terms that recall his character's oscillation between barbaric hope and disillusionment. While he was in Paris, he exhibits an unmistakable North African pride. He mentions that once he arrived in Paris he "left behind a world" that was usually portrayed as "barbaric." Once in the metropolis he understood that this barbarism was "infinitely more human, more fraternal and even more refined" than the French "hard and egotistic universe only concerned with self-benefit."[34] When he returned to Tunisia, however, he became disappointed. He joined the barbaric alliance and next to Muslim Tunisians developed an influential journal, *Jeune Afrique* which he uses in the struggle for decolonization. Yet, after political liberation, he was allegedly excluded. While most of his Muslim comrades were appointed to the government he was not. In a later interview he acknowledged that this discrimination was a clear consequence of his Judaism.[35] For Memmi a different solution needed to be found for the barbaric Jew.

Memmi may have been disappointed that Jewish liberation could not take place in his homeland, but he does not abandon the positive re-appropriation of barbarism. He re-imagines its interpretation. After sending his character to the Global South, he settles back in the metropolis. In this context he further engages in the exploration of diverse forms of domination in order to find "a solution" for the barbaric Jew outside of the Maghreb. He finds several interlocutors and, inter alia, engaged in a dialogue with Africana thinking. This openness to a broadly conceived Africa, some may argue, was already apparent in his novel and encapsulated by the very same scene where he re-claims his barbarism. Memmi "returns" to positive barbarism after witnessing his mother's presence at a spiritual gathering. This gathering is defined as a dance influenced by "a tribe" in the Maghreb that was "an offshoot of Negro Africa." He further clarifies the central role of Sub-Saharan artists at the Magrhebi gathering.[36] Memmi will re-evaluate Jewish liberation from the narrative of barbarism operating within a broader Francophone Africanist perspective.[37]

After being disappointed with the fate of Jews after Magrhebi liberation, Memmi settles in Paris. During the 1960s, the overriding objective of his work was devoted to unveiling the patterns of domination and potentialities of liberation that interrelate barbarians and others experiences of oppression. In a series of articles, including "Negritude et Judeite" ("Blackness and Jewishness"), Memmi elucidates the importance of analyzing different forms of domination and liberation which occur in parallel. The Black experience is by far not the only comparative source for Memmi, but it is an important means to analyze Jewish liberation within the aforementioned Africanist perspective. His (non-exclusive) exploration of the Black experience as a comparative choice was likely determined by a number of factors. He may already have chosen these particular dialogue partners because they could provocatively contribute theoretical sources or because they intended to represent a broader understanding of Africa. It may similarly be true that his intention was to analyze "Global Judaism" (including European) from a Maghrebi Jewish perspective and not just his local community. For this reason he may have understood the need to engage in dialogue with networks that were formed in large diasporic contexts which, despite their internal geographical realities, still collaborated with other specific political liberations.

By the 1940s–1950s, Cesaire and Memmi had already re-appropriated the term barbarism. In the 1960s Memmi commenced the aforementioned article, recognizing the theoretical strength of the decolonial strategies of the Negritude movement. This includes not only the literary affirmation of Cesaire but also the positive appraisal of the politics of Leopold Senghor, the first president of Senegal, who aspired to a large African commonwealth.[38] Memmi explicitly acknowledged the influence of the re-appropriation in his formulation of the Jewish condition and sought to further advance these conceptualizations. Memmi confirmed that both experiences arose from the same need to combat systemic structures of racialization, often inextricable from colonial designs.[39]

But parallelism does not mean an existential reduction to the same experiences. Jewish transatlantic enslavement or attempts at total Africana annihilation, he argues, are historically scarce. The relation between Jews and Blacks, however, can shed important light on mechanisms of oppression and liberation. Memmi contends that the collaboration among "dominated" barbarians can be, of course, political. Nevertheless, he is more interested at this early stage in exploring a shared epistemological decolonization. Memmi explains that, at the "psychosocial" level, Blacks and Jews have a common condition to respond to their oppression. Since all political strategy is premised on a critical analysis of reality on the ground, each community can benefit from learning from each other and subsequently think of ways out of the patterns we have defined as coloniality.[40]

In conversation with the diverse experiences of oppression, among them Africana models, Memmi developed theoretical tools that will be mobilized in the service of the Jewish question in the following two decades. Perhaps one of the most important was his tripartite model of barbarian reaction to oppression: self-rejection, self-acceptance, and liberation. This is not merely relevant because it influenced the portrayal and liberation of Jews but also because it enables Memmi, as we shall see soon, to differentiate between European and barbaric (i.e., Africa), Jewish decolonial models that intended to account for the same reality. Memmi, already in his late 1950s *Portrayal of the Colonizer and the Colonized*, had advanced insights about these models. But it is not until the 1960s that he elaborates this three-fold schema.

The model can be found throughout different texts written during the decade. Echoing Cesaire's veiled stage, Memmi explains that after being dominated, the oppressed always commence with a period of "self-rejection." Exhausted from the experience of suffering exclusion by means of a derogatory discourse, the individuals intend to assimilate by refusing to accept, at a particular juncture, the position that the racial system has allocated them. The system, however, is being built upon the same racial construction that the individual attempts to undermine. As a consequence, this attempt at assimilation would invariably find a rejection by the very system that requires the racialization in the first place. Following these attempts of assimilation/self-rejection, the proverbial scales of the individual's eyes begin to fall. Now conscious of race relations, the "self-acceptance" stage is able to commence. The border thinker is able to revisit the tradition but now with intimate knowledge of not only normative society but its vast limitations. The acceptance of her pejoratively construed identity, the "return" à la Cesaire, causes the intellectual to invest time and effort into raising consciousness in learning about the vanquished identity (for herself and other barbarians). This struggle represents, to paraphrase in Third-Worldist language, a "flag for liberation" for the negated and scorned communities. Liberation, for Memmi, is a third step that follows stages that all the barbarians share. This liberation becomes specific to the kind of oppression that each was suffering. Returning to African examples such as Senghor, but also to the Magrhebian process, Memmi states that in the twentieth century, this liberation is inflected almost exclusively in national terms.

The interconnection between self-acceptance and liberation is the turning point whereby we can appreciate Memmi's proposal within a Global South dialogue. The most iconic European supporter of decolonial struggles, Jean-Paul Sartre, had offered years before an a priori similar model investigating Jewish and subsequently Black oppression. In this model, however, Sartre expresses that the period of self-acceptance (or the "authentic avenue") is only a negative move that prepares the barbarian to dissolve her identity and join a positive Humanist-Socialist revolution.[41] Memmi, after his Jewish experience in the Maghreb, rejects this future dissolution. For Memmi, explicitly siding with Negritude, the process we call border thinking (the return, the self-acceptance, the re-appropriation, the counter-narrative) is already a move with a positive content that constitutes a community. He denounces the insistence of a "false Humanism" that qualifies non-European cultures as negative mediations that would only serve to dissolve in an all-inclusive pan-human solution. For Memmi this simply reproduces the epistemological and political asymmetries of power limiting liberation to a unique path. The mistake is not only a problem because becomes functional to the old colonial epistemology but also because the colonized mistrusts the intellectuals who intend to follow this path. This was the fate of a decolonial Africana icon, Fanon, who shared "the fate of those Jewish intellectuals who declare themselves universalists and are suspected of cosmopolitanism and even treason."[42]

Memmi anticipated and preempted criticism of mythical nativism by suggesting that positivity already existed in the re-appropriation of cultural values. He drew from old and new generations of Africana thinking to explain that this communal re-affirmation is not an attempted ontological return to an ahistorical golden age. It is, on the contrary, a "community condition" formed in consequence of a history which seeks to undermine a "structure of conscience" that coloniality had imposed. The communities do not naïvely retrieve the past, but are future-oriented political projects that have a very modest goal. They intend to recast "the whole structure of the universe." In other words, the self-acceptance that leads to the re-affirmation of identity represents an attempt to decolonize the total system of theory and praxis.[43]

Although he personally does not favor them, he understands how a-historical myths are employed with imaginative and even progressive intentions. Conscious of his desire to envisage a global Judaism—including the European—Memmi draws from Africana communities in the Fourth World to further elucidate his philosophy. Going beyond Francophone boundaries he identifies the discursive power of Afro-American Muslim Malcom X who challenged the anthropology and theology of racializing Christianity by asserting that "the first man was black and the man of the future will be black" and that "even God himself was black." This should not be seen as a historical claim. It is a rhetorical move—Anglophone Postcolonialism may gloss it as "strategic essentialism"—which is deployed in the interest of propagating "an exact counter-myth to Christianity."[44]

Throughout the 1960s, therefore, Memmi avails himself of a comparative structural analysis which transcends the Magrhebi region. In his encounter with the broader Africa, he draws particularly from the Negritude movement and its relational projects in other parts of the word. In conversation with the Black experience, he acknowledges the influence they had on his own re-appropriation of colonial language, further elaborates a tripartite model of liberation, and rejects the essentialist reading of these communities by, inter alia, avoiding the discursive pitfalls of Euro-Humanism.

The application of the structure to the Jewish case was written in parallel and particularly well developed in his two-volume *Portrait/Liberation d'un juif* (*Portrait and Liberation of a Jew*, 1962/6). *Pace* scholarly interpretations that currently defy the existence of a unique Jewish people, Memmi insisted that as there is a global Black condition, and that there is a general Jewish condition shared by global Jewry. He defined this as an "inescapable fate" and explained this condition drawing examples from both the Maghreb and Europe. In virtually every case, he follows the three-fold process governing decolonial networks: self-rejection, self-acceptance, and finally a particular liberation that could be a provisional step in the broader, barbaric-wide, emancipation.

For Memmi, the West had been portraying Jews as antithetical to its own self-understanding. This discourse made Jews share a common "misfortune" with other members of the network such as Blacks, Muslims, and others.[45] Emphasizing the central role of the narrative of barbarism, Memmi chose Voltaire as a particularly provocative exponent of this discourse and explained how this paradigmatic figure of liberal thinking "ill disguise[d] his hatred" when he referred to Jews as "barbarous people."[46] The description of the Jew follows the traditional narrative. She is politically, economically, and physiologically deficient unable to overcome her/his condition. According to Memmi, against classical Zionist interpretations, a cursory look at the historical record gave the lie to such a facile and patently false understanding. But the narrative created its own reality by magnifying a perception of Jews, as a whole, who became an incorrigible race of barbarians unable to achieve civilized status.[47]

The prototypical individual Jew, as conceived within this understanding, first reacts to this narrative negatively, rejecting her own identity and striving toward assimilation. These are attempts at rendering Jewish barbarism "invisible" to the eyes of mainstream society. The avenues of escape, however, fail for two reasons that by this point are easily anticipated. First, hegemonic society has a well-established mechanism which requires the myth of Jewish natural limitations. While a certain segment of Jews would undermine the basis of this systemic identity, a further rejection would only serve to reinforce the structure. Furthermore, this active attempt to elude an existential condition creates a psychological tension in the conscience of a Jew. She lives in the eternal agony of being discovered. Her overcompensation leads to a faster and deeper unveiling of her true ontology. This attempt, "far from liberating" Jews, further "contributes to their oppression."[48] In his analysis of self-rejection, Memmi deploys parallel European and North African examples. While he does emphasize experiential diversity, he establishes that both follow parallel mechanisms which ultimately culminate in the same condition.

The barbaric Jew, however, can opt for an alternative path: self-acceptance. Drawing on his interpretation of the Africana movement, however, he rejects any essentialist claim that does not intend to use this path expressly for the purposes of subversive politics. Memmi dismisses alternatives such as physical or cultural segregation (*Ghetto/Hara* return) and a Messianic justification of suffering. He explains that this attempt of "separation" makes them unable to perceive the structural depth and magnitude of racialization and "disarms the oppressed" by theodicically placing them in an apolitical "state of artificial sleep."[49] Most of the examples Memmi employs follow the common practice: The Jewish communities of the Maghreb and Europe have different paths but adhere to a common trajectory and terminus. There is, however, at least one exception. He explains that while some Western Jews dreamt with the apolitical Ghetto, Tunisian Jews predominantly lived in the Hara. When the decolonial movement erupted, Magrhebi Jewry, formally politically asleep, became well aware of the political dynamic at play and the potential consequences for their community. They made metropolitan Jewry aware of the potential danger. But the call remained largely unheeded.[50]

This is one of the few moments in his analysis of Jewish liberation that Memmi makes a distinction between Jews in Tunisia and the metropolis so it deserves a closer exploration. While Tunisian Jewry was better acquainted with their surrounding to understand the politics to come, it is also true that there were reasons for trusting the movement. The vast majority of Tunisians admired Bourguiba and Memmi himself joined the movement. Yet, the "artificially-asleep" Jewry seems to be able to understand the drawbacks of decolonial liberation better than their "awake" counter-parts of the metropolis. Two questions arise from this situation. The first question is whether or not the Tunisian and the French community indeed had the same objectives. Second, one could ask whether or not Memmi implies there is a geo-political privilege of the Tunisian Jewry that even when politically asleep can understand what the Humanist French Jewry cannot. Memmi avoids making an explicit enunciation about either conclusion. This would have undermined his project to speak for global Jewry. Memmi, conscious or not, decides to continue developing a Tunisian perspective of the collective.

Memmi argues that there is a second ill-advised path for self-acceptance of the part of barbaric Jewry. While the first option emphasized difference, the second emphasizes Jewish attachment to civilization: the contribution to universal culture. Memmi does not critique the content of the contribution itself, but points out that it represents a failure as a Jewish escape from her condition. If the individual is not able to overcome the myth of parochial provincialism, the contribution will never be seen as universal. If she does, by practicing self-censorship, Jewish sensitivities are expurgated but the portrayal of a Jew remains inalterable. As one might expect, Memmi uses Magrhebi and European exemplar interchangeably and the European Kafkas, Mendelssohns and Freuds achieve normativity in the process. This path ultimately gets the worst of both world, terminating in simultaneous self-acceptance and self-rejection. Memmi then clarifies that, within the "current structure[,]" there is no solution for the Jewish condition of barbarism. In order to break with the system the Jew should follow the example furnished by other networks and engage in a "radical revolt."[51]

Failed Positive Revolution

The way through this impasse is ultimately neither via self-rejection nor apolitical self-acceptance. The answer, rather, resides in a self-acceptance of the positive potential of the incurable barbarian changing the system through total revolt. Memmi is ready to break with any aspirational alliance with the civilized West. Since this political break arises from an existential need, he finds literature an apt space by and through which to explore it. In his second novel, *Agar* (translated as *Strangers)*, he narrates the failed marriage between a Catholic French woman and a Jewish Tunisian man. When their romantic dissolution is imminent, the European protagonist explains that, despite her deeply Humanist intentions, "the world is divided in two: in the upper part of the globe" one finds "Northerners, [who are] clean and orderly, civilized." The "lower part," in the contrary, is inhabited by colonized "Southerners." This group includes a disparate number of parochially deficient groups with pernicious characteristics including Jews and Africans defined by their "barbarity." Initially, the African Jew was surprised at being included in ranks of this motley collective. It is not only he was a barbarian, but also that he was suddenly "responsible for Jews and Arabs, for Negroes and [revising geographical designs] Chinese." Soon after, however, the barbarian is able to achieve self-acceptance. He thenceforth understands himself as forming an integral part of this barbaric "South" and acknowledges the bond the narrative has created. Even when this acceptance defies common geo-political sense to fully include Jews among the Southerners.[52]

The only solution for Jews is to break fundamentally with the narrative by self-acceptation. This cut cannot be achieved by a self-rejecting assimilation to Western society. The break will be facilitated by a Southern self-acceptance in a revolutionary network with other barbarians. Prior he had understood Europeans, like Sartre, to be limited in their understanding of the positive role of self-acceptance. He now advances in a challenge to European Marxism. The total revolt, he argues, cannot be European. Memmi, loyal to Third-Worldism, is suspicious of classical Marxism. While Jews have been historically predisposed to join Marxist struggles, the school is still trapped in a material reductionism that considers ethnic or national struggles to represent superstructural epiphenomena of the material conflict. Following a classical interpretation of Marx, his followers claim that they can make anti-Semitism disappear simply by making the barbarian Jew disappear as well. The limited perspective to engage with the barbarism of civilization in dialectical materialist theory becomes an obstacle for the Marxist revolution to be a self-accepting liberationist project for Jews.[53]

Memmi refuses to base Jewish history in European social theory and, instead, seeks wisdom from Africana experiences. He asks other Jews whether, for example, they think that the liberation of the "American Negro" can be just reduced to class struggle after centuries of racialized slavery.[54] Jews should follow the examples of the other barbarians, all the while understanding that their struggle cannot be solely explained in terms of material reductionism. In contraposition, it is a struggle that requires Jews to realize the national and racial components of their project. Memmi, therefore, re-places the Jewish liberationist struggle outside the European mandate and interprets it according to broadly conceived Africana frameworks. As he already anticipated, during the twentieth century, the liberation from racial/material oppression in Africa has taken the form of national liberation. Contradicting classical Zionism, he explains that this does not mean the national liberation is a natural or even preferable model of emancipation. It is rather the case that every contextually impossible condition requires a specific solution and in the current context the national path was normative. Following Magrhebi, Black Africans and other self-proclaimed barbarians, Jews ought to support the "most vigorous and political manifestation of Judaism." In the twentieth century, he argues that this is Zionism. For Jews, the only space in which Jews can recover their "dignity" and have a positive political self-acceptance is via the State of Israel.[55]

Memmi's defense of Zionism is achieved by re-interpreting the ideology from a decolonial perspective. After dismissing Sartre's negativity vis-à-vis self-acceptance and the Marxist reduction to materiality, he critiques liberal Western sociologists who reduce the idea of the nation-state to ideal types established around already constituted civilized European nations. The academicians lack the imagination (or the political will?) to realize that Third World liberation movements, inclusive of Israel, are forging alternative types of nation-states. The political self-acceptance, he remembers, is not the constitution of an ontological nation, but a construction of those who suffer a similar condition of oppression. Zionism is a decolonial movement that responds to the condition of global Jewry. As a consequence, it should be interpreted as a movement of the "national liberation of Jews on par with other liberation movements, in the Maghreb, in Africa and elsewhere in the world." Following his analysis of the conjunction of European/Magrhebi sources, he explains that Israel became the political aspiration of "an entire people," of "global Judaism" in search of liberation.[56]

Memmi understands that he is espousing a polemical position. For this reason he further explains that throughout the 1970s, the Jewish state—having undergone the wars of 1967 and 1973—had already predominantly lost much of the early support in had garnered in Left circles. In this series of articles he admits that his position could concern many barbarians. The Third World could see the Jewish State as a European Jewish settler state that displaced Arab Palestinians. He raises, however, two objections to this reading:

The first objection is the presumption that this is only a European program. He explains that the reasons behind the creation of the State of Israel do not simply lie in the continent. Knowingly contradicting historians articulate the position that Jews "lived very badly in the Arab-dominated countries. The State of Israel did not stem solely from the unhappiness of European Jews."[57] The "colonized Jew" needs to "reconquer" the national dimension in order to achieve full-acceptance of his or her barbaric self. He is not reticent, however, to admit that the Zionist movement may have committed censurable acts and he identifies, for example, the 1948 attack against the Arab Village of Der Yassin that become a symbolic act in the Israel/Palestine conflict, as a case in point. Memmi, however, intends to place these acts within a larger context, insisting that Jews have "undergone a hundred or thousands of Der Yassins." Preempting the criticism that this claim is very European, he adds that these similar attacks took place "not only in Russia, Germany or Poland, but also at the hands of Arab people."[58] The State of Israel, for Memmi, is a national solution for global barbaric Jewry.

There is a second objection to the Third World formulation of Israel as a state that displaced Palestinians. Memmi admits that they constitute an "awkward problem" for his reading of Israel. He acknowledges they are "dominated" and rightly "unhappy" with this situation.[59] He suggests, however, that if Israel committed any mistake it was failing to integrate them more quickly within the Jewish state. He asks the readers not to be "naïve" analyzing the situation. Palestinians were not "wronged" by "Zionists" but by their own Arab Muslim allies who collaborated in and reinforced their displacement.[60] This does not signify a recantation of his early support for Arab nationalism (e.g., the

Tunisian). He recognizes both Arab and Jewish nationalisms as legitimate political aspirations. If there is a conflict, he argues, it is because of the decision of Arab Muslim leaders to avoid the acknowledgment of the double legitimacy. This is where his reading of Arabs could be represented as a pathology. He observes that the Arab leaders are "obsessed by Israel's existence and genuinely want to see Israel wiped off the map." As a consequence they make Israel "the Jew of the Arab countries." Returning, unfortunately, to a Eurocentric perspective of Judaism that acquired renewed resonance in a post-9/11 context, Memmi explained that "Israel no more endangers the Arab world than the Jews of the time endangered the Reich." He construes those who are unable to acknowledge the legitimate aspiration of Jews to have a state as "destroying" Israel "symbolically," something analogous to paving "the way for its real destruction."[61]

Memmi effectively included Jewish liberation among the various barbaric decolonization efforts. He agrees that the barbarians may have competing demands. He insists, however, that these are historical "conflicts" and not perennial "contradictions"; as such, they can be solved. The rivals just need to acknowledge that Israel is not a Western "settler state." Zionism is a "movement of national liberation" that reproduces the same aspirations one finds in the "decolonial movements" of "Arab or Black peoples of Asia and Africa."[62] This re-placement of Jews in the barbaric front enables us to pose the question of the future of his project. Is Memmi, as is the case with Levinas and even Senghore, intending to create a trans-national project of liberation that can gather all barbaric forces? A reading of the end of his most classical text, *Portrait of the Colonized*, may suggest an openness to this possibility. In a Third-Worldist tone he clearly indicates that such political national liberation is "only the prelude to complete liberation." The work just starts with the "liquidation" of colonization.[63]

There may be, however, two objections to this understanding of Memmi. The first is his disagreement with Sartre. He explains before that one of the mistakes of the iconic existentialist is to presume that the liberated nations were just a negative step toward a different project, a more peaceful socialist world. Memmi pointed out the danger of claiming the "abandonment of identities in struggle" because this generally presumes an incomplete stage that national movements can achieve. The second objection returns to Africana thinking in the Magrheb. In a piece highly critical of Fanon, Memmi evaluates the proposal of the Afro-Caribbean about the new world that could be created by Third World forces. The Tunisian dismisses this proposal as idealist and finishes by asking whether this was an actual political proposal or just a "dream." For Memmi the project was simply "messianic prophesying" because there is "no indication" that there existed sufficient material or sociological conditions to achieve this project. In a move analogous to Jewish Marx confronting Christian utopian socialism, Memmi construes this idealism as ineluctably reproducing the same system that is under criticism. Therefore, his attempt to see national liberation as an incremental step in larger project and his rejection of idealism represent objections to our reading.[64]

These two objections notwithstanding, in the late 1970s Memmi seems to mature in his understanding of an idealized world in which a barbaric front could be realized. In his last chapter on "Jews and Arabs," he analyzes possible solutions to the conflict. Simultaneously undermining his critiques of both Sartre and Fanon he writes "we are entitled to dream of what a completely socialist Middle East would look like, where there would actually be fraternal collaboration, a binational or even anational symbiosis."[65] This statement contains a surfeit of riches. First, he not only allows himself to idealistically envisage a peaceful future, but he also calls this a dream. Second he recognizes the possibility in an intra-barbarian context, which could surpass the nation-state paradigm as a possible solution, as well as solve all of the problems the nation-state itself has caused. Third, he terms the project Socialist even before he categorized this particular reading of Socialism as a trap of European Humanism. Memmi, therefore, creates the circumstances necessary for himself to think in an extra-national barbaric space.

Nevertheless, after the early 1980s his project took an alternative direction and this potential path seems to be abandoned. The question as to why the barbaric option was aborted remains open. In an interview in the 1990s Memmi analyzed the current situation of dominated people and identified the Jewish historical experience. When asked if Jews were a good example in the twenty-first century he admitted that the "Jewish example is no longer enlightening." Jews, today, are indeed "integrated" within mainstream civilization.[66] Beginning at that time, Memmi discourse shifts, some critics have argued, more toward the center-right of the political spectrum (albeit in a mode moderate way that the French Jewish intelligentsia).[67] In his final writings he accused the colonized of blaming colonization for their endemic corruption, nepotism, and lack of creativity, and understands the problem of the Palestinians, defined as the "foot soldiers of the Arab world," to have been magnified as part of an anti-Semitic enterprise.[68] He furthermore critiques the mediocrity of the intellectual Left supporting the claims of both groups.[69] The barbaric project is, therefore, abandoned. The only question left is the relationship between Memmi's acknowledgment of Jewish integration and the actual abandonment of the barbaric project post-1970s. This is one of the questions to be answered in the last part of this book.

CHAPTER 6

Barbaric Paradoxes: Zionism from the Standpoint of the Borderlands

One of the most iconic stories of Western political Zionism is its founder's alleged "conversion" to a nationalist project. Just prior to the turn of the twentieth century, Theodor Herzl, a young journalist from central Europe, was canvassing one of the most notorious cases of modern anti-Semitism: the Dreyfus affair. According to the now-legendary narrative, Herzl left Paris shocked by the case we discussed a few chapters hence. A perfectly assimilated individual, very much like himself, was not only singled out as a Jew but also falsely condemned through recourse to a pernicious narrative of barbarism. The same society that had shed blood to achieve liberty, the same political system that fought for equality, and the same nation that promised universal fraternity was demonstrating its fierce loyalty to a narrative which supposedly undermined each of these humanitarian ideals. Notwithstanding all the service he had provided to the modern European state, Dreyfus, an assimilated Jew par excellence, was accused of having participated in a seditious plot to destroy the most universal of the Western nations.

Following the affair, and in accordance with a portrayal he explicitly nourished, Herzl decided to revise his early support for Jewish assimilation as a means by which to confront anti-Semitism. Reducing the solution to the options imposed by coloniality, he became the father of Western political Zionism. In the immediate aftermath of the trial he published the manifesto *Der Judenstaat* or *the Jewish State* (1896). In his proposal, as should be expected, he engages with the narrative of barbarism. Instead of repudiating the accusation or reinvesting the term with new meaning, he reaffirms it. Disregarding epistemological alliances with other barbarians, he insists that the solution for Jewish barbarism was perfectly in keeping with Western ideological objectives. He announces his intention of creating a Jewish State in Palestine that would represent a "rampart of Europe against Asia," or even more clearly, "an outpost of civilization as opposed to barbarism."[1]

The reproduction of the narrative of barbarism may not surprise contemporary readers. Zionism is still a highly contested discourse in both academia and the public sphere more generally. Very few, however, would deny that Israel has come to fulfill the role of a Western representative in the Middle East. Supporters proudly argue that Israel had contributed well beyond its share to the West. It established the "only" democracy in the Middle East and developed key technological advances that are indispensable to the daily lives of Westerners. Such narratives insist that these already impressive political and commercial advancements reach the status of quasi-miraculous given the fact that they occurred under the unremitting threat of barbarism, from both within and without. Detractors of Zionism energetically denounce Israel as a colonial settler state in the Middle East that has successfully and hypocritically inflicted the same atrocities perpetrated on European Jews during the twentieth century. These strategies, Western in ideology and praxis, perpetrated programs of ethnic cleansing or genocide that continue to this day. Moreover, they continuously point out that the alleged success is not product of Jewish genius but of expropriation and exploitation of Palestinian resources, non-Western (including Arab Jewish) labor, and the exorbitant economic largesse continuously received from Western powers.

This chapter follows the latter orientation. This particular line of thinking is diverse in tone and discourse and is driven by perennial debate and contestation. One such point of disagreement is the temporal turning point for the Zionist adoption of a colonial mentality. Some date it to the nineteenth century with the emergence of Western political Zionism, others to 1948 with the displacement of Palestinians and the mistreatment of non-European Jews, and still others to 1967 with the conquest and occupation of territories well beyond those stipulated by the United Nations in the late 1940s. In this chapter, I consider previous scholarship which canvasses all of these options in order to appraise continuities and ruptures between theory and praxis. I am interested in exploring how a program that started in the nineteenth century was applied in its extreme in the 1940s and since at least the 1970s has reinforced systemic patterns of domination and ultimately naturalized the Jewish state as a Western outpost against barbarism. In its assimilation and reproduction of this narrative, Israel clearly gives expression to normative Jewish incorporation into civilization and its interrelated racial transformation into mainstream society throughout the world.

This civilizational portrayal is embraced by Israel's detractors and supporters alike. This consensus signals a paradox for decolonial Judaism. In the previous chapters, we discussed diverse counter-narratives. The projects that identified Jews as colonized peoples and positively re-appropriated the concept of barbarism subsequently supported a nation-state commonly identified with Western civilization. In Levinas's project, Israel leads the community that faces a civilization destined to condemnation, but the contextual Israel he supports is an ally of the same imperial civilization he seeks to attack. In Memmi's counter-narrative, the Jewish state represents the ultimate liberation of global Jewry, parallel to other global barbaric liberations. This state, however, would reproduce the same oppressive narrative from which he was hoping the barbarians, Jews among them, would ultimately be liberated. Some may argue that there were some ambiguities in the relationship between Israel and Third-Worldist proposals in the 1940s and 1950s. Both authors, however, end their proposals in the 1970s and 1980s, well after the traditional turning points of the nineteenth century, 1948, and even 1967. While Levinas seems oblivious to these configurational changes, Memmi acknowledges the integration of Jews within Western society and, instead of changing his underlying position vis-à-vis Zionism, seems to abandon the barbaric project altogether. Paradoxically, the only counter-narrative that did not engage in conversation with the Global South was that produced by the Frankfurt School. Though this proposal appears to be free of this charge for a temporal reason, this exculpation is premature.

This chapter explores the paradox of the positive counter-narratives. On the one hand, they understand and represent themselves as supporting a decolonial project. In different ways they integrate Jews into a cohort of barbaric forces contesting Western colonial designs. On the other hand, the particular way they propose to integrate Jews into this project is through the State of Israel, established by a specifically political Zionism that by the 1980s could not be identified with anything other than Western civilization. The identification is not simply reducible to propaganda generated by the disputing factions in question. The State of Israel largely employed the same narrative of barbarism that the counter-narratives hoped to undermine. In this chapter, we explore not only the paradox of the counter-narratives but also the conceptual reasons behind their historical limitations.

Decolonial Barbarism

Between the 1940s and the early 1980s, Jewish intellectuals problematized the narrative of barbarism, one of the central tenants of Western colonialism and coloniality. On the one hand, the context could not have been more propitious for Jewish resistance. Jewish intellectuals had more than enough reasons to distrust Western designs during the Post-Holocaust and Postcolonial eras. Their resistance represented a confrontation with the memory of oppression, displacement, and annihilation from Frankfurt to Kaunas to Tunis. On the other hand, the context also militated against Jews confronting Western society. From Paris to New York to Tel Aviv, the same Jews who had traditionally been considered barbarians were transiting a last step in the re-articulation of their identity. They were normatively incorporated into the Judeo-Christian civilization in what would soon been construed as exculpation from the horror of the Holocaust.

The counter-narratives emerged as options by means of which to confront the incorporation of Jews into civilization. These programmatic proposals, like many constructive projects, contain problematic paradoxes. But before leveling a direct critique, it is important to acknowledge the decolonial features which are responsible for the paradox in the first place. In the last three chapters we explored each project individually. It is now time to consider the lessons learned from the previous analysis and elucidate the decolonial nature of the proposals. I will do it by returning to the discussion I opened in chapter one and explore how the conceptions of hybridity and border thinking can (or cannot) illuminate the decolonial features of the counter-narratives.

Postcolonialism employs diverse strategies to describe the intellectual subversion of imperial projects, but none of them rivals the potency of "the hybrid." This category, coined in its current incarnation by Bhabha, intends to disrupt binary oppositions (colonizer vs. colonized, civilized vs. barbarian) by focusing on the ambiguous existence of those in-between, occupying a via media and constituting a third space. This location is illuminative when analyzing the discourses of some colonized peoples who struggled to adapt to the society of the colonizer but were restrained by a racial stratification that prevented them from accomplishing this objective. The imposed mimicry is undermined by the subversive efforts of the colonized to transform the imposed imitation into creative mockery. This mockery, however, does not intend to re-affirm the standpoint of the oppressed. Instead literature mobilizing

Bhabhian persuasion tends to be more interested in combating dualisms by imploding any kind of polar argument than exploring alternative knowledge negated by Western discourses.[2]

The most frequently employed Anglophone conception of programmatic intellectual subversion significantly illuminates diverse colonial experiences. It does not, however, shed light on the Jewish counter-narratives we have explored. It does not explain the way the authors of the counter-narratives are portrayed or portray themselves. In other words, the Jews who are analyzed in this book are neither existentially nor programmatically hybrids.

The members of the Frankfurt school wrote the negative counter-narrative toward the end of the Holocaust. During this time, Jewish ancestry—however remote or imagined—would earn the body of a European (and, in more limited way, Magrhebi) Jew a place within the gas chamber. This anxiety, which helped give expression to the most extreme incarnation of the negative counter-narrative, was born of an existential condition of complete polarity. It is true, however, that Benjamin, Adorno, and Horkheimer considered themselves Europeans and, in different ways, assimilated Jews. But far from fully embracing this ambiguity, they reacted to their racialization by replacing the polar racialization with a reading that privileges the standpoint of the oppressed. The counter-narrative not only blames the West, the Enlightenment, and capitalism for being barbaric and exculpates Jews from the accusation; but is also locates alternative optics with which to critique the rationality of Western action from within the Jewish textual heritage. The members of the Frankfurt school confronted Western designs by retrieving Jewish commandments such as the prohibition of fashioning images or prognosticating the future. Neither the condition nor the conceptual proposal of the proponents of the first counter-narrative fits the description of a hybrid.

In a similar fashion, Levinas was neither existentially nor programmatically a hybrid. The Lithuanian philosopher wrote the transitional counter-narrative under the presentiment of the Holocaust and described the experience as unique in representing a complete destitution and annihilation. This condition, however, was not just a memory, including the nostalgia of his disappeared Lithuanian family. It was re-enacted during his time in Paris, and discussions of Jewish barbarism deeply divided French society throughout his life. He reacts to this polar existential condition that acknowledges the created binarism and elaborates his response as an alternative option and not as a convivial hybrid space. Early in his work, he describes the barbarism of the

West, and he, more than anyone else, reinterprets in a contemporary key Jewish modes of thinking reproduced over a millennium as an alternative thereto. In his late work he explains that the only possibility of recovering transcendence is through the plural knowledges of those he identifies as barbarians, residing at the margins of the West. His reading calls the colonized on the margins of the West to become a community with the mission of inaugurating the Messianic era through a confrontation with the rejected imperial West. This alternative proposal therefore resists the analysis of the deconstructive Bhabhian persuasion as well.

Like the two previous counter-narratives, Memmi cannot be interpreted by an ambiguous condition or proposal. As a Jew, African, and Arab/Berber, he experienced multiple, overlapping, and contradictory regimes of racialization on a quotidian basis. He did not, however, describe this existential condition as ambiguous. Fully aware of the power of racial stratification, he described it as an impossible condition not because of its ambiguity but because of its overlapping polarities. He is triply objectified. Although the logic of French colonialism placed him, as an elite colonized, in an ambiguous space, he repudiated this identification and pursued the only possible exit for his subaltern condition: national liberation. First he engaged in a creative support for Tunisian liberation and subsequently, Jewish liberation. Contradicting European Humanists, he insisted that his national partisanship cannot be disbanded in favor of a cosmopolitan project that intends to establish a single synthesis. The hybrid, the most popular Anglophone category that describes intellectual decolonization, is therefore a misfit for the interpretation of the Jewish decolonial counter-narratives.

While hybridity is arguably the most important category of contemporary Postcolonialism to describe subversive intellectual projects, it does not accurately interpret the existential condition and the conceptual program of our counter-narratives. Nevertheless, there exists another set of resources that can illuminate the decolonial features of Jewish experiences and proposals. In the previous chapters, we explored the project of Jews who re-appropriated the accusation of barbarism in conversation with Francophone and Hispanophone Postcolonialisms between the 1940s and 1980s. Since then, and in parallel development with Anglophone Postcolonialism, the same barbarians who were in conversation with Jews elaborated alternative theoretical frameworks. Given the historical interrelation of these frameworks with Jewish thought, this alternative space understandably represents a more welcoming option for the conceptual analysis of the Jewish counter-narratives in particular and Jewish decolonialism in general.

These alternative theoretical frameworks also provide a number of categories that help to understand the decolonial features of intellectual resistance to Western narratives. Border thinking stands out among them as the framework that can illuminate the decolonial aspects of the Jewish counter-narratives that the hybrid is unable to recognize. Mignolo coined the term by combining the two linguistic theoretical frameworks that were in conversation with barbaric Jews. He is a Latin American trained in France who elaborated his category of border thinking by combining definitions previously made by the Francophone and Hispanophone literary theorists, Moroccan Abdelkebir Khatibi and Chicana Gloria Anzaldua.

In chapter one, we explored the construction of the concept of border thinking. It is now important to elucidate the differences between this model and Bhabha's hybridity in relationship to Jewish counter-narratives. The border thinker is an intellectual who may be forced to integrate the zone between "the West and the rest" where Bhabha puts his hopes to create a Third Space. Cognizant of the dark side of modernity, he/she is conscious of his/her own subject-position, and thus acknowledges the colonial difference, and selects a preferable option for the side of the colonized. This proposal overcomes three of the central limitations of the conception of hybridity. In the first place, it acknowledges the asymmetry of power between parties in the struggle. Second, it does not seek to playfully deconstruct the polarities. The border thinker constructs an alternative by prioritizing the colonized epistemologies thereby breaking with the two central features of the narrative: her/his racialization and the presumption of the inexistence of alternatives to Western thought. Lastly, it enables the integration of the modern Jewish experience as a decolonial programmatic project. This includes Jewish voices from the sixteenth to the twentieth century. In this book, it also includes the counter-narratives of barbarism.[3]

The counter-narrative of the Frankfurt school is significantly illuminated by the category of border thinking. Mignolo, it is important to clarify, acknowledges the limits of theory emergent from Europe.[4] Yet, he explicitly associates "Jewish" Frankfurters with the emergence of "barbarian theorizing" and argues that the second generation of the institute, led by non-Jew Jürgen Habermas, abandoned the existential condition that made the Frankfurt School such an intellectual watershed.[5] As previously mentioned, the context of the Holocaust made assimilated Jews, who otherwise could have been hybrids, recognize the asymmetrical relationship between the discourses supporting Western patterns of domination and the decolonial discourses of its victims. In their counter-narrative, following the previous Marxist tradition, Jews are relocated among the colonized.

It is true, however, that members of the school—especially Adorno and Horkheimer—possess a clear limitation. They are chary of positive constructions of identity, such as the re-appropriation of barbarism. Since they presume a dialectical reading of history they are afraid that any positive proposal can easily and logically morph into its antithesis. What they miss, mostly for minimizing other non-European experiences, is that the system they are critiquing did not turn from enlightenment to genocide. It aspired to the elimination of the barbarian from the outset. While their dialectical method is historically limited, their proposal is able to conceptually break with the narrative. Their European hermeticism may not have enabled them to acknowledge the historical roots of coloniality, but they confront one of its stages by retrieving the sources negated by the system. The Frankukters opt to confront the totalitarian West with the limitations and possibilities inherent in Jewish maxims. Retrieving Jewish prohibitions as an alternative to the barbaric West, which was barbarically annihilating Jews in the gas chambers, demonstrates their strong support for the epistemological prioritization of the negated side of the colonial divide. If classical Marxism located universal consciousness in the victims of capitalism, the Frankfurt School understands this consciousness as arising from the victims of fascism, allegedly the most extreme (but not the only) of its forms. The retrieval of Jewish sources reveals the acknowledgment of the asymmetry, the affirmation of the existence of alternatives to Western thought, and finally the explicit preference of the latter beyond classical dialectical formulations.

Levinas's counter-narrative is also illuminated by the category of border thinking. Following in the trajectory of the Frankfurt School, Mignolo also points out that Levinas "opened a slot" in Western thought to announce the existence of a non-Westerner, the Jew, who resists being reduced to the same.[6] Indeed, Levinas recognizes the asymmetry between Athens and Jerusalem, the ego and the other, the criminal empire (barbaric civilization in the early work) and the decolonial margins (barbaric community in the late work). He explicitly reflects on the imperialism of the former entities over the latter ideal types and emphasizes the lengthy resistance of the (Jewish) other to the (Christian) self. Following both existential and epistemological conditions, Levinas clearly supports an asymmetrical reading of the colonial divide.

More than any of the other proposals, Levinas's counter-narrative retrieves Jewish sources, especially those taken from rabbinical texts, to confront the constructed dualism with the strength of the ethics, rationality, and cosmovision of the vanquished. For Levinas, the barbarians are the only constituencies with the right to judge history given their general ethics and their history of oppression. The Jew, first alone and later accompanied by other colonized, appears in Levinas's project as the centerpiece of a program prioritizing the oppressed, first as victim and later as the party responsible for political and existential liberation. Problematically, while the decolonial project is identified with the margins of the West, civilized Israel appears on the vanguard of the Messianic community.

The concept of border thinking also illuminates Memmi's positive counter-narrative of barbarism. Memmi, a Jew who lived under a colonial regime, explains better than anyone else the asymmetry that exists between the powers of the civilizational colonizer and the barbaric colonized. He takes a clear stand in favor of the latter by positively re-appropriating the concept of barbarism and supporting the national liberation of not only Jews but all the oppressed, including Arab nations. His support for Zionism as a response not only to European but also to Arab Jewish history presents the project of national liberation as addressing the problems arising from global Jewry and not just European Jewry (despite the fact some Arab Jews will soon disagree with this reading of their past).

This national liberation, decolonialists may argue, can be seen as an emancipatory project that re-affirms the Western cosmovision as the only possible frame-of-reference. Memmi, however, insists that his liberative proposal breaks with the patterns of domination consistent with coloniality. He argues that the communities in struggle should not be disbanded even after the construction of national states. While he favors a Third-Worldist future, he acknowledges that that particular struggle cannot be seen as a negative step on the way to achieving a positive Humanism that again presumes the need of a unified global path of development. Memmi, therefore, adopts a partisan decolonial perspective vis-à-vis national liberation as a way of denouncing two sides of the same Western coin: the criminal colonial enterprises and the fake civilizational Humanism. Authentic national liberation, for Memmi, includes an epistemological decolonization of organizational structures and teleological readings of international relations. The problem, as we shall soon explore, is that Memmi intends to build a future world with a Jewish representation that reproduces, rather than combats, the narrative of barbarism. Jewish integration into Western society, with Israel serving as the chief global litmus test, eventually causes him to abandon the project.

Let me conclude by elucidating the reasons that lead us to describe the counter-narratives as Jewish decolonial proposals. On the one hand, if we were to analyze the projects under canonical categories of English-speaking Postcolonialism, the counter-narratives would neither be adequately illuminated nor respond to decolonial structures. On the other hand, if we explore them according to the alternative theory emerging from their own dialogue partners, Hispanophone and Francophone decolonialisms, the results are very different. The category of border thinking illuminates central features of the counter-narratives. The authors were able to confront the basic tenants of the narrative by offering a re-affirmation of the values discarded by the modern/colonial project. Paradoxically, the proposals that have gone furthest in the dialogue with the Global South and in the positive re-affirmation of barbarism ultimately support an apparent contradiction. They endorse the integration of Judaism into a barbaric space through a formation that is seen by both supporters and detractors as a civilizational political entity.

Zionism and Barbarism

The analysis of the Jewish counter-narratives through the optics of border thinking sheds important light on Jewish resistances. Some of the most radical proposals effectively re-appropriate the concept of barbarism. The positive counter-narrative, elaborated by an Eastern European and an Arab Jew in conversation with (or as part of) Global South networks, rejected the denial of rationality and found a place for Jews within a decolonial ensemble of the colonized. The problem, however, is that the affirmative counter-narratives support a particular integration of Judaism into an assemblage of nations that became historically unviable and conflicts with its own discourse. I refer to the integration of Jews through a State of Israel, which reproduces the narrative of barbarism.

Jewish Studies scholarship has analyzed the relationship between Zionism and colonialism in a variety of ways. Since the establishment of the State of Israel, some pro-Zionist scholarship programmatically insisted that Zionism was a movement of national liberation inspired by Third-Worldist discourses. This trend, which has lost traction in recent decades, still disregards the situations of Palestinians and "Oriental"

Jews as accidents that can be solved within a flexible Zionist structure.[7] With analytical subtlety, a second scholarly contingent understands the local history of Israel as a hybrid between colonial and liberationist features that ambiguously offer arguments to both sides of the colonial divide. Yet, we might suspect that the balance is challenged by the geo-political Western support for the State of Israel that spans the Cold War to the War on Terror.[8] A third trend emphasizes the origin and development of Zionism within a European age of imperialism that perpetrated atrocities committed against European Jews in the past. This trend focuses on the continuity between theory and praxis in order to explore the reasons behind the colonial turns in the construction of Zionism.[9]

This section is informed by the last critique but focuses on one aspect of the problem. Here I do not intend to analyze the multiple patterns of domination and racialization that are reproduced in or at play in Israel and Palestine. There are several schools of thought, including early Palestinian historians and revisionists Israeli scholars (including *New Historians* and *Critical Sociologists*), who have expended a great deal of scholarly labor on the issue. Here I limit myself to employing some of these sources to comment on the tension between the civilizational narrative of Zionism and the decolonial counter-narratives of barbarism that were in play when Memmi and Levinas were undertaking their projects.

Though debates on barbarism are not foreign to "political" Zionism, they, unlike Jewish decolonialisms, reproduce an adaptation of the narrative. The movement, which originated in late nineteenth-century Central Europe, is the hegemonic branch of the most pragmatically successful Jewish movement of national liberation. The general movement, however, is far from monolithic. Other Zionist alternatives preceded, followed, and rivaled its general philosophy and orientation. Examples include cultural and material-dialectical Zionism on the Left and Revisionist nationalism on the Right. Scholarship in the area, however, suggests that when Zionism started to gain traction among global Jewries in the 1940s these trends were not viable alternatives. The options on the Left were disarticulated under National-Socialist or Communist boots, reduced their ideological potency, or were co-opted by mainstream political Zionism. By the time of the establishment of the Jewish state, an Israel Prize awardee of political science argues, the differences between the mainstream and the Revisionist right "was a struggle over the methods of implementing national objectives, not over the objectives themselves."[10]

To elucidate the objectives of the movement, I follow previous scholarship interested in its intellectual sources. Herzl's oeuvre is an excellent point of departure. For a movement that takes pride in its pragmatic grassroots organization, the location of bourgeois Herzl at the center may appear paradoxical. Some of the most articulate examples of pro-Zionist scholarship, however, explain that Herzl became "one of the most powerful elements of the Zionist creed," his life "acquired legendary proportions," and "his portrait" under which the State of Israel was declared became "one of the trademarks of Zionism." According to this literature, Herzl's contribution inhered not in his intellectual capacity or originality. It was, rather, his ability to broaden the appeal of the project from "obscure" circles (read non-Western European) to more mainstream "public opinion" (read unambiguously Western).[11] It is not only that the project emerged in an era of nationalism—a view that Postcolonialists initially suggested, and is now widely accepted. It was a project that first and foremost intended to and succeeded in a "breakthrough" to Western audiences.

Among Herzl's written records, the two most important published works shed important light on the relation between Zionism and the narrative. I refer to his programmatic manifesto (i.e., the aforementioned *Jewish State*) and his novel (*Altneuland* or *The Old New Land*). The combination of the two texts reveals that this Zionist proposal restricts the options to the possibilities established by coloniality and reproduces the same Eurocentric narrative of barbarism that we canvassed in the second chapter. This is a teleological project of colonization that theodically justifies the subjugation and/or annihilation of a community with natural limitations (sub-human, inferior and/or incorrigible). By asserting that there only exists a monolinear path of development, the narrative obscures its genocidal practices, appealing to a common good that obscures Western material and epistemological interests. As such, it creates a programmatic tension for the decolonialists who intend to integrate Jews into the Third-Worldist collective through the State of Israel.

Herzl's political program, elaborated in *The Jewish State*, is without any doubt one the most popular texts emanating from political Zionism. For the father of the movement, the central problem of world Jewry is anti-Semitism, and the cause of hatred against Jews is their abnormality compared to "other" Western nations. While all civilized nations had a nation-state, Jews lacked a homeland. Critics argue that Herzl's "conversion" never took place. He did not pass from assimilationism to nationalism, but from trying to make Jewish Westerners to create a

Jewish Western state.[12] Herzl, not surprisingly, dogmatically accepts not only the diagnosis of the Jewish problem from Western sources but also its solution. The portrayal of Jewish barbarism (and/or Jewish barbarism itself) would be resolved if Jews, like any other Western people, established a state and became a civilized nation among civilized nations. The geo-political location of the Jewish people, therefore, became a central difference between the positive counter-narratives of barbarism and the Zionist project. Herzl, following the portrayal of Zionism as a European project, reproduces the imperial mentality that would be soon denounced by decolonialists. First he flirts with the establishment of a Jewish homeland in two traditional colonial locations, Africa and Latin America. He finally settles for a third colonial location, the Middle East (i.e., Palestine).

As in many allegedly utopian projects, he offers an extremely detailed program of action. Zionism would be realized by a curious amalgam of Western and Eastern European Jews. While the former civilized Jews would found a colonial trust, the later pauper Jews would be brought in as cheap labor to prepare for the arrival of Western middle classes. Following the Holocaust and the Soviet restrictions on Eastern European immigration, "Oriental" Jewry would replace the pauper Europeans but would permanently confuse ideological roles.[13] These were, ironically, the two allegedly "pauper" locations from which Levinas and Memmi elaborated their counter-narratives. From the very beginning some critics denounced Zionism as a project of the financial capital that was leading non-Western Jews by "their noses" to labor for the benefit of Western Jewry. For Herzl, however, the Jewish state was not just a service to Jews of the West. It was (also) a service to the West. Herzl, underplaying that it was the same European civilization that would make Jews leave the continent, makes his contribution to the narrative of barbarism. The future of the Jewish homeland, he prophesied with propagandistic flair, will be a "rampart of Europe against Asia, an outpost of civilization as opposed to barbarism."[14]

In contradistinction to the positive counter-narratives, the Zionist founding father envisaged the movement as a colonial project led by European Jews who sought to create a Western bastion in the Middle East against the barbarism of Oriental peoples. In this programmatic manifesto, however, he hardly mentions the identity of the barbarians. While in his personal correspondence, as we shall see later, he recommends a "discrete transfer" of these populations in his literary contribution,[15] the novel *Old Land/New Land*, he gives voice to a "local Arab," a Palestinian. Reducing Jewish identity to the European paradigm, the novel is narrated through the eyes of two Westerners, an Austrian aristocrat and a young, Central European Jewish intellectual. The couple is traveling to the Pacific and visits Palestine on two occasions spanning a decade.

The description of the first visit overlaps almost perfectly with Cesaire's portrayal of his Caribbean homeland when he was still gazing at it through his white veil. The land is stuck in time. It is desolate, unproductive, and petrified. It is shamefully barbaric. It is, as Zionist slogans would later pronounce, "a land with no people" that was awaiting "a people with no land." The second time, however, the description undergoes an inversion. Palestine is a miraculously flourishing land. This is due not to a European acquisition of a new inner vision of the positivity of barbaric depth similar to Cesaire (who, we recall, develops his influential counter-narrative through recourse to his new optics). It is that the people with no land had triumphantly settled, colonized, and, in Herzl's terms, "civilized" Palestine. Jews had brought financial and cultural advancement to a barbaric society that was, in the best of Orientalist narratives, petrified in time.[16]

Herzl, however, was more sophisticated than the publicists who succeeded him. He does not deny that the land possessed prior occupants.[17] During this second trip, a sympathetic local "Arab" under the name of Reshid Bey, is integrated into the story. In his script the Palestinian intends to dispel any concern that Westerners (including Jews and non-Jews) might harbor about Jewish action. In practice, however, it represents the same rhetoric used today to defend Jewish settlements. Bey ignores the most traditional consequences of colonization that would take place in the history of Israel/Palestine and were already taking place in settler colonies: occupation of lands, displacement of inhabitants, structural racism, political persecution, and state violence. Furthermore, coinciding with the traditional narrative, the native is depicted as intrinsically unable to articulate any political aspiration. As such, Herzl could not imagine a nationalist movement emerging from the local Arabs that might eventually resist (or be an alternative to) the establishment of the colony. He simply expresses gratitude to Western Jews for having brought the barbaric land to the Western path of economic and cultural development.

The Europeans, however, remain vindicated and self-righteous. As self-appointed judges, they insist on asking the Palestinian whether he found the Jews to be colonial usurpers. In response, the Palestinian explains that Europeans are unable to understand that Jews and Arabs enjoy a venerable tradition of cooperation and camaraderie. The Jews have done nothing but attempt to enrich everyone by divesting the land of its barbarism. They are, as Herzl mentioned in his program, a civilizing force that settled in the land for the common (Western) good of everyone (in the West).

Reading the manifesto and the novel retrospectively, Herzl portrays both non-Western Jews and Arabs in a similar fashion. Both are unable to forge the conditions for their own betterment. They require the illumination that only Western programmatic leadership can provide. The colonization of Palestine is a Western project that explicitly intends to combat barbarism by ignoring any political ethos beyond the West. It is true that Herzl allegorically intends to convert the barbarian. This is not a surprise for readers acquainted with the narrative of barbarism and the intentions behind the civilizational mission. The barbarian could avoid the judgment of historical evolution by acknowledging her/his inferiority and accepting the enlightenment conferred by colonizers. As such she/he would become a pliant cog in the capitalist machine. The colonizer would exploit her/his labor and resources justified by the promise of an elusive integration that would be heavily regulated. Zionist scholarship has unapologetically and even proudly emphasized this integrationist feature of the proposal. Such literature contends that Herzl may have been "naïve" and "simplistic," but his openness demonstrates that he was indeed a truly Humanist.[18] The founder of political Zionism simply intended to bring the most generous version of Western designs to barbaric lands and peoples.

I propose to re-read Herzl alongside and by means of Memmi's acknowledgment of coloniality and critique of Humanism. We recall that on his path to the positive re-appropriation of barbarism, Memmi rejects Eurocentric Humanism. Memmi explains that this tradition reproduces a conception of the natural limitations of the colonized. The school is unable to acknowledge a positive political ethos already present in the community and seeks to abandon parochial or national identities in favor of a global status of civilization. He adds that this project actually paves the path for colonialism by ideologically erasing and operatively fragmenting local particular aspirations. One alternative could be a dialogue among the oppressed cultures. This humanist logic for the barbarian contradicts both Levinas and Memmi. Levinas would accept Jewish leadership of the barbaric movement but not the reproduction of a model that promotes a Western illuminist reading of history. Memmi, as we already advanced, would resist the lack of acknowledgement of the political ethos of the barbarian and refuse to repudiate political liberation. Following the Tunisian writer, the reproduction of the narrative of barbarism would place two barbarians, the Palestinians and the cheap-labor, non-European Jews, in an *impossible condition.*

In 1948, the State of Israel was established under the aegis of political Zionism. Two central aspects of Herzl's proposal, the alignment of Israel with civilizational powers and the reproduction of the narrative of barbarism, were further entrenched.

On the international scene, Israel began to be viewed with deep distrust by most global South constituencies. This was especially true after the Israeli alliance with Britain and France during the Suez crisis in 1956 and the occupation of territories in 1967. Since that time Israel has been impervious to geo-political changes and has received, from the *Cold War* to the *War on Terror*, remarkable support from Western powers led by the United States. These resources helped Israel to combat its geographical isolation, develop its economy, build one of the most powerful armies in the world, block international initiatives against its actions, and foster technological advancements that qualifies it as a highly innovative, cutting-edge civilization. On the global scene, Israel has ineluctably become part of Western civilization. During the same period of time, non-Western powers have increasingly deepened this identification by engaging in military and non-military violent confrontation against Israeli and global (allegedly) pro-Israeli Jewish targets, establishing economic and diplomatic blockades against the Jewish State, and delivering international declarations identifying Zionism with racism and imperialism. It is clear that Herzl's dream of creating an image of a Jewish fortress against barbarism in the Middle East became a self-fulfilling prophecy.

From the beginning, however, there was a hope that these internal practices could help Israel become a model for other newly liberated nations. After all, it was a population that fought for independence from imperial Britain and accomplished a "desert boom" using "communitarian" strategies (i.e., Kibbutzim) that could have been "exported" to the decolonized communities of Asia and Africa. The international role of Israel as well as its internal policies, however, increasingly damaged this reputation.[19] At this time the second part of Herzl's proposal took a radical form well beyond any pretense of Humanism and reproduced the narrative in the body of two of Herzl's secondary actors, the Arab Palestinians and the Jews of Asian and African extraction.

Anglophone Postcolonialism is particularly illuminating with respect to the Jewish reproduction of Manichean dualism. To explain this problem, I engage the voices of two victims of the Zionist reproduction of the narrative of barbarism: Palestinian Said and Shohat, an Arab Jew. In the last decades of the twentieth century, they published two related articles entitled and subtitled "Zionism from the Standpoint of its Victims" (1979) and "Zionism from the Standpoint of its Jewish Victims" (1988). These two voices are particularly important because their timeframes overlap with the last stages of the positive counternarratives. Memmi writes the above-quoted *Arabs and Jews* in 1978, and Levinas publishes "Israel among the Nations" in 1986. I explore these voices in order to understand the implications they may or may not have for the French debate with which Levinas and Memmi were engaged on the other side of the Atlantic.

With incisive lucidity Said and Shohat denounce the basic features we associated with the narrative of barbarism, not only in the ideological discourse that preceded the establishment of the State but also in the construction of the State itself. It is true that these voices, many times self-defined as cosmopolitan, do not re-appropriate the concept of barbarism. They do, however, employ lenses able to denounce the intricate use of the narrative. Before starting this exploration I would like to clarify, once again, that the following paragraphs are not primarily interested in an exploration of the multifaceted reality of Israel/Palestine in the contemporary moment. Since at least the 1940s and until the present day, different narratives overlapped and competed to best describe Zionism and its discourses. In the spirit of these intellectual guides, I here point out the existence of a thread to barbarism that unifies its victims until late 1970s or early 1980s (the timeframe of Memmi and Levinas). I do acknowledge, however, that this represents a very partial account of the problem.

Both authors describe the movement as a product of the age of European imperialism and not a parallel process to Third World movements of liberation. Said clarifies that political Zionism never "spoke unambiguously as a Jewish liberation movement." On the contrary, it understood itself as "bringing civilization to a barbaric locale."[20] It is no surprise, therefore, that pre- and post-political Zionist discourses generally sought European support for this enterprise. While in the 1860s Moses Hess trusted in French tutelage, in the 1910s Chaim Weizmann—later first president of Israel—secured British approval of the plans stipulated in the Balfour declaration. Herzl, in his published works, already understood the Western nation as an outpost against barbarism. Said indicates that in his diaries he not only wanted to get rid of barbarism but also the barbarians. Pace the position articulated in his novel, he here recommended a discrete "expropriation and removal of non-Western populations."[21] During the actual events in 1948 the "ethnic cleansing of Palestine," as the process has more recently been identified, was not an excess of war.[22] It was an attempted, systematic military-led annihilation of a people who would come to constitute a significant obstacle for an illuminist Zionist vision. By the end of the conflict over three-quarters of almost million of Palestinians were either massacred or forced to flee the country as refugees.

A contemporary of Said explains that Israel practiced an "internal colonialism" in Palestine. This is defined as the imposition of a capitalist economy over another mode of production that creates an asymmetrical relationship between the settler and the native society. This dualistic construction of (communitarian) capitalism verses peasant economies justified the portrayal of "Arabs" as unable to understand the laws of economic development that could secure a more promising future.[23] This strategy of domination is not foreign to readers acquainted with the patterns developed by coloniality. This conception of Arab inability to "appreciate" its own land was based, Said suggests, on a frequent colonial justification of the conquest of an "empty land." This discourse did not require the colonizer ignore the existence of natives in the area. It rather reproduces their natural inferiority by denying a political ethos justified by the economical asymmetry. It implies that given the inability of the Native to understand the laws of economical development, her "sovereignty" over the land is denied. Therefore, the limited Jewish ownership of land in 1948 (calculated to six percent) was not an obstacle for the declaration of the State. Nor was this a problem for the imposition of a juridical system negating prior Palestinian ownership of land.[24]

The description of "the Arab" followed the classical colonial narrative. It was portrayed as an irrational collective unable to foster the conditions of its own development. They were only unified by their inability to overcome their natural limitations and their hate for civilization. The displaced inhabitants quickly became a "synonym of trouble- rootless, mindless, and gratuitous trouble."[25] Said clarifies, however, that the Palestinians did not resist colonization because they irrationally opposed development. They resisted because, like most colonized, they were unable to view the expropriation of their lands and the denial of sovereignty (let alone their humanity) as positive developments. This construction of an Orientalist "Arab mind," however, was also justified scientifically. Studies of "Arab pathology" were ubiquitous in Israeli universities. Palestinians were investigated as an "unregenerate" "race" whose barbaric attacks on Jewish national building were "essentially unmotivated."[26] The ideological apparatus furnished well more than just university classrooms and laboratories. Even in large newspapers Arabs were defined as a collective who, unable to "integrate itself to a world of efficiency and progress," disregarded "all what is sacred to the civilized world."[27]

It comes as no surprise that Palestinians were usually referred to as Arabs denying their constitution as a people and, soon later, their representation. The Palestinian Liberation Organization (PLO) was accepted by large constituencies of Palestinian constituencies and closely scrutinized by them. Furthermore, within a decade of its existence, the PLO gained international recognition, reaching the position of observer in the United Nation in 1974. Israel, however, refused to accept their political ethos: first to acknowledge the identity of Palestinians and later on its representative organization. In the contrary it was until only recently defined as a "terrorist organization" whose only objective was to destroy the State of Israel. Even in the celebrated peace treaty of 1979 between Israel and Egypt, Palestinian representation was arrogated to the two states and the Unites States.[28] While it is true that this position formally changed in 1993 with the Oslo accords, the description may have well been transferred to Hamas, governing Gaza since 2007, negating the political rationality of a large number of Palestinians.

Israel, portraying itself as a "Western outpost" or the "only democracy" of the Middle East, has always understood itself geographically and ideologically as engulfed by barbarism. The Palestinians were thus denied their sovereignty over land as well as national political representation. They were, above everything else, described as an irrational force, unable to overcome its limitations, and with the only objective to destroy the advance of civilization. It is true that a small number of Palestinians became second-class citizens and, in the aftermath of 1967, Israel took over territories with over one million Palestinians (over two and a half million today). While "toleration" of the "docile" Palestinians became a possibility at this time, the majority of Palestinians under Israeli subjugation still qualified as barbarians. They have suffered continuous harassment, structural discrimination, dismantlement of their organization, confiscation of land, and destruction of their homes, usually justified by their alleged support of Palestinian terrorism. Palestinians, pacified or not, are continuously portrayed as barbaric terrorists and generally defined as incorrigible. When Memmi and Levinas were penning their pro-Israeli barbarism scholarship in the 1970s, Abraham Avidan, an army central command's rabbi, was recommending soldiers (i.e., most of the adult Israeli population), to kill all non-combatants they found to be in their way. Replicating the traditional narrative, this was a justified because "under no circumstances should an Arab be trusted, even if he gives the impression of being civilized."[29]

This employment of the narrative of barbarism was not exhausted with the barbarization of Palestinians; rather, Said acknowledges, the colonial discourse affected both "Palestinian Arabs and Oriental Jews" originating mostly from the Maghreb and the Middle East.[30] The narrative affected non-Western Jews in two a priori contradictory ways. On the one hand, their integration into a unique Jewish people was a requirement for the European Jewish elite to legitimate its leadership in the construction of an Israeli identity and state. This assimilation provided a key ideological function feeding the narrative of Palestinian barbarism. If the Oriental Jew was for centuries living a static and powerless life under Muslim subjugation this could only mean that the Arab had an eternal, gratuitous, and irrational hated for Jews. On the other hand, justified by their alleged primitivism, Oriental Jews were placed at the bottom of society for economical and ideological reasons (i.e., it was feared they could Arabize the European settlement). As previous barbarians before them they were perceived as naturally inferior and when they protested their condition they were denounced as barbaric threats to the state and the national unity. Furthermore, conspiratorial fears, fomented by Israeli jingoists, described an imminent an "Oriental" alliance among Palestinians and Oriental Jews, which could barbarically defy the European settler elite and ultimately destroy the state.

The original plan of political Zionism was to support a massive migration of Eastern European Jews. The plans changed following the Holocaust, the restrictions behind the Iron Curtain, and the unstable situation of Jews in the Muslim world after the establishment of Israel. Shohat points that the groups of different origins were subsumed in one single denomination (*Sephardim/Spaniards* or *Mizhraim/Orientals*) and, from the very beginning, placed as a "future-less bottom" of the society. Despite the discourse of national unity, the distinction between the two sections of Israeli society (a minority European and a majority "Oriental") was striking with respect to political participation and socio-economic status. The national narrative explained this "gap" largely in functionalist terms. Jews from Islamic lands had been living in backward societies without access to modernity and under constant persecution. The State of Israel, then, becomes the savior not only rescuing them from their oppressors but also introducing them to modern society.[31]

Shohat explains this was only a myth of national construction. On the contrary, a significant segment of the "Oriental" constituencies lived comfortably in Islamic societies and were largely urban communities able to access economic advances and social status. If we compare the modernization of some of these communities with the situation of Eastern European Jews who became the leading elite in Israel, the balance would easily favor the Jews of the Islamic world. The reason for the "gap," therefore, was not their Oriental origin, but the construction of the Oriental in Israel herself. From the very beginning, they were treated as disposable lives in order to create a subjugated and pacific pool of cheap labor. In comparison to Eastern European immigrants, they were treated inhumanly in transit camps, sent to development and border towns, and restricted in their education and work opportunities. The gap, therefore, was a consequence of the reproduction of the patterns of coloniality in general and racial stratifications in particular. It was not a consequence of their alleged backwardness. Time only reinforced the division that, going beyond Shohat, reached our days.[32]

Writing in a North-American context, Shoat explores the common root of the oppression of Palestinians and "Oriental" Jews in comparison to the colonial experience in the United States. To the colonial European elite, Palestinians were equivalent to the annihilated Natives as Oriental Jews occupied the functional labor equivalents of Blacks. Her reading is not just a conceptual comparison made from across the ocean. The first prime minister of Israel, David Ben Gurion, had already compared the "Oriental Jews" with "blacks who were taken to America as plantation slaves."[33] Following popular acknowledgment of the association between Blacks and Oriental Jews, one of the most striking grassroots protest movement took the name of the Black Panthers.[34] Shohat Provocatively acknowledges that Jews were simply repeating a common discourse that we have already identified as key in the narrative of barbarism. If Jews in Europe were usually described as Blacks, in Israel they "imposed the civilizing thesis in their own blacks."[35]

The national myth required the construction of a single society and the possibility of Oriental assimilation to civilization was vital. Yet, even the highest members of the Laborist political spectrum (hegemonic until the 1970s) became increasingly suspicious of the potentiality of Oriental Jewish assimilation to and collaboration in the construction of the state. Ben Gurion, in office for most of the period between 1948 and 1963, had compared Oriental Jews with Black slaves, pointed out they had no "trace of Jewish or human education," and showed his fear that the "Arab spirit" could corrupt this Western outpost against barbarism.[36] The second Prime Minister, Moshe Sharett, emphasized that only civilized Jews could truly fashion Israel. He mentioned that was "not a question of number of people, but their quality" indicating that Israel "cannot depend upon the Jews of Morocco to build a state, for they are not qualified to do that." This role could only be taken by "Jews of Eastern Europe [who] are the salt of earth."[37] Golda Meir, one of the most virulent anti-Mizrahi chiefs of government, significantly surpassed her predecessors. In power between 1969 and 1974, she compared Russian and Arab Jews, welcoming the former asserting that only Yiddish speakers were "real Jews." Subsequently she publically questioned the responsibility (or even possibility) of the Jewish state "to elevate" the barbaric *Mizrahi* populations to "a suitable level of civilization."[38]

The impossibility of full correction and, even more important, the danger of Oriental Jewish contamination of the European character of Israel, was further corroborated and undergirded by other sources emanating from the right. Already before the creation of the State, Vladimir Jabotinsky, leader of the revisionist faction and traditionally second political force in Israel after the Laborists, opposed intermarriage between European and Oriental Jews and called for the dissolution of the "spirit of the Orient." While Memmi was writing his Arab Jewish support for the State of Israel, Kalman Katznelson published his *Ashkenasi Revolution* (1964). In this text he advocated the irreversible genetic inferiority of the *Mizrahim* and structured a series of recommendations to preempt a majority Sephardim rebellion against the European elite. He expressed himself clearly: "they look like Arabs, and think like them, and hence Ashkenazim must prevent them from uniting against the European minority" that would mean the "racial decline" and "ultimate disintegration" of Israel.[39]

Was there a legitimate reason to fear of an alliance between the Palestinians and the Arab Jews—two naturally limited (inferior/incorrigible) barbarians par excellence? This was prima facie unlikely. While large communities of Jews largely lived at peace in the Islamic world, their history was re-inscribed within a "European pathology." In other words, different historical dots were aligned to justify the description from "pogrom to pogrom" and securing the liberationist character of Israel. This explanation was a necessary myth and constructed not only an image of the irrational timeless hatred of Arabs for Jews but also the figure of the fanatic Jew of Arab land who only wanted to take revenge for past suffering. Furthermore, the borders' "unsafe" towns were usually residence to the "Oriental" communities making the everyday fight for lands and jobs serve to reinforce the historically rooted ill-will between these communities.[40] While the reframing of history and the internal subjugation of the *Mizrahim* reinforced the narrative of Palestinian barbarism, the fear of the barbaric alliance seemed to be unfounded.

On the other hand, some *Mizrahi* collectives severed the historical distance between the communities and were at the forefront of largely ignored attempts of conversations with Palestinians. From the early community until the 1980s, both moderate and radical movements tried to mediate between the parts in conflict. Some even protested the Israeli massacre of Palestinians and intended to initiate conversations with them. But most attempts were rejected by the Zionist establishment. While a more careful analysis of each circumstance may be in order, the repeated rejection of these attempts may, according to some critics, be attributable to the fear that Palestinians and Muslims could forge a common front and challenge the settler European hegemony. In other words, critics argue, European Jews may have come to believe their own reification of the narrative. This categorization of Oriental Jews as a barbaric threat was not restricted to center-left Laborism or right-wing revisionism. Even long-term leaders of the Left, such as Shulamit Aloni, referred to Oriental Jews as "barbarous tribal forces."[41]

The fact is that Oriental Jews did resist their subjugation and the patterns of domination imported from the long-standing coloniality. Their protest was seen many times seen as a barbaric reaction that challenged not only Jewish unity but also the civilized character of Israel. From the early establishment of the State (ca. 1940s–1960s), they took the streets and governmental building for the lack of opportunities for their communities and the asymmetry between the resources provided to Europeans and themselves. In the 1970s, one of the most striking groups, the Israeli Black Panthers, stormed onto the political scene, reclaimed their affiliation to the Orient, and asked for more than just welfare. They demanded radical changes in the social and political system. Following the traditional oscillation, the state sometimes treated the rebellious forces as primitives, disciplined them with paternalist rhetoric and actions, and tried to disarm them through co-option or the extension of welfare. At other times, they were treated as barbarians, severely repressed, infiltrated, and dismantled. The latter strategy, critics argue, exploited the same resources and techniques perpetrated against Palestinians by the Jewish state. This is not unsurprising given that the narrative of barbarism affected both populations.[42]

The aforementioned denunciations of Anglophone Postcolonialism were written at the same time as the last writings of the counter-narratives of barbarism. The final constructions of the counter-narrative of barbarism and the full identification of Israel with civilization both happened between the 1960s and 1980s. Both insist on the barbarization of Palestinians and the *Mizrahi* Jews. The positive counternarratives of barbarism that are decolonial in nature may have similar theoretical concerns, but they insist on describing Israel as the path to the integration of Jews into a barbaric Third World community. This is probably the central paradox animating our analysis. How is it possible that the decolonial counter-narratives support Jewish integration into the barbaric concert through a project that in theory and praxis reproduces the same narrative of barbarism that they are confronting? More importantly, is this paradox the reason behind the ultimate failure of their projects?[43]

Re-Evaluating Decolonial Barbarisms

In the second half of the twentieth century, Jewish intellectuals disrupted one of the most important colonial narratives: the Manichean dualism between barbarism and civilization. In conversation or within Global South networks, they reclaimed the barbaric capacity of Judaism. The path for integration or dialogue would be a Jewish entity they called Israel. Problematically, the contemporary political definition of Israel could not be disassociated with the Jewish state founded in the first decade of this period. Paradoxically the Zionist movement that founded the state was in theory and praxis reproducing the same narrative of barbarism they were confronted and sought to undermine. The decolonial nature of the project, therefore, was challenged. There exist two means by which to confront this problem. The first is to exculpate the counter-narratives, disregarding or bracketing the significance of the contradiction. The second is to acknowledge the tension and explore the reasons behind these problematic proposals. Let us explore these two possibilities.

The first approach to the problem disregards the tension that exists in the dual support for barbarism and Zionism. A post-modern intellectual could argue that Zionism has never been monolithic and that within the diversity of Zionism, one can find alternative proposals to mainstream political Zionism. It is true that other proposals preceded, followed, and rivaled the movement that led to foundation of the State of Israel. One could argue that Memmi and Levinas are attempting to retrieve Zionist or nationalist options beyond their immediate contexts. Unfortunately, this option cannot adequately account for the tension that the two counter-narratives present. If Levinas had intended to present an alternative barbarism that defied political Zionism, there was no reason for him to exculpate Israel or state idolatry; he could have recognized Palestinians as an-other other and not necessarily a third party. The case of Memmi is even clearer. He explicitly proclaims that the product of political Zionism, the State of Israel, is the only way out for the Jewish condition and expressly supports its national claims, abundantly citing Herzl in the process. Memmi, in contraposition to Levinas, recognizes the suffering of Palestinians and Arabs Jews, but he reduces them to an internal "social question" that can be solved within the current State of Israel and never delegitimizes the political structure developed by political Zionism.[44] This exculpation, therefore, is hard to maintain.

Allow me, however, to venture yet another possibility. A good historian of ideas may argue that Levinas and Memmi lived in pre-1990s Paris. In this context, the possibility of a pro-Zionist decolonialism cannot be readily dismissed. This is not to say that the protest against actions of the State of Israel was unknown in France. While a number of politicians, scholars, and activists strongly objected to actions undertaken in Israel/Palestine, part of the decolonial establishment did not. For example, the most iconic of French public intellectuals, Jean-Paul Sartre, maintained an alternative position. I do not argue that Sartre necessarily influenced the counter-narratives (though very few would contest this in the case of Memmi), but that between the 1950s and 1980s in France—the immediate context of both Levinas and Memmi—a pro-Israeli decolonialism was not out of the question.[45]

Let us explore the possibilities and limitations of this exculpation through the eyes of Said himself. In 2000, Said wrote a short article recalling an encounter with Sartre in Paris. The meeting took place just before the Palestinian-American published *Orientalism* in 1978 and two years before Sartre passed away in 1980. Sartre had marshaled a group of international scholars to discuss the situation in the Middle East. The meeting took place in the home of Michael Foucault, and Levinas was likely listed among the distinguished catalogue of guests. As Said notes, Foucault, to the surprise of many, was already a strong supporter of Israel following his teaching experience in Tunisia. For his part, Sartre had cultivated an unimpeachable record in the French public arena. He was the iconic personification of the engaged intellectual, and his record of support for decolonial struggles was unimpeachable. His writings endorsing liberationist struggles, especially but not limited to the Maghreb and South Asia, came to serve as the metropolitan source of legitimation for these struggles. It is hard to imagine a more provocative encounter than that of Sartre and Said, but the Palestinian intellectual left the meeting disappointed. He was uncomfortable not only with the explicit points of discussion but also with the silences. The Arab-Jewish problem was discussed, but reflections on the Palestinian situation were silenced. Said reflected retrospectively that Sartre, the iconic French decolonial intellectual, "did indeed remain constant in his fundamental pro-Zionism."[46]

Memmi and Levinas wrote their decolonial counter-narratives between the 1950s and 1980s in the context of the French debate. The iconic decolonial metropolitan intellectual during this historical moment was not Said, but Sartre. Said reads Sartre's position with aplomb and insight. Sartre advocated for the Jewish struggle against the British mandate and defended, even in court, the pro-Israeli Jewish right of armed struggle. He "rejoiced" in the creation of the State of Israel, calling it "one of the most important events of our era," and envisaging it as one necessary step (let's remember Memmi's proposal) in the elaboration of a more inclusive pan-Humanism. On several occasions he worried that the fortune of the Israelis against the "Arab mercenaries" would not continue. In the following years he confronted the official discourse of Charles de Gaulle, perhaps the only public figure that could rival him in popularity, and who, referring to the Arab-Israeli conflict, reproduced anti-Semitic stereotypes.

We cannot forget, however, that Sartre formally declared himself neutral, supported Arab national struggles, and on some occasions sanctioned what others would consider terrorist attacks. But intellectual Parisians largely perceived Sartre's position on Israel as consistent with Said's account. Sartre remained firm in his pro-Zionism and demonstrated this stance by his defiance to the supposed neutrality. Toward the end of his life, Sartre accepted a doctor *honoris causa* from the Hebrew University of Jerusalem. While his Cold War neutrality led him to decline the Nobel Prize in literature (arguing he would also reject a Soviet equivalent), his neutrality in the Israeli-Arab conflict did not lead him to the same conclusion. He described his acceptance as a "political choice."[47]

Sartre, the leading metropolitan force of decolonial struggle within France, was not only pro-Israeli but also supported Israel in terms of a national struggle of liberation. In judging Sartre harshly, one might consider the extent to which we are mobilizing anachronistic or contextually unreasonable standards with respect to the positive counter-narratives. I am not exculpating their blindness to Palestinian or "Oriental" Jewish suffering. I am simply entertaining the possibility that the pro-Israeli decolonialism they practice seems to have had a place within the context of metropolitan Francophone Postcolonialism. The contextual exculpation, however, does not solve the problem. We can salvage the decolonial nature of Memmi and Levinas by implying the existence of a pro-Israeli decolonialism in Sartre, but we should also remember that Sartre did not contemplate a positive reclamation of barbarism as a subversive practice. Sartre's position may have been blind to the realities of the situation, but, as a non-Jew, he never claimed the existence of a dualism that placed Jews in a barbaric space. Levinas and Memmi, on the other hand, contradicted historical perceptions of the role of Zionism and supported the Jewish barbaric representation in a political entity called Israel. The contextuality of the counter-narratives can save the decolonial feature of Levinas and Memmi, but following this record we cannot exculpate the contradictory role of the positive appreciation for barbarism.

Since the historical exculpation only partially explains the problem, I would like to venture a second option, namely the acknowledgment of the contradiction and its explanation. It could be argued that the transformation of Global Jewry during this period limited the contextual possibilities for the decolonial function of the projects. In other words, given their new existential conditions, Jews were challenged to generate a decolonial project. Nevertheless, there are problems with this reading. In the first place, the counter-narratives do disrupt one of the most important Manichean dualisms of Western thought and are influenced by or expressed within a Third World community. Furthermore, they pass a successful test of decolonial features when analyzed through Spanish/French-speaking decolonialism. A critic may argue, however, that given its spatial concern, the latter decolonialism may be blind to the problem in the Middle East. Here I contend that, on the contrary, the same decolonial theory that influenced Jewish writings will also manifest the very reasons for the contradiction in the first place. While English-speaking Postcolonialism was able to point out the contradiction, the decolonialism that emerges from the interconnection between the French and Spanish versions complements this identification and explains the misstep of the counter-narratives.

In an article written in the early 2000s, parallel to Said exploration of Sartre's decolonialism, Dussel complements Mignolo's proposal of border thinking by exploring the steps border thinkers engage in developing what he entitles "Transmodern conversations." Like Mignolo, Dussel also constructs his proposal by drawing from French- and Spanish-speaking Postcolonialism (Moroccan Mohammed Abed

Al-Jabri and Guatemaltecan Quiché Rigoberta Menchu). He describes three steps that border thinkers of each tradition engage in an intra-cultural conversation that does not require passing through main-stream European thinking. The first step is the re-affirmation of the barbaric identity; the second is the critical re-interpretation of the tradition; and the third is the actual conversation among critics of the scorned traditions to create an alternative framework of think-ing beyond the monopoly of European rationality. When we explore the structure of the positive counter-narratives of barbarism, we real-ize that the partners of conversation of the Jewish counter-narratives not only illuminate the decolonial features of the proposals but also explain their limitations.[48]

Neither Levinas nor Memmi have problems with the first step of Dussel's process (the re-affirmation of barbaric identities), but their contradiction appears in the third step (the global engagement with other traditions). Levinas offers one of the most compelling retrievals of the Jewish textual tradition. The records of struggle became an alter-native to Western imperialism. The problem appears in the conclusion when the engagement with other traditions finds Israel, contextually civilized, leading a barbaric community that faces a Western imperial-ism destined for destruction. Memmi, for his part, after analyzing all possible escapes from the barbaric condition, understands that Jews have an identifiable core, a common condition that, once affirmed, should lead them to a national exit. The problem is that the integration of Jews into a barbaric space depends on an entity that would be increasingly identified with civilization and not barbarism. His late abandonment of the alternative to Humanism seems to adhere to this understanding of the impossibility of the project.

Between the first successful step and the problematic dialogue that extends beyond the tradition, there is an in-between misstep. I argue here that the problem for both Levinas and Memmi is this second step: the internal critique of the tradition. What is the internal critique they are unable to develop? Let me make the following suggestion: the bar-baric spaces created by Levinas and Memmi are unable to acknowl-edge the normative re-positionality of Judaism and instead mobilize anachronistic resources that blind them to the reality that was already ongoing (and of which Israel was diagnostic). These resources include descriptions of textual sources and the existential conditions of perse-cution. This is not to say that both projects support the same path of a barbaric justification of the Jewish state, but that both fall into the same misstep while constructing the projects that result in this fashion.

Let us take a closer look at each one of the options before returning to the common blindness. Levinas represents a tradition which remains central to current interpretations of Jewish thought. This scholarly/philosophical trajectory understands Judaism to be an ethical tradition that, either based on revelation or history, represents an alternative to the West. The problem with this paradigm is not exegetical per se, but rather the insistence on considering Jewish records as timeless sources of wisdom instead of an archive of struggle. Let me explain this point with an example. In the last Talmudic text we interpreted (Pesahim 118b), Levinas reaches a crescendo when he retrieves a medieval textual interpretation of the original text. This interpretation was likely written during or following the first crusade. In this context the interpretation, the welcoming of other barbaric communities to the anti-imperial community of Israel, was not an attempt to subsume resistances in the Jewish experience, but an aspiration to find new allies for Jews during Christian persecution. Levinas, however, retrieves this interpretation in 1986–1987, just months before the first Intifada, making his interpretation problematic (to say the least).

This is one among many examples of the consequences of employing the same method of interpretation after the contextual re-positionality of normative Judaism. Some of the texts that are employed to justify the new position emerged from very different contextual circumstances. Since there is a presumption of the timelessness of the text, however, the contextual difference is discarded as a variable. The text becomes a guide for Jewish action independent of the changing contexts. If we apply these caveats to the case in question, Israel ought to represent an alternative to the West. It may have represented an alternative in the first context, but a quick analysis of the second places the timeless wisdom of the source in jeopardy. The problem appears when in the second context the reality (the colonizing State of Israel) defies the ideal (the community of Israel as the primacy of ethics).

An idealist could answer in two ways. She can acknowledge the clash and, realizing the change of context and re-positionality of normative Judaism, could level a critique of the real by means of the ideal. But if it is necessary to save the timeless wisdom of the sources, she can avoid recognizing the clash that is brought by Jewish re-positionality and describe the ideal as a potential and not a reality. Levinas follows this latter option by continuously arguing that Israel was not an immediate fulfillment of the Messianic project, but it becomes its potentiality through the application of the social law. Levinas's inability to understand the clash between Israel as a source of alternative barbarism and Israel as a reproduction of Western designs stems from a tacit favoring of the latter option. In short, the mobilization of anachronistic resources—in this case, texts as repositories of timeless wisdom—tends to create a set of circumstances unable to acknowledge normative re-positionality.

Memmi represents a second trend that appears in the exact opposite space of Levinas but reproduces a parallel tension. A priori the justification of the State of Israel is not about its timeless ethical potentiality, but its historical reality. Integrating the history of European and Arab Jewry, he describes the Diaspora as an impossible condition. The only possibility of solving the problem is via national liberation. He recognizes that there is no ideal situation, but instead of confronting the problem, Memmi declares them transitory tensions and the responsibility of the state is downgraded. Palestinians and Mizrahi Jews, for example, may be undergoing suppression. But these are just "internal problems" that would be solved in time. In concrete terms, the former are largely victims of the Arab neighbors and the latter comparison to Afro-Americans is hyperbolic at best. Memmi, as Levinas before, ignores the reproduction of the same narrative they denounce, places the State of Israel within a decolonial context, and ends by vesting trust in the future to solve the problems.

Memmi, however, lives for longer than Levinas and, after the 1980s, becomes unable to support this vision for the State of Israel. Even before the transformation, he resisted the formation of a barbaric front which included Israel. During this later period he still believes that Israel is a young nation, but he largely overlooks her previous placement among postcolonialist regimes. This is not to say that he qualifies Israel as a colonial state, but he undermines the liberationist character he saw earlier in the Postcolonial states rendering in-transcendent the collectivity. What can explain this sea change in Memmi's position? There is one fundamental change in Memmi's perspective. In the first stage he considered Jewishness an impossible condition and was unable to acknowledge the changing global conditions of normative Judaism. In the second stage, he acknowledges (and celebrates!) Jewish integration within the West, acknowledging that his previous understanding of the impossible condition of Jewishnness was attributable to an anachronistic narrative of persecution that no longer (and perhaps never) existed.

Memmi, in this new situation, is confronted by a difficult situation. One of his central arguments he has advocated throughout his work is that the defense of the oppressed does not follow identification with them but a frank rejection of oppression. In a first stage his support for the barbarians and Jewish solution was not a contradiction because Jews needed a solution for their oppression as well. As a "double colonized" (Tunisian and Jewish) man, this position was not a problem in this first stage. In the second stage, however, he recognizes that Jews have lost that barbaric condition that had theretofore defined them. Therefore, it does not seem to constitute a compelling reason to support the Jewish struggle anymore, especially when it is confronted with and persecutes those defined as currently oppressed. Yet, he decides to continue his defense of the Jewish position in both France and Israel. If one reads his comments, especially those advanced with respect to Palestinian and Maghrebi immigrants, two factors are immediately noticeable. He does recognize their domination and loosely hopes for a solution, but does not engage in the struggle and aligns himself with normative Jewish interests now in a Western framework. After the 1980s, Memmi still recognizes oppression, but the re-positionality weakens his aforementioned preference for the oppressed.

During the transitional period spanning to the 1980s the two positive counter-narratives of barbarism failed to advance an internal critique of Jewish re-positionality. Their analyses mobilize anachronistic resources to justify a normative Jewish presence among the underside of history to which current reality was increasingly giving the lie. The entity they defended as representative was not combating but reproducing the same narrative they were critiquing. Their lack of acknowledgement of progressive change in the racialization of normative Judaism resulted in their inability to recognize, let alone confront, the contradiction. Taking refugee in anachronistic readings of texts or existential conditions, they became conceptually limited in their ability to offer a plausible project of the new normative positionality that was opening in front of their eyes. The most important failure, however, was not just conceptual. After the period the acknowledgment of the re-positionality would lead to the abandonment of the project. Furthermore, as we shall see in the next chapter, their historical legacies in a post-9/11 context would use their records to support the opposite project: a narrative of neo-barbarism. This made the positive counter-narrative of barbarism fail twice: first during the transition and second in its aftermath.

CHAPTER 7

After 9/11: New Barbarism and the Legacies in the Global South

In 2004, the central Jewish community of Argentina, then under labor leadership, published a book entitled *La cuestión Judía vista desde la izquierda* (*The Jewish Question Through the Eyes of the Left*). A priori, the book was promising. Marcos Aguinis, the author, boasted a long-term record of social engagement and activism. He was part of the opposition to the aforementioned dictatorship that disproportionately targeted Jews in order to secure the advancement of civilization in the South. After the return of democracy he would become the secretary of culture to the democratic government that brought the perpetrators of genocide to justice. Explicitly influenced by Memmi, Aguinis's book not only reflects on the narrative of barbarism but also addresses "decolonial" constituencies, with the principle objective of engaging in a uniquely Jewish reading of global politics "from the South."[1]

The actual content of the book, however, is a testimony to Jewish re-positionality. The Argentinean reframes Jewish history explaining to confused revolutionaries, including survivors of the persecution, how former friends—their own comrades—have been not only enemies, but unabashed anti-Semites as well. He accuses the Left of having entered into an alliance with the Fascist right and Islamic fundamentalism, vesting responsibility for the history of anti-Semitism largely in these new barbarians. While he recognizes persecution of Jews in the Western hemisphere, he exonerates his reified understanding of the West of this atrocity. He glosses this political formation as a staunch proponent of the same "human rights" that the "democratic" or "liberal" West denied to Argentinean Jews in the 1970s and 1980s. Aguinis concludes his book naturalizing the Jewish alliance with

Western civilization, which paradoxically represents the antithesis of Memmi's original objective.[2]

Aguinis's reading was not exceptional. An analogous discourse, which identified a similar alliance of geopolitical formations and constituencies as a threat to the West and as responsible for the historical suffering of Jews, existed throughout America, Europe, and Israel at the time. Some propagandists, not surprisingly, identified the alleged phenomenon as an alliance of three "barbaric movements," Marxism, Islam and Fascism.[3] This new narrative not only dominated Jewish normative discourses around the globe but also deeply affected the resistances under examination in this book. Both the first and second positive counter-narratives had an almost identical fortune. Bernard-Henry Levy, a Maghrebi intellectual whose family joined many Algerians fleeing to France, largely appropriates this understanding. BHL, as he was known publically, supported the revolutionary fervor of the late 1960s and later became one of the most famous self-appointed heirs of Levinas. With other intellectuals, largely disappointed Jews, he inaugurated a long-lived tradition of renouncing the Left and, after 9/11, accusing his former comrades of entering into an alliance with "Islamofascists." Uniting the three movements conceptually, he follows Levinas in articulating a "prayer" of destruction. Drawing on the imagery and symbolism furnished by the rabbinic tradition, Levinas imparts his hope for the defeat of the empire, while BHL energetically prays for the West to make an unequivocal "stand against the new barbarism."[4]

In this concluding chapter, I venture beyond the era with which this book is first and foremost concerned (1940s–1980s) in order to analyze the current debate on barbarism. Specifically, I explore the narrative of new barbarism. To be sure, Jews still occupy a central place within this narrative. This time, however, Jews not only serve as discursive subjects, but the normative voices become also responsible for the articulation and propagation of the narrative itself. That is, Jews and Israel are not only incorporated into Western civilization, but the latter is understood as inconceivable without express Jewish support for this integration/collaboration. The Southern heirs of the failed positive counter-narratives of barbarism incorporate features of Levinas and Memmi and adapt them to this new option. In so doing, they reproduce some of the same limitations of their predecessors and contribute new paradoxes by recanting the aspiration for a positive barbarism. In this way they cause the counter-narratives to fail twice: first by their blindness to the contextual limitations of Jewish incorporation within a decolonial struggle and second by the reproduction of a new narrative of barbarism, attendant upon the abandonment of the aspiration for a positive contribution.

It is important to note, however, that the existence of this normative Jewish understanding and deployment of barbarism does not mean that all Jews subscribe to this narrative. To provide a sense of the diversity of perspectives, I here analyze a contemporary Global South reinterpretation of the negative counter-narrative, which derives from the same geopolitical context that produced Aguinis. An exploration of Ricardo Forster's "Notas sobre la barbarie y la esperanza: Del 11 de septiembre a la crisis Argentina" ("Notes on Barbarism and Hope: From 9/11 to the Argentinean Crisis"), allows for the analysis of the possibilities and limitations engendered by the re-positionality of Jews through the civilization/barbarism dualism.[5] This analysis will culminate in a discussion of whether it is preferable, in the current context, to abandon the positive counter-narrative of barbarism altogether or whether some of its more promising and radical features can be recovered and retrofitted for future generations.

Narrative of the New Barbarism

It may be objectionable to take September 11, 2001, as the point of departure to discuss the currency of the narrative of barbarism. On the one hand, the explanation for the attack against the World Trade Center is discernible well prior to this time. A provocative decolonial theorist will point out this was a resistance against a new articulation of the patterns of domination of coloniality that have been in play since the sixteenth century. A meticulous historian would likely explain it as a reaction to the European colonization and subsequent Euro-American neo-colonization of the Middle East, which began in the eighteenth century (if not prior). An articulate political scientist may explain it as an unintended result of American Cold War political tactics, which provided resources to Islamic groups to engage in proxy warfare against the Soviet Union. An avid international relations scholar may explain it in terms of an American quest for a global rival, largely absent since the implosion of the USSR. On the other hand, 9/11 did inaugurate a new era in the international scene. While the systemic roots can be found before this time, the events of 9/11 served to crystallize a long-term geopolitical discourse that required the reinforcement of Manichaeisms in general, and the dichotomy between civilization and barbarism in particular.

The current consensus among international relations experts is that 9/11 was indeed a watershed with respect to the popularity of Manichean dualisms. This is not to say that the discourses did not exist during the years following the Cold War, but they needed to share their space with vocal prophets who were announcing the end of history and the ultimate triumph of Western capitalism.[6] The post-9/11 era, however, witnessed the re-instantiation of one of the oldest, if pernicious, features of coloniality: the narrative of barbarism.[7] For example, American president George W. Bush identified members of Al-Qaeda very early in the process as "barbaric criminals."[8] A year later he defined the Taliban regime in Afghanistan as "one of the most barbaric regimes in the history of mankind."[9] Throughout the first decade of the century, different European leaders, like Silvio Berlusconi, pledged to guarantee the superiority of "Western civilization," a coalition that explicitly comprised Europe, America, and Israel.[10] In his last year in power Bush condemned Hamas's strike against the Jewish state, by qualifying it a "barbaric and vicious attack," which paved the way for his secretary of state to declare the "barbarous act had no place among civilized nations."[11]

The political rise of the narrative was simultaneous to and concomitant with its formulation in technical circles. Robert Kaplan is one of the most influential proponents of a theory of new barbarism that was widely used after 9/11. Notwithstanding many conspiracy theories to the contrary, this is not to suggest that Jews or Judaism in general are responsible for current geopolitical outcomes. It simply means that the change in racial configuration positioned normative Jewry among the necessary enunciators of a geopolitical perspective that perforce employs the narrative of barbarism. Kaplan is an American-born consultant who joined the Israeli army in his youth and was deeply influenced by the Jewish state's military history. He became a prolific journalist, specializing in national security and serving as lecturer at several institutions including the US Naval Academy in Annapolis, the CIA, and the FBI. His expertise was broadly recognized not only by Republican but also by Democratic administrations. Clinton declared Kaplan's argument influential in his position regarding Bosnian Muslims and the Obama administration appointed him to the Defense Policy Board in 2011. His rising stardom was recognized by Foreign Policy magazine, which included him among the "top 100 Global Thinkers."[12]

According to Kaplan, current debates are stymied by a "social-social science" which seeks to use socio-economic phenomena to explain political situations around the globe. In lieu of this procedure, he insists that the behavior of certain collectives primarily inheres in their "natural," "environmental," or "basic" structures. Several societies that have not been illuminated by Western values lack the civic ethos that can ultimately trigger their development. Their social context (e.g., chronic mass poverty, epidemic diseases, political instability, etc.) is a direct consequence of their inability to achieve civilized development. The inhabitants of these societies engage in irrational violence, against themselves and against their perceived exterior enemies, as a way to canalize their "frustration" in a mistaken path to liberation. This traps them in a vicious cycle of violence, in which the promised freedom remains unachieved and illusory. At first glance, this understanding bears a striking resemblance to Samuel Huntington's *Clash of Civilizations* theory, perhaps the most renowned neoconservative manifesto of the late twentieth century.[13] Kaplan, however, differs in one key aspect. Huntington qualified (or constructed) non-Western collectives as alternative civilizations that rival and sometimes offer stronger core formations than the West. Kaplan, however, understands these same formations as peopled by anarchical barbarians unable to achieve a normative civil ethos.[14]

Kaplan's new barbarism, critics argue, merely serves to naturalize the consequences of global dynamics. Disregarding the social, political, and economic consequences of geopolitical designs, Kaplan fails to acknowledge the role of global capitalism in the formation and perpetuation of the social conditions obtaining in these societies. Furthermore, the monomaniacal quest for fixed "environmental" sources of poverty and violence seems to offer a complete unbalanced negotiation between the incorregibility of the barbarian and the civilized mission. These barbarians, unable to understand civic virtues, irrationally reject adaptations of modern values and remain immersed in a constant spiral of violence. Kaplan further supports his position by asserting that there exists no historical indication of the possibility (and, implicitly, the desirability) of the exportation of Western values to non-developed societies. The irrational peoples of Africa, Asia, and Latin America are, as the narrative understands them, intrinsically unable to divest themselves of their barbarism.[15]

In several passages of his work, Kaplan appears to hope that the barbarians will die of starvation, epidemic, or intra-fraternal struggle. Indeed, this "top global thinker" became the prophet of the most extreme of conditions. Remarkably following Coetzee's presentation he predicts the coming of an anarchical era in which civilization will perilously exist surrounded by threatening barbarians. Both the State of Israel and civilized Judaism play a determinative role in the geopolitical landscape to come. Israel, for example, assumes a role which exceeds that of ally to Western powers. Inverting the current description of Israel surrounding Palestinians, Kaplan argues that given the "violent youth culture of the Gaza shantytowns," the Jewish state will become a Western "fortress" among a "volatile" sea of barbarism. Israel, however, is not only the functional equivalent of a geographic wall against Islam, as previous generations beginning with Herzl imagined it. It represents, rather, a symbolic and confirming force proving that it is possible to cultivate civilization despite being surrounded by barbarism.

For this reason Israel ought to be seen as exemplary of a democratic civic ethos and functional capitalist economy. Muslims (Palestinians, Taliban members, Iraqis, Iranians, etc.), for their part, are portrayed ipso facto as irrational barbarians who resort to violence due to their intrinsic inability to develop either a democratic ethos or capitalist economy. Israel is thus portrayed not simply as a strong militaristic border, constantly besieged by the threat of barbarism. It is to remain the only democracy of the Middle East demonstrating that it is possible, in the coming world, to develop a Western polis and capitalist economy despite the unfortunate and ubiquitous presence of barbarism in the region. Israel becomes then the gurantee for the survival of coloniality.[16]

Barbarism is a phenomenon that exists not only in the Global South proper. The existence of growing minority populations in civilized nation-states threatens both the comfort and stability of civilization in developed nations with venerably civilized values. This description implicitly includes both immigrants (Muslims, Africans, Latin Americans) and racialized groups (Latinos/as, Natives, and Afro-Americans/Europeans) in America and Europe. Euro-American Jews, in this context, fulfill a second role: the confirmation of others' barbarism, simply by instantiating an unbreachable and unimpeachable model community. It is true, Kaplan argues, that in the post-war era Jews, who previously had not been generally considered civilized, were able to assimilate into mainstream American society. Even Huntington, who doubts if Israel belongs (or is just an ally) to Western civilization, confirms the remarkable adaptability of Jews to American society.[17] Kaplan implies that Jews exhibit a profound solidarity vis-à-vis these disenfranchised communities and routinely attempt to teach them strategies of adaptation to Western society. Nevertheless, the minority communities, including but not limited to Afro-Americans, decide irrationally to reaffirm their identity and reject the advice of those who successfully adapted to society. The irrational rejection of this path to assimilation is proof of their thoroughgoing barbarism (not to mention their anti-Semitism).[18] Across the Atlantic, public intellectual Alain Finkielkraut misreads post-war French history in a fashion similar to Kaplan. Finkielkraut is the son of Eastern European survivors of the Holocaust and one of the most popular public intellectuals in France. He explains that Jews after the Second World War were received by French society with "open arms" due to of their lack of "resentment" toward Europe, a general "gratitude" to the society, and "openness" to assimilation. Nevertheless, current immigrant communities—largely but not limited to Muslims/Africans—irrationally reject said adaptation, justifying their "barbaric costumes" by, inter alia, appealing to "identity politics." He describes the reaffirmation of the identity of the barbaric colonized as a residual heritage of European Fascism. This strange liaison between right-wing xenophobic groups and immigrants from Africa, Asia, and Latin America is supported by a "naïve Left" that misuses historical resources to justify what is variously termed "Islamofascism."[19] The alleged rhetoric of anti-Semitism employed by this supposed alliance is a fundamental component of the portrayal of Jews in twenty-first century narratives of barbarism.

The narrative that depicts the new barbarians supported by the Right and the Left, the Fascists and the Marxists, is in wide circulation throughout the English-speaking world. Daniel Pipes, an American Jew who founded "Campus Watch" to denounce barbaric activities in American universities, goes a step further than Finkielkraut. In a public debate in London, as if the cross-North-Atlantic symbiosis needed to be emphasized, he explicitly rejects the pre-9/11 Huntingtonian argument (as articulated in *Clash of Civilizations*) to explain the War on Terror. What is at stake for Pipes is a struggle "between civilization and barbarism." The first is represented by a "civilization" centered in the United States, Israel, and Europe. The latter, the enemy, is represented by the three usual suspects of Fascism, Marxism, and Islam. He identifies them as nothing other than three "barbaric movements." The commonality among these parties is the usual description of barbarians: natural limitations, rejection of Western rationality, desire to regress history, and senseless homicide of millions of innocents.[20]

The integration of the enemies of the Second World War, the Cold War, and the War on Terror, finds some of its most articulate exponents in public intellectuals and scholars belonging to the school known as the "New Anti-Semitism." The school can be found in America, Europe, and Israel and is not new. Since at least the 1980s it has espoused the position that anti-Zionism is equivalent to anti-Semitism. 9/11, however, brought a "new atmosphere" and dynamism to the problem. Due to the extraordinary advancements in the transmission of knowledge and speed of communication, a "new mutant strain of Anti-Semitism" has steadily been acquiring force and momentum. This "frightening coalition at a Global scale" finds "the extreme right and extreme left working together with immigrants of Arab descent and terrorist organizations."[21] This "unlikely" (as they explicitly recognize) unholy alliance employs a discourse of anti-racism in order to make Israel the equivalent of the Jew in international politics. Israel, according to this logic, is to barbarians what Jews were to Europe. Furthermore, they ask the West to be attentive to these attacks. The Palestinian cause became the rally of operations against the West, and an attack against Israel represented not simply an attack against all Jewry, but an attack against the whole West. Making Islam the center of their concerns, they echo voices that call for a full-fledged struggle against "barbarians who clothe their criminal deeds" with fanatic religious "canonization."[22]

This reading, naturally, is replete with paradoxes. To name a few requires only the phrasing of a few questions: how is it possible that the same narrative that led to the oppression of Jews is now represented as a guarantee of their very survival? How much does the Euro-American ability to enunciate a triumphalist discourse depend on the transference of its guilt? To what extent is a repackaged version of the same narrative likely to create alternative geo-political results? These important questions notwithstanding, the purpose of this section is not to deconstruct the internal logic of the argument. While the narrative of barbarism has not been central to their concerns, other historians and theorists have analyzed interrelated questions and elaborated provocative answers.[23]

Here I attempt to show that in the post-9/11 Global North, the narrative of barbarism has been re-enacted and Jews still hold a central role. But they nonetheless find themselves on the other side of the equation. The new narrative of barbarism elaborates several roles for Jews. Israel and the Jewish community are portrayed as eternally Western and in some narratives even the guarantors of Western survival. Any attack against Israel, furthermore, represents an assault against world Jewry as well as the entirety of the West itself. The locus of barbarism inheres in an unlikely alliance among xenophobic Fascists, anti-racist Marxists, and terrorist Muslims. Lastly, the barbarians cannot be redeemed and should be destroyed.

Failed Legacies in the Global South

Jewish participation in the new narrative of barbarism is as paradoxical as it is persuasive. In the interests of full disclosure, I admit that when I began research for this book I hoped to reach the opposite conclusion. Following some of my previous work, I imagined I would demonstrate the existence of a barbaric Judaism that would likely emerge in the Third World. While Jews with origins in the Global South, for existential reasons, have a higher potentiality for reclaiming barbarism, many have nearly fully assimilated the new reclassification of Judaism. As I demonstrate in the following paragraphs, they reproduce a narrative of barbarism that puts them at odds with the possibility of integrating Judaism within a community of barbarians.

Only months before 9/11, a group of self-appointed heirs to Levinas established *L'Institut d'Études Lévinassiennes* in Paris and *Ha-Makon Lelimudei-Levinas* in Jerusalem. The founders of these research centers were former Left-wing activists who became disillusioned after 1968 and eventually found a political alternative in Levinasian philosophy. In the last few years, these scholars and activists made discussions about barbarism a central aspect of their work. In these accounts, the problem is not the magnification of the tension that was already in place in Levinas's work, but the fact that, in the context of the new narrative of barbarism, the transitional step toward a positive barbarism is largely forgotten. The previous section canvassed the reproduction of the narrative of barbarism produced by an Eastern European co-founder of the institute, Alain Finkielkraut. Here I would like to focus on the failure to pursue the counter-narrative by an heir to Levinas who was born in the Global South and had an early participation on the Left: Algerian-born Bernard-Henry Levi (henceforth, BHL).[24]

This public intellectual wrote two books analyzing the problem of barbarism. In the second one, a reflection written for the American public after 9/11, he concludes by elaborating (as the subtitle indicates): "A Stand Against the New Barbarism." The argument, as we might anticipate, forgets the positive contribution of his mentor and grapples with some of the contradictions with the narrative of barbarism. He trades in some of the predictable tropes of the contemporary discourses of coloniality, presupposing the existence of a Marxist/Fascist/Muslim barbaric alliance against the West and the inexistence of a political ethos in what he terms "Islamofascism." BHL, however, takes this one step further. Not only, in his estimation, are all attacks against Israel/Jews ipso facto attacks against the West, but attacks against the West itself can similarly be read as anti-Semitic attacks against Jews. In the post-9/11 context, BHL's anti-barbaric stand attempts to overcome the limitations of Levinas's counter-narrative with the new narrative, dismissing the "positive" contribution advanced by his mentor.

Before taking his twenty-first century stance against the new barbarism, BHL wrote a book in the middle of the Cold War entitled *La barbarie à visage humain (Barbarism with a Human Face)*. The text formed part of an ensemble of manifestos produced by a group of young—largely Jewish—intellectuals who were disappointed with Marxism after 1968. The title of the book alludes to the famous Czechoslovakian program of reforms, "Socialism with a Human Face," which was repressed by the Soviets. The book contains compelling insights on Levinas in particular and the negative counter-narrative in general. One of his central themes in his analysis is the limitations of Marxism. He explains that this political program and philosophy of history, along with Fascism and the Enlightenment, are faithful to a Western idea of progress that traps them within a "double standard." On the one hand, the movements promised liberation by critiquing the oppressive actions of competitive projects. On the other hand, they reproduce the same barbarism by teleologically justifying their totalitarian acts as the only paths by which humanity can be saved. Up to this point, he faithfully follows Levinas's critique of the West that was framed in large by the negative counter-narrative of barbarism.[25]

Contrary to the second Levinas, however, BHL limits the possible emergence of positive barbarism. This abandonment of his mentor's contribution would be further explored in his post-9/11 text. In his early text, the Algerian argues that given the power of the projects described above, "there are no more barbarians condemned to marginality."[26] Here we witness a paradox in his use of the term barbarism, and a confounding of the narrative and negative counter-narrative. On the one hand, he contends that the advance of the Western project has teleologically incorporated everyone into a Western framework, rendering the barbarians (metaphorically or actually) extinct. On the other hand, he (prophetically) proclaims that barbarism will come to dominate the world. The world to come, the new *Pax Romana*, will be an era of "triumphant" and "tragic" barbarism (i.e., socialism). Perhaps ironically lost in the texts of Marx, he advances a critique (on which, see chapter three) which entirely neglects the contribution of the late Levinas. Let us recall that central to Levinasian philosophy of the early 1970s was the conviction that there existed an irreducible alternative to Western thought which he identifies as residing at the "barbaric margins of the

West"—something BHL rejects in 1979. While for Levinas positive barbarism has the (latent) potential to affect a regeneration of humanity, BHL understands barbarism in exclusively pejorative terms, emerging from an unwieldy ensemble of variously described totalitarianisms.[27]

Despite BHL's prophetic proclamation, Marxism—the ultimate barbarism in a world without barbarians—did not triumph. Following the implosion of the Soviet Union and the explosion of the Twin Towers, the argument intensified. In *Left in Dark Times: Taking a Stand Against the New Barbarism* (2007), BHL adopts a decisively partisan posture. He not only dismisses the possibility of any positive counter-narrative, but he also rejects the counter-narratives altogether by reproducing the new narrative of barbarism.

The book represents a continuation of his previous monograph, attacking Marxism for its support of barbarism. His argument, however, goes well beyond this attack against the Left. Situating himself in a post-9/11 global context, BHL re-appropriates an old dualism, giving it a new twist. He identifies attacks perpetrated by Muslims against Americans and Israelis in New York, Jerusalem, and Baghdad as "barbarous acts." He invests the term barbarism differently. Barbarity, according to his usage, does not principally inhere in brutality and the impulse to destroy innocent life. Of course they were brutal, but all "good" revolutions (e.g., that of American independence, the Israeli War of Independence, and the French revolution), were only successful because of the use of necessary and liberative violence. For BHL the fact that these attacks were perpetrated without a political ethos, without the ability "to come up with a coherent project, a discourse" not even a "wish list" renders them, in the final analysis, barbaric.[28]

While the assimilation of barbarism to violence is common in popular consciousness, the understanding of barbaric violence as resulting from the lack of political ethos is a particular characteristic of the narratives of both barbarism and new barbarism. BHL's formulation of this understanding, however, adds some tension in his long-standing formulation. In the 1970s, BHL still shared a negative counter-narrative of barbarism with Levinas. At that time he categorized Fascism/Marxism as barbaric because it subscribed to a program that teleologically justified brutality as a means by which to achieve a political end. After 9/11, however, barbarism acquired a different meaning. He thenceforth incorporates Muslim "terrorists" into this old alliance. Following a classical reading of the narrative, he explains that they are barbarians because they lack the political ethos by means of which to forge a coherent and persuasive alternative. While it is true that an author can change his mind over thirty years of work, an alliance between barbarians who were constituted as such for contradictory reasons ultimately makes his proposal suspicious. In the 1970s, Marxism and Fascism were barbaric because they implemented a political project. After 9/11, Muslims qualify as barbaric because they do not. While the first book framed BHL within a Levinasian negative counter-narrative of barbarism, the second book, written in the post-9/11 era, contextualizes the *pied-noir* within the same narrative of new barbarism espoused across the Atlantic by Kaplan and his ilk (i.e., Pipes, Finkielkraut, Taguieff, etc.). It is within this context that the positive contribution of Levinas is lost in his heir.

BHL's reproduction of the new narrative is not incidental but central to his text. He fully acknowledges similarities between the three barbaric movements (to adopt Pipes' formulation). He explains that for him it is "hard to differentiate between a brown (Nazi), red (Stalinist) or Green (Islamist) despot."[29] He alerts the barbaric threats are using the same rhetoric to justify their "appetite." For example, just as Hitler used Versailles to justify the need for restitution after a series of perpetrated injustices, Muslims use colonialism as an excuse to launch the most barbaric of terrorist actions. The congruence BHL perceives is both discursive and historical. BHL goes so far as to suggest that Muslims plotted with Nazism to annihilate Jews during the Holocaust. The current Arab-Israeli conflict represents no more, according to BHL, than a continuation of the barbaric alliance.[30]

If Muslims appropriate Fascist rhetoric, the Left takes this same discourse from the Muslims. The Left, which has always been anti-Semitic, now uses anti-Zionism to issue "fatwas over world liberalism" in support of the barbarians. This New Left perpetuates hoaxes accusing Jews of all world evils, spanning the colonial slave trade to the Palestinian genocide. Proof of this reality is, closing the circle, that Left-leaning self-hating Jews such as Chomsky and Butler, recover fascist Schmittian politics confirming the bond that links Hitler, Stalin (and now Khomeini?). While BHL's argument is very thin, a thorough analysis of his logic is beyond the scope of this book. If it were not, I would engage the place of race that makes the reaction against Versailles and colonialism completely different rhetorical structures as well as the profound divisions among the Left that make it impossible to issue fatwa-like proclamations. My objective here, however, is to demonstrate how this heir-apparent to Levinas disregarded the negative counter-narrative in the first book to support the new narrative of barbarism in the second. Levinas's positive understanding of the barbaric is entirely neglected in the process.[31]

Jews appear in the post-9/11 era as the victims of a perverse Muslim/ Marxist/Fascist alliance of new barbarians. Jews, however, are not alone. In a statement that adopts the rhetoric of the early Levinas but completely neglects his subsequent work, BHL explains that "as Levinas predicted Christians are becoming the Jews' strongest allies."[32] In a world in which "Anti-Americanism is a metaphor for Anti-Semitism," Christians are the guarantors of Jewish survival in an "increasingly anti-Semitic" world. We have seen how the narrative of new barbarism considers any attack against Israel an attack against the West, but BHL takes this construction even further. He explains that when the barbarians "say American imperialism," they actually mean "Jewish power, domination and conspiracy."[33] BHL is not only decisively situating Jews in the West and discarding his previous critiques of the European Enlightenment; he is making Judaism discursive representation of the West.

BHL concludes his project by asserting, against the early and mature Levinas, that there is no safe haven outside Euro-American discourse. In the 1970s, he explained that the West was all that existed. In the 2000s, he recognized barbarians but accused them of not having a political ethos with which to forge a viable alternative. While there exists a tension between both discourses, there is also a common thread. The only possible political truth emerges from the naturalized alliance between Athens and Jerusalem. In his "Stand Against the New Barbarism," the Algerian Jew reproduces Kaplan's formulation arguing that there are two poles: on the one hand, civilization represented by the ideals of democracy and human rights and barbarism represented by violent terrorists without a political ethos on the other. He misreads the history of colonialism arguing that the earliest anti-colonial discourses emerged from European individuals [Francisco de Vittorio (sic) and Bartolome de las Casas] who protested the excesses of colonialism. Of course, he neglects to mention that Amerindians (and African slaves, etc.) protested the geo-politics of racialization before the Europeans. BHL, overlooking the positive turn of Levinas's barbarism, understands knowledge to be legitimate only when emanating from civilization.[34]

Notwithstanding the limitations that led to the failure of his proposal, Levinas exhibited an openness vis-à-vis a positive barbarism at the margins of the West, and understood Judaism within this ensemble. After 9/11 his Maghrebian heir, however, forsook this contribution. Memmi will have a similar destiny in post-9/11 Buenos Aires.

The reception of Memmi's Jewish Postcolonial theory was widespread in Latin America. Several of his books were translated and his interviews quickly sold out. There are multiple testimonies of the elective affinity between Memmi and the local intellectuals. Bernardo Kliksberg, who in time would become a leading voice in development ethics at the United Nations, attests to this connection. In one of his several studies about this affinity, under the title "Latin American Judaism and Albert Memmi," he reports a "spontaneous" "opinion block" shared by Latin Americans and Memmi in gatherings of Global Jewish intellectuals. Kliksberg reflects on the reason for this "enormous interest in the ideas of the Tunisian writer" among Latin American Jewry. He argues that Memmi's problematization of the position of Jews in colonial societies offered a compelling vocabulary with which to reflect on the struggles of the local community against the patterns we identified as coloniality. Latin American Jewry employed Memmi's ideas and discerned a natural "correlation" between Jewish experiences of colonization in the Maghreb and Latin America.[35]

One of the most prominent authors influenced by Memmi is the aforementioned Aguinis. Since he may be less known among English-speaking audiences, I will here provide a more extensive introduction. Aguinis is a public intellectual whose work was restricted during the military dictatorship in Argentina (1976–1983). Eventually he became the national secretary of culture after the return to democracy. Aguinis's writings, like Memmi's, mobilize literature and social theory in their reflection on the role of Jews within the Global South. Usual topics include Global Jewish politics, the Israeli-Palestinian conflict, and the role of religious difference in Latin America and the Middle East. In one of his most memorable novels he amalgamates, appropriately or not, Ashkenazi and Sephardic cultures. He navigates a Latin American perspective of Judaism emerging from a semi-fictional history of crypto-Jews persecuted by the Inquisition during the era of Spanish colonization.[36] While early in his career, he seemed to follow what might be understood as a typically Leftist persuasion, in recent decades he defined himself as a "liberal" (in the European sense) espouser of "liberty" and joined the ranks of other Latin Americans who followed a similar trajectory, such as Nobel laureate Mario Vargas Llosa, in "the conservative" (in the American ideological sense) *Freedom Foundation*.[37]

Aguinis published his readings of *Judaism Through the Lenses of the Left* three years after 9/11, basing his text on *Judaism Through the Lenses of the Third World* a manuscript he drafted over a decade earlier and witness the ideas. This shows that the gestation of the ideas well preceeded 9/11.[38] The publisher of the last version was the central Argentinean Jewish community. In the text, Aguinis promises a Southern perspective on Jewish history and politics. The book, indeed, employs decolonial language of explicit Memmian provenance. The work does, however, ultimately replicate the typical mainstays of the new narrative of barbarism. These include the reproduction of the naturalization of Jews as contemporary Westerners, the enemies portrayed as an alliance among Fascists, Muslims, and Marxists, and anti-Zionism as an ideological mask to hide anti-Semitism. In his abandonment of Memmi's early political project identifying Jews with positive barbarism, he also undermines a central claim of Memmi's project: the acknowledgment of the legitimacy of Southern competitive aspirations. Instead, this intellectual hews closely to the narrative of new barbarism, insisting in the natural limitations of the barbarians and negating any political ethos emerging from their adversaries.

Aguinis, after citing the strength of Memmi's argument, takes as his interlocutor a prototypical "Latin American intellectual" who "is enrolled in a firm decolonial stance."[39] He partially follows the spirit of Memmi's central arguments. He defines the "utility" of "Latin American lenses" in analyzing the role Jews are capable of fulfilling within an international setting. This Global South perspective helps to challenge the "centuries of imposed European cosmovision" that "conceives progress as a straight line of development that emerges from barbarism and finishes in the luminous center of the European metropolis." Denouncing Euro-centrism, the Argentinean Jew explains that Westerners "could never imagine alternative paths of creation and development" which did not originate in their own midst. Incorporating the prototypical Jew, especially the European Jew, among other barbarians, he explains that the "the Natives of America, the Blacks of Africa, the peoples of Asia, [and] the Jews of the ghettos" all share an experience of colonial racialization. The oppression, Aguinis agrees with Memmi, was justified by a narrative that describes all of them as simply "backward," "unsettling," and "barbaric" communities.[40]

Still following his Tunisian forerunner, Aguinis identifies Zionism as the path for Jewish liberation. He admits that Zionism possesses a staggering diversity and heterogeneity. But he quickly recognizes that Herzl's political Zionism, the same that defined the Jewish state as an outpost of civilization against barbarism, has attained primacy over other ideological alternatives. The formulation of this support is where the Argentinean departs from the Tunisian. Memmi's positive construction, before being abandoned, contained two elements that made the argument distinct—both are lost to Aguinis. In the first place, Memmi identifies his African Jewishness—that which justifies his Zionism—with a positive re-appropriation of the term barbarism. In the second place, he argues that the national movement toward Jewish liberation should, first and foremost, acknowledge competitive demands and, second, be seen as a step toward a larger liberation that does not disband the communities fashioned from the struggle. Both arguments, once again, are lost to Memmi's heir.[41]

Though Aguinis explicitly engages the logic and persistence of a European lexicon that perpetuates a Manichean dualism, he does not appear interested in problematizing this in any fashion. Barbarism is acknowledged as a narrative that racializes Jews, among others. But he does not develop a counter-narrative. He does not re-appropriate it (like Memmi or Levinas), re-deploy the accusation negatively (like the Marxists), or tear it asunder (like the European dissidents). He leaves the accusation intact and employs it with the effect of amplifying the new narrative. In the second place, he does understand the role of national Jewish liberation according to traditional Zionist politics and not (despite an explicit acknowledgment) in a fashion similar to Memmi. The state emerges from a need for liberation framed by a national construct. Aguinis, however, soon abandons the possibility of integration to "the dream" of Memmi, a Third World space that acknowledges competitive demands and does not require the abandonment of identities. He does mention a hope for future alliances but calls into question the political ethos of Arab and Palestinian nationalists who, along with Marxists and Fascists, blocked Israeli integration into the decolonial community.

For Aguinis the geo-politics of Judaism can be accurately perceived in terms of global relations with Israel. He argues that Israel could have been a partner in Third World struggles. It is indeed a movement that holds more "social inquiries" and "decolonial potentials" than many other movements and could export its creativity to the Third World. But this integration has been blocked by an alliance that includes, not surprisingly, Muslims and Marxists reproducing a "Hitlerian" or Fascistic rhetoric. Aguinis, in contraposition to BHL, does acknowledge that there may be cognitive dissonance for the large number of Jews who explicitly identify with the historically oppressed and downtrodden. He recognizes that it may be strange for someone coming from the Left to see former "friends turned into our enemies." His answer, however, fully overlaps with BHL. He seeks to take a closer examination of the Marxist theory undergirding the new stage. He argues that the intellectual history that invariably culminates with Stalinism and is reproduced by new Left movements has always been anti-Semitic. It is this construction of the Left that blocks Israel from the Third World.[42]

Aguinis explains the situation historically. Since 1948 "Arabs" have been drawing from "Hitlerian" anti-Semitic techniques and arguments in order to "erase Israel from the map." Until 1953, however, their global support was limited. The USSR portrayed itself as a friend of popular democracies, including both Arab states and Israel. After the middle of the 1950s, however, the USSR changed policies and only supported the aspirations of the former. The Soviet change in policy, in keeping with a traditional anti-Semitic perspective that climaxes in Stalinism, helped the Hitlerian discourse articulated by Arabs to attain new heights and persuasiveness. Since that historical moment, the narrative not only insists that Orthodox Marxism would eventually implode with the USSR but also that this political ideology was in service of different and successive movements identified with the "New Left." While they paradoxically have cut ties with orthodoxy, they have widely reproduced the Arab slogans taken over by "Hitlerian" factions ideologically under-girded by a "Stalinist" doctrine. These "forced arguments," Aguinis argues, recall the "times of the Hitler-Stalin pact."[43]

Though the historical justification of the alliance may sound out of step with the times, it is important to note that it represents the identical interpretation that was provided to justify the attack against the Argentinean Jewish headquarters in 1996, (between the publications of the two versions of this piece [1986 and 2004]). It is thus important to analyze both the logic and the implications of this construction. He insists that the problem of the Left is the reproduction of a Stalinist orthodoxy that was, inter alia, reflected in the pact with Hitler. He does analyze Stalin's ideology and policies in detail. He fails to mention, however, that when the USSR supported Israel (1948–1953 according to his reading) it was Stalin who was in power. If there was a change of policy following the second half of the 1950s, this belongs squarely to the era of de-stalinization. In all fairness, it is possible to argue that the Soviet Union did not undergo full de-stalinization after 1956. His construction still needs to take into account that, independent of state crimes perpetrated by Stalin, he was in power when the Soviet Union sustained the friendship, which Aguinis identifies. Aguinis still requires the ghost of Stalin to represent orthodox and heterodox Marxists alike.

Why is it necessary for Aguinis to identify the broader Left with orthodox Stalinism despite the dubious historical accuracy? It achieves four interrelated objectives. First, it disqualifies any moral high ground for "the cowards," as Aguinis names them, to discuss human rights violations within Israel. Any discussion of the topic will be preempted by an accusation/mention of the dreaded Gulag. Second, it textures an imaginary that understands the enemies of the Second World War and the Cold War as eternally allied and essentially homologous. If Stalin once entered a pact with Hitler, there is no reason to believe it cannot happen again. Third, it shows that the enemy of the Cold War is collaborating with the antagonists of the War on Terror to accomplish the task that was inaugurated in the Second World War. In other words, the Arab/Palestinian attack against Israel represents an attempt to complete the Holocaust. And finally, it shows that the new enemy, the non-European, the barbaric terrorist, lacks the political ethos and thus the wherewithal to initiate a project of ideological coherence and persuasiveness. The "Arab" barbarism is merely an attempt to translate the Hitlerian project into the "mystical" language of "Jihad."[44]

Aguinis, therefore, is successful in renewing the patterns of domination set by coloniality by reproducing an alliance defined by contemporaries as the new barbarism. He furthers his explanation of the barbarian's natural limitation—the lack of a political ethos—in *"La Invención del Pueblo Palestino"* ("The Invention of the Palestinian People"), an op-ed penned several years later. The main argument advanced in this piece contradicts Memmi's positive conception of communities in struggle. Memmi understands the Palestinian conflict to be magnified. Aguinis, however, follows the narrative of new (and old) barbarism negating its political ethos. For him the collective we call "Palestinians" is a recent Arab invention that was formed as an irrational proposal of those who, lacking the political and economical ethos to secure development, only use it as an ideological shield by which to veil their anti-Semitism.[45]

The author starts with a historical account showing that there was a geographical area that changed names several times, but for political reasons was re-named Palestine in the last centuries. In the best Herzelian/Caesarian fashion, he describes this land as "deserted and desolated." Since the turn of the twentieth century, the "energy" of Zionism began to develop, and the place petrified in time. After the "heroic" struggle of Jews in defense of the allies in the European wars, the West understood the importance of the place for the Jewish people and decided to part with the land. Jews were always eager to share the place with other inhabitants (of the previously "deserted land"?) but the barbarians irrationally rejected this humane proposal.[46]

Aguinis does not simply reject the Palestinian representation by declaring it magnified (like Memmi) or corrupt (as is common in some mainstream Western media). He denies a political ethos, on the basis of which an actual people can form. The group now called Palestinians chooses as the central "objective of their struggle to eliminate the Jews who were bringing progress" instead of working toward the construction of a (democratic) state or a viable (capitalist) economy. He goes ventures beyond Stalinism as a nexus between Muslims and Fascists, and echoes BHL in describing a timeless and quasi-mystical alliance between Fascists and Muslims. Like his Algerian peer, he remembers that the Mufti of Jerusalem had an indispensable role in his alliance with Hitler to eliminate Jews. The "mythological" Palestinian people, in Aguinis's perspective, are an invented collective that exist only to impede progress.[47]

He corroborates and complements this narrative in a third text, Las Redes del Odio (The Networks of Hate), published between the two aforementioned texts. In this monograph, he insists that if the Palestinians do not have a nation state, it is the Arabs who are fully responsible for this state of affairs. If the mythically constructed Palestinians today engaged in barbaric terrorism, and decided to protest their lot/engage in national self-determination, they should direct their efforts at the Arabs who never trusted in their political ethos. If Israelis have one responsibility, it is to follow Herzl's design even more rigorously and "teach" Palestinians what they can "learn" from the Israelis. Here Aguinis recapitulates the same narrative of new barbarism with the same strategy firmly intact. While in some parts of his analysis it was the barbaric alliance (Arabs/Marxists/Fascists) that prevented the possibility of Jewish political collaboration with the Global South, now it is the barbarism of the Arab countries that disenfranchised Jews along with the imagined collective of Palestinians who made the development of a Western democracy and capitalist economy problematic at every juncture. Jews in the first case and Israel in the second are exculpated of any responsibility.[48]

Aguinis, in Buenos Aires, bears some commonalities with the early Memmi. He soon enough loses the central thread of Memmi's thought: the positive affirmation of Jewish barbarism as a way to integrate Jews into a Global South community. In turn he finishes reproducing every step of the new narrative of barbarism: anti-Zionism as a cover for anti-Semitism, the Marxist-Fascist-Muslim alliance against Jews, and their natural inability to develop a political project. Memmi did offer a positive barbarism that, albeit limited and contradictory, sought to incorporate Jews within a Global South struggle. His heir in Buenos Aires would abandon both this framework and the intention underlying it.

In conclusion, the legacy of the positive counter-narrative fails in the Global South. While the early projects had complications, the re-positionality of Jews led the heirs to betray the central aspiration of the project: the positive adoption of barbarism and the desire to create a barbaric space inserting Jews within a decolonial struggles. On the contrary, the heirs of the positive counter-narratives reproduce virtually every central aspect of the new narrative of barbarism. This includes the representation of Jews as Westerners, the construction of a new barbarian, and the barbaric alliance among Marxists, Fascists, and Muslims. Above everything else, they portray the barbarians as unable to overcome their own natural limitations. The positive counter-narratives of barbarism, therefore, were defeated twice by Jewish re-positionality. First, when their context conflicted with their attempt of re-inserting Jews in a decolonial struggle; and second, when the heirs forgot the positive contribution and wound up using the basic framework to reproduce a new narrative of barbarism.

Beyond Positive Barbarism?

While normative Judaism may have trapped a number of Jewish voices, not all counter-narratives have been abandoned. The legacy of the negative counter-narrative has been adopted in Aguinis's context with a different outcome. Though the legacy of the Frankfurt School thus represents a hopeful departure, it leaves us wondering what is lost by the final Jewish abandonment of the positive counter-narrative of barbarism.

In this spirit, let me introduce a third voice into the discussion. In 2006, Ricardo Forster published *Notas Sobre la Barbarie y la Esperanza: Del 11 de Septiembre a la Crisis Argentina* (*Notes on Barbarism and Hope: From 9/11 to the Argentinean Crisis*). Forster is an Argentinean public intellectual with abiding connections throughout the Americas. Holding degrees from Mexico and his homeland, he has been a visiting professor in various American universities. Working with other intellectuals, he founded the intellectual advocacy group *Espacio Carta Abierta* (*Open Letter Space*) in 2008 to support the wave of center-Left governments in Latin America. This coalition of governments has been traditionally thought to deify American political barbarization of non-Western powers by welcoming Venezuela and establishing powerful relations with Cuba and Iran.[49]

Forster applies traditional negative dialectics to understand the new social order, as well as the place of Judaism and Jewish resistances therein. Starting with Benjamin, he queries the extent to which 9/11 should be understood as an historical watershed. In the post-Cold War context, the theories of the clash of civilization and new barbarism were competing with a powerful philosophy that identified the fall of the USSR as the end of history and the ultimate triumph of capitalism. But the events of 2001 seem to have broken this alleged idyllic culmination of history. Drawing on Adorno, Forster explains that the events did not ultimately change the foundations of the modern system that historically and conceptually preceded the Cold War. On the contrary, the conflict between two apparent nemeses only served to re-enact "the old Manichaeism built upon the pair civilization/barbarism."[50]

The dualism was not reproduced because the two rivals were different but because they had the same point of origin. On the one hand, the American empire, fearful that it was the beginning its inevitable decline, reacted by "relapsing into barbarism." This meant dividing the world dualistically and establishing a state of exception to annihilate the barbaric forces of terrorism. While in other historical opportunities the construction may have been more sophisticated, this time the "poor politics" was executed in a "Far West" fashion.[51] On the other hand, the presumed liberationist forces were no more than a proverbial "boomerang" of the West. Forster acknowledges that these are not the old Third-Wordlist voices that were once the main hope for decolonization in the Global South. They were a regressive reaction of constituencies manufactured during the Cold War by the same West. They were not employing new ways of understanding politics. They were connecting the techniques inherited from the former patrons with archaic theological rhetoric in order to reproduce the same violent dualism. "From barbarism," an Adornian Forster concludes, "can only follow barbarism."[52]

Forster critically engages with intellectuals supporting both sides of the spectrum and identifies both with negative barbarism. On the one hand, there is a group of "hypocritical" intellectuals that could easily fit the model of BHL and Aguinis. They have abandoned the Left and placed "barbarism outside of civilization." They portray the United States as a "naïve" lover of freedom shocked by incorrigible fanatics disregarding their responsibility not only for genocide and colonialism but also with the dialectical development of the now regressive barbaric forces. Forster urges Westerners to acknowledge that the promised "horizon of hope" dialectically led to a world dominated by injustice and violence. He concludes, in the best of the negative counter-narrative fashion, arguing that the "price" the West paid to defeat barbarism was to "relapse" into barbarism itself.[53]

But Forster also critiques the "bankruptcy" of the intellectuals who, staying on the Left, welcomed the barbaric terrorism represented by Al-Qaeda. His special target is some of the heirs of the 1970s movements of liberation that share his background. He clarifies that some of the inheritors of these movements blindly support an "Islamic Fundamentalism" confusing the meaning of its struggle. While the intellectuals usually represent the terrorists as liberationist or progressive movements, the movements are actual failures of the civilizational process that intend not only to stop imperialist advances but also to cause their own communities to regress. Their reproduction of the same Western dualism led them to fall into historically problematic mistakes. The reproduction of the dualism creates paradoxes. Bin Laden, for example, "identifies the West with Judaism," when the Jewish people were actually "her great victim."[54]

If neither the West nor Islam represents a viable alternative, what is the answer according to Forster? Forster argues that the Holocaust, the "most extreme" action of the barbaric civilizational process, dialectically generated its own self-introspective process that led to a critical theory that should serve as a model for the post-9/11 era. It is essential to clarify that in other texts, Forster does welcome non-European critiques, and in this text, he insists recognizing that the Nazi machinery also annihilated people beyond Jews.[55] Yet, when he is discussing the conceptual alternative, he retrieves the post-Holocaust critique as the model for post-9/11 consideration. His proposal, therefore, coherently follows the Frankfurters. There is a special place for the Jew in the history of Western persecution, and, in its extreme situation, Jews such as Benjamin, Adorno, Levinas, Arendt, or Primo Levi generated an internal critique to the West that now becomes exemplary of critical inquiry itself. A non-Western Jew who also suffered the Holocaust, Derrida, is included, and at the same time Jewish life in Muslim lands is represented in the same continuous fashion of persecution after persecution. "Our critique," Forster clearly argues, "was born from the interior of the bourgeoisie culture."[56]

Forster takes this reading one step further by engaging with Israel. In the same spirit of his previous statements, he is quick to recognize contextual problems. For Forster, global Jewry is in a very compromising situation, especially after 1967. The policies of the State of Israel that have continuously negated the "historical rights of the Palestinian people" created a wound that only helps to support the forces of fundamentalism. Yet, to assert that Israel is the "axis" of the problem is "disingenuous." Palestinians are responsible for complicating the peace process, and pre-Israeli Arab regimes are responsible for historically utilizing their Jewish communities as "scapegoats." He prognosticates a "dark future" for the Jewish people. Replicating Levinas, whom he also cites, he presents Jews at the crux of history and shows his fear that Jews would become, once again, scapegoats in this process. Especially, (here recall his critique against Israel) when in the West itself there are voices emerging that mask their anti-Semitism with Anti-Zionism.[57]

It is important to appreciate the strength of Forster's argument of resistance. In contradistinction to the two aforementioned legacies, he constructs a faithful adaptation of the original aspiration to contemporary politics. Furthermore, he is able to defy the other counter-narratives not only by making a strong critique against the practices of Zionism but also by reflecting on the implications this can have for Israeli Jews, global Jewry, and global Jewish thought. In another article published recently he takes this critique on step further again.[58] The adaptation of the negative counter-narrative is a persuasive and balanced piece with which to confront the narrative. But the persistence of the central features of the negative counter-narrative also limits its perspective. Forster indicates that the locus of the resistance's emergence is bourgeois European culture. While he never makes racial suffering an exclusive feature of the Jewish people, he privileges the European Jewish experience as the model for alternative thought. Reading modernity as arising from this experience he insists on the dialectical reading that presumes that the enlightenment was a process of liberation that turned into barbarism instead of a project of global dominance with clearly genocidial programs from the outset. This is not to say that the negative counter-narrative fails as it is able to denounce central features of the narrative. But the radical Southern features of the positive counter-narrative are generally absent from what becomes one of the most balanced post-9/11 global south barbaric proposals.

Shall I propose, therefore, to elaborate a new stage in the Jewish positive narrative of barbarism? I resist offering a simple answer. If we remember Dussel's construction in the last chapter, this step would be complicated. Prior to any positive reclamation of identity, there should be a contextual and external objectification. Today the re-positionality of normative Judaism limits the possibility of initiating even this first step. Yet, there are some Jewish communities, certainly within the minority, which are objectified from both the inside and the outside for being unable to fit in the normative portrayal. Some of them have been expounding resistances that are still resonant today. These communities have the potential to reclaim their barbarism. I am not necessarily proposing that voices emanating from racialized Jewries appropriate a legacy that encountered geo-political difficulties and contradictions. I am, rather, proposing an analysis of what particular features of the positive counter-narrative can serve to complement contemporary possibilities in a context that does not present itself as especially encouraging for critical Jewish thought.

In the first place, the counter-narrative enabled a relocation of the conceptual center of discussion. Under these lenses, the connection among different barbarians is not limited to their common history of suffering under the yolk of colonial discourses and powers. It particularly illuminates the interrelated epistemological struggle that arose from these patterns established by colonial discourses and perpetuated by coloniality. This feature is largely abandoned in the contemporary options we examined above. These interpretations particularize the Jewish experience and create an independent understanding of its resistance(s). In the best of cases, this is presented as a model for other experiences. But the acknowledgment that this option arose from the interior of centers of power and knowledge a priori calls into question the viability of this transference. The positive counter-narrative, however, has the potential to go beyond the particularization of Jewish resistances and destiny, realizing not only common historical roots of suffering but also the common generation of critical alternatives.

The positive counter-narrative enables a relocation of not only the conceptual center but also its geo-political core. Since the most perdurable uses of racialization take place outside the centers, the Southern lenses possess an epistemological privilege vis-à-vis the margins. It is no surprise, therefore, that a Southern intellectual either influenced or directly elaborated the positive Jewish participation in barbarism (Dussel and Memmi). The epistemological presupposition contained in the narrative, however, is largely abandoned in the latter debate on barbarism. This shows that a Southern location may be a necessary but insufficient condition for the elaboration of a radical critique. The positive narrative of barbarism tends to go beyond the orthodox privilege of history and resistances elaborated at the centers of power and knowledge. In this way it not only provincializes their knowledge but also fundamentally inverts the role of universal consciousness in the elaboration of the critique itself.

The last contribution is a lesson learned from the failure rather than the success of this endeavor. The positive counter-narrative became diagnostic of the passage of Jewish re-positionality between the opposite poles defining the civilized/barbaric dualism. The same discourse presented prior to or following the transitional period could yield radically different results. I here reiterate that I consider the deconstruction of the dualism a corollary of this project. Yet, if the dualism between civilization and barbarism is imploded, the Jewish passage between one and the other is as well. As a consequence, responsibility for discourses of victimhood mobilized during moments of empowerment vanishes. Strategic participation within the dualism offers a telling window through which to gauge not only the discourses themselves but also their functions in changing racial realities.

Am I proposing, therefore, to recover a positive counter-narrative of barbarism? Not necessarily. This particular positive counter-narrative was located in time and space and had geo-political tensions that cannot be overcome unless there is a future re-positionality of Jews (as Forster suggests). Nonetheless, given the persistence of coloniality and the strength of some features of the counter-narrative, it would be interesting to imagine the role that the conceptual, geo-political, and strategic partisanship can have in future Jewish engagements with global politics. The legacy of Jewish barbarism may or may not be in the re-affirmation of barbarism, but one may want to take note of the central features that a failed history can provide for the future of critical Jewish thought.

EPILOGUE

Duped by Jewish Suffering
(Analectical Interjections)

Devil Borders

"Santiago," the armed man asked haltingly, "Santiago...Slabodsky?" he read back to me. His question frightened me. In all likelihood he was wrestling with the cognitive dissonance engendered by the encounter with my first and last name. He surely anticipated a Jacob, Noam, Micah, or even a Paul. Santiago, however, was unexpected. His X-ray eyes, endowed by the Department of Homeland Security during employee training, suddenly began to comprehensively inspect me. I could only answer him by avoiding eye contact, attempting to occult my raising anxiety.

The agent finished his inspection and earned time drinking water. He next posed a question I was not expecting: "Are you...I mean...are you...Jewish?" I could have anticipated such a query in a different time and place, but it came as a surprise in early twenty-first century JFK International airport. Though my mind managed to escape the migratory boot, fearing the worst, my body was too afraid to follow her lead. Suddenly I had one of those lucid moments that come all too sporadically and infrequently. I decided that running away from the border agent in July 2002, less than a year after 9/11, was not a good idea.

I needed to answer the question. I tried to look as confident as I could. Yet, I could only whisper my answer in a question form: "Yes, I am?" Immediately after I closed my eyes, fearing the worst. If the portrayal of Jewish history as a chronicle of eternal and continuous persecution had any merit, I could only anticipate a terrible outcome. Yet, after ten long seconds I could still hear my accelerated respiration. I decided to open my eyes. The agent had stamped my student visa and handed the passport back to me. He smiled and announced my unexpected success: "Welcome to America!" Something did not fit in the history of Jewish victimhood. Yet, I decided not to question my luck.

I smiled, retrieved my passport and began walking away. After I left the boot, the agent shouted something to my back. My English was very deficient and I thought I heard "go devil!" Until today I am almost certain he said "go devil!" I had no idea why in twenty-first century America an officer would relate the medieval European association of Jews with the Devil. It seems that the guard was somehow relating me with the "red evilness" that in modernity had nourished the portrayal of Jewish Left-wing barbaric agitators. In my experience this was a given among armed forces in Argentina and I had reported in my interminable visa application my affiliation to activist organizations. But, I decided not to confront the apparent insult/praise. Surprised I had achieved two moments of lucidity within ten minutes I realized that having crossed the border was enough excitement for one day.

A few hours later I arrived at my new university in North Carolina. A Colombian doctoral student in history was generous enough to pick me from the airport and give me a tour of campus. It was a gorgeous summer day in Durham when she stopped outside a stadium and asked me in Spanish "do you want to visit the basketball court? It is the house of the famous Blue Devils!"...blue devils, go devil...I started laughing at myself and took a few minutes to stop and explain the border story to my friend. She laughed loudly and with playful condescension started teasing me: "I am sorry. I know you Jews only talk about your persecution and your paranoia may be well justified. But the guy was probably just wishing you a good season for Duke. You know, you are not a red, but a blue devil now." I was indeed a blue devil from the very same moment I arrived in the United States, even if I had never attended Duke.

This is not to say I never experienced discrimination in North America. As someone with a Visa perpetually nearing expiry, a precarious legal status, a heavy Spanish accent, and a face that is normally confused with Maghrebian, Southern Italian, or (even worst!) Persian, life can be complicated. This is especially true if one lives in Durham, Waco, Saskatoon, or Claremont (Toronto and San Francisco were somehow better). This daily struggle against exterior objectifications may indeed represent the underlying reason why I gravitated to a study of the narrative barbarism. Yet, every time my Jewishness is unveiled, this serves to offset my other barbaric characteristics. At that point, the interior perception of one's affiliation (in my case Latinos/as or Arabs) is

effaced. The experience at JFK becomes more normative than exceptional. The border, a space of fear for historically racialized people,
becomes a secure passage for many Jews. The blue devilness saves them
even if this disrupts my vision of what a Judaism per se should look
like.

Complicity

If I learned the lesson, why does this book insist on framing history
according to Jewish persecution? Looking back at each author who built
or abandoned the various counter-narratives canvassed in this book,
all of them reproduce the chronicle of victimization. This is true for
Europeans (Frankfurters and Levinas), Magrhebis (Memmi and BHL),
and South Americans (Aguinis and Forster). Their works, naturally,
cannot be reduced to this narrative arc alone. Yet, no proposal can be
conceived which is completely shorn of the portrayal of Jewish history
as a narrative of victimhood.

My own framework does not transcend this limitation. I did focus
on subversions and their ultimate abandonment that lead to the Jewish
reproduction of colonial designs. Furthermore, I insisted throughout
this book that Jewish victimhood is not exceptional but should be interpreted through recourse to a common systemic root defined as coloniality
ity. But, in a context where civilized Judaism seems to structurally offset
other barbaric traces of Jewish identities, I should consider whether
there exists a clear tension between my reproduction of the narrative of
suffering and the current re-articulation of Jewish positionality. I argue
that the positive counter-narratives failed because they were unable to
make an internal critique of the new Jewish status. May I be falling
into the same trap by being unable to make an internal critique of the
chronicle of Jewish persecution? Am I collaborating with the relativiza-
tion of current racialization by insisting on and helping to undergird an
anachronistic reading of Jewish history?

If one were to reflect on this question reading some of the most innovative work in Jewish studies, the answer would be affirmative. For several decades, radical intellectuals have tried to critically appraise what
precisely underlies this history of Jewish persecution. They generally
explain that Jewish history is a reified historiography developed in the
nineteenth century during an age of rampant nationalism. European
Jewish historiographers, Shlomo Sand denounces, weave together
fragmentary pieces to create a genealogy that ultimately justified the
national solution. The norm in Jewish diasporic life was persecution

and Israel thus served as a solution to two thousands years of an alleged genealogy of calamities.[1]

This reading, the new critics argue, contains and obscures a Christian and/or European reification of Jewish peoplehood. It naturalizes the Christian myth of Jewish exile as a form of punishment. While this was originally used by Christians to convert Jews, it subsequently became trapped by its own narrative negating the value of the diaspora outside persecution. It also reproduces the racist coloniality inherent in some European nationalisms by creating an inexistent "blood-link" between the mythical and current Jewish populations, ipso facto claiming not only an ahistorical cohesion but also ownership of a territory their ancestors never inhabited. Arab Jews and Palestinians became the victims of the first and second mandate. Is it possible, I would like to ask, that we attempted to make a critique of Zionism all the while reproducing a Zionist construction?

A generous reader may help exculpate such a reading. Of course different features of the critique can and have been contested. For example, while it is important in the context of its formation, there is no modern community that was not imagined. It may be true that there was no sense of one unique history. Yet, it is impossible to negate the existence of networks of solidarity and a literature that did privilege some historical events over others and did give central relevance to Jewish persecution. Furthermore, Augustinian Christians did elaborate a myth of Jewish suffering to favor conversion, but the topic was already existent in Jewish texts and grew in dialogue—many times conflictive—with other traditions.

Others may be more generous, but I am not interested in exculpating myself so easily. In the introduction I decided not to follow the challenge to a single Jewish history because I wanted to analyze the counter-narratives according to their own failed logics. I am, however, a contemporary of the challenge and my employment of Jewish history should undergo a re-examination. After all, I do share with the counter-narratives the same framework that runs from the Inquisition to the Holocaust passing through Eastern European pogroms. This record not only sets Jewish history in a European locale (adding exceptional moments of persecution in other parts to justify the unique reading) but also presents the diaspora as a space of persecution that needed to end for the well being of all Jews. Yet, not all Jews experience this history or were benefited by this historiographical construction.

This is an argument Jewish scholars developed from material of Ottoman imperial provenance. Levantian Ammiel Alcalay reflects on the role of the well-known myth of the persecuted, wandering Jew. He argues that this obscures the fact that for centuries Jews in the Islamic world were considered natives and not foreigners.[2] Iraqui Ella Shohat adds that the universalization of the persecuted Jew led Israel to eradicate communities like hers, of venerable millennial ancestry, who had a strong status in the society until the Zionist activities started in the country.[3] Both of them, implicitly or explicitly, agree that the Spanish Inquisition not only lead to the Holocaust. This phenomenon also reinforced the Jewish spaces in Muslim lands where Jews kept developing a largely neglected culture in permanent conversation with Muslim cultures. The chronicle of Jewish persecution, however, overlooks these histories.

This series of critiques should be taken seriously. First, they denounce the reproduction of the patterns of coloniality in Jewish epistemologies. Second, they challenge the exceptional character of Jewish victimhood. Third, they explain Jewish minimization of other's suffering by comparison to the length of Jewish persecution or the magnitude of the Holocaust. And finally, they reveals that some of the most carefully developed arguments against Zionism may serve to further re-silence the same non-European Jewish populations that were marginalized by colonial designs.

Another Reading

Am I therefore, duped by Jewish suffering? I likely am. But there is always an underlying reason for our chosen opium. I would like to explore why I cannot abandon the framework by appealing to another South American voice. After critiquing dialectical methods, I would finish arguing that the model developed in Europe may look differently when it is interjected analectically with sources from the Global South.

This second story also took place at an airport. Just a few months before my departure to the United States, Argentinean Juan Gelman was arriving to Ben Gurion International Airport in Israel/Palestine when an "accident" occurred. Gelman is not just another South American Jew with a curious mismatch between his first and last name. He is a son of a social revolutionary who participated in the 1905 revolt in Russia, became disillusioned with the movement and eventually, like Memmi's character 50 years later, escaped to the last place on earth, Argentina. Juan became an essayist and poet in the service of some of the most radicalized Third Wordlist groups during the 1970s. Right before the *coup d'etat* he was forced into exile. While he was proscribed from entering the country, the military government kidnapped and "disappeared" his daughter, son, and pregnant partner. Only the first of the young adults would re-emerge.

During his exile he wrote poems in Ladino, effecting a re-encounter between Eastern European Jewry and Arab Jewish culture. This placed him at the forefront of a loose collective of Latin American (Arab and Euro-) Jews who claimed a literary affinity with "the lost world of Andalusia." He struggled, in his words, to rationally articulate the reasons for the move. Being expelled from a continent built upon the violence of 1492, he intended to recover the negated and exiled languages he admired. Upon the return of democracy he became one of the iconic fighters to bring the genocidal perpetrators to justice. His socially-committed essays, poems, and editorials were translated into multiple languages and awarded some of the highest honors of Spanish letters, including the Pablo Neruda and the Miguel de Cervantes prizes in 2005 and 2007.

In 2001, the famous poet was traveling to Israel for the funeral of a family member when he was detained for hours after an Israeli officer, in a symbolically laden flight on British Airways, overhead a conversation and alerted the authorities to the presence of a critical voice. After this occurrence, Gelman returned to Argentina and published a newspaper editorial entitled "Israel." As a poet Gelman had already linked the Spanish expulsion with Latin American Jewish life. He now textures a history of Jewish suffering that may be familiar to North American and European Humanist critics of Israel. Yet, it contains a surprising twist. Reflecting on the Israeli "siege of one million of Palestinians," he writes:

> How is it possible that the besiegers of a whole people are the sons/ daughters, grandsons/daughters and great-grandson/daughters of, like my mother and her siblings and her father rabbi, suffered the Czarist siege in the ghetto, and later, like my cousins, the enclosure of the concentration camps of the Nazis. At the age my mother witnessed how the Cossacks burned the family home and my grandmother was rescuing her kids from the fire, but could not help her 2-year-old daughter that disappear under the flames. Now the decedents of the persecution build ghettos for the Palestinians, dynamite their houses, starve them, destroy their olive trees, and lay waste to their cultivation, and usurp their lands just because they bother in their development plans... Is there really a relation between Judaism and these politics of the State of Israel? Jews have been always persecuted, never persecutors; discriminated, never

discriminators; marginalized, never marginalizers. At this point there is no relation between the State of Israel and the Jewish tradition, the most democratic of the world, created from below and perpetuated throughout centuries. I know these opinions will be qualified as anti-Semitic ... the tactic to confuse the critiques to the State of Israel with anti-Semitism recalls me to the pretension of the last dictatorship in Argentina, that called an "Anti-Argentine campaign" the denouncements against their crimes. I have a particular sadness for the genocidal politics of the State of Israel because I am truly Jewish. Because when I was a kid and was sick with a high fever, my father used to sit in my bed to read me in Yiddish the story of Sholem Aleichem, It was called "Das messerl" (the little knives) and related the tales of the pains of the ghetto.[4]

Let me attempt to analyze what Gelman is accomplishing with this op-ed. Yes, he is indeed reproducing the chronology of Jewish victimhood that culminates with the State of Israel. If we take into account his previous work, he is no doubt creating a throughline that connects Spain to Central/Eastern Europe and Israel. Furthermore, he is describing it as a single family portrait and depicting it as an idealized Jewish community with eternal life under persecution. I will nonetheless argue that this reading is different. Before the final jump to Palestine, he interjects the experience in Argentina, a source for an analectical analysis. Intimately acquainted with the extreme limits of the coloniality of the nation-state, he explains the existence of a similar rhetoric between the regime that persecuted Latin American Jews and Palestinians (anti-Semitic/Argentine campaigns). Said himself, let us recall, was careful enough to add to the same argument already in 1979. In the same article in which he critiques the displacement of Palestinians and relates this to the abuse against Arab Jews, he identifies the luck of Argentine Jews. He asks why Israel, the functional equivalent of a rhetorical a guarantee that Jews would undergo a second genocide, had being silent about the luck of the local Jewry when still engaging in business as usual.

I do not claim that Gelman's proposal is original. Today, after decades of silence, scholars, activists, and the general public are increasingly challenging policies of the State of Israel. Some of them do claim, as Gelman, the paradoxical relation of the oppressed becoming the oppressors. What Gelman does accomplish, however, is the creation of a through-line between Jewish suffering and Global South experiences. As articulated in the introduction, colonial rhetoric can be applied everywhere, but its crude extremities take place in the Third (and occasionally Fourth) World. For this reason its inhabitants, especially persecuted, can more lucidly understand, theorize and marshal some of the most meaningful protests against such rhetoric. Gelman's evocation of South American history in light of Palestine, not only preempts meaningful explanations but also helps to underscore one of the most powerful features of old and new colonial narratives: the assimilation of anti-Zionism with anti-Semitism. This is accomplished by presupposing the same historiography that needed to be negated. Gelman's solidarity does not emerge out of an idealist humanist experience, but from the experience of Jewish struggle in a location under the designs of coloniality. Without the chronicle of Jewish victimhood, proposals like Gelman's would be missing the strength of their discourse.

Open Reflections

This books ends, perhaps, with a question that could have preceded it. What are the conditions according to which one could undertake a Jewish decolonial reading of the geopolitical scene? What is clear is that there is no single answer. Some Jewish discourses will need to deconstruct the narratives that establish the peoplehood in order to show the perversity of a model that has achieved a normative positionality. Other Jewish discourses will re-appropriate old narratives to re-claim a forgotten or overlooked normative core that shows the historical betrayal of the new positionality. Only a critical dialogue between such strategies, perhaps one that exceeds the limits of academia, can show the possibilities and limitations of such a project.

The acknowledgment of not only the new positionality but also the failure of projects that attempted to confront it requires learning historical lessons. Westerners, either in the North or in neocolonial locations, should recognize that the Jewish presence does not guarantee the unveiling of current conditions of oppression. On the contrary, this often can serve to reproduce the very same coloniality that construed large Jewish populations as past victims. As a consequence it is important to question the role the token normative Jew takes by representing an alterity that cannot recognize suffering outside the parameters of a Euro-American discourse. Some Southerners, for their part, might find it helpful to explore the role postwar anti-Semitism plays in their own reproduction of colonial constructions. They should proceed with a critical engagement in order to understand what features of their discourses about Jews help or limit their own epistemological challenges. In consequence it is important for them not only to question the actions of a former ally-turned-enemy. They would also be well advised to contest the integrationist project that leads friends to become rivals.

Jews, for their part, have a challenge confronting them. In the context of Jewish diversities there is a long record of protests that reach our day and have resisted the racial re-classification. Today, more than ever, there are protests against the consequences of Jewish re-positionality. The normative portrayal of Jews, however, has left little space for a geopolitical challenge that can emerge from the barbaric instead of the civilized features of Judaism. The historical reality ultimately challenges the location from which Jewish discourses are allowed to emerge. As fragmentary as the decolonial Jewish proposal may seem at this point, it contains a few features that can, in collaboration, help end the problem. The exit, however, needs to revise its own logic. The Eurocentric philosopher, convinced of the only path to development, may have tried to change history. But he may have forgotten that we also needed to judge it.

Notes

Introduction   The Past Was Worse (and We Miss It)

1. Albert Memmi, *La statue de sel* (Paris: Gallimard, 1966), 145. Edouard Roditti, trans., *The Pillar of Salt* (New York: Beacon Press, 1992), 165. As we will explore in the next chapters, pre-Islamic North-African populations have been glossed as Berbers in both Muslims and Western discourses. Memmi idiosyncratically employs the terms berber (*berbère*) and barbarian (*barbare*) in his novel, with only the latter serving to qualify his incurability giving a global connotation to his argument.

2. After democracy returned, a commission of notables was commissioned to investigate the genocide perpetrated by the dictatorship. The fate of Argentinean Jews is emphasized in the document itself. See CONADEP, *Nunca Más* (Buenos Aires: Eudeba, 1984), 59–63. Ronald Dworking, et. al. adapt, *Nunca Más Never Again* (New York: Farrar Strauss Giroux and London: Faber and Faber, 1986), 67–72. To understand the role of anti-Semitism in the construction of the project of a Christian civilization, see David Rock, *Authoritarian Argentina: The Nationalism Movement, Its History, and Its Impact* (Berkeley and Los Angeles: University of California Press, 1995), 222–237.

3. An account in English of the intellectual implications of this attack and the negotiation of narratives can be found in Edna Aizenberg, *Books and Bombs in Buenos Aires* (Hanover and London: University Press of New England, 2002). There is an extensive Hispanophone bibliography that sheds considerable light on the construction of the new narrative. In particular, I recommend Juan Salinas, *AMIA, el atentado* (Buenos Aires: Planeta, 1997) and Gustavo Bossert et al. *AMIA. doce años despues: jornadas de reflexión* (Buenos Aires: Editorial Mila, 2006). A reproduction of the narrative can be found in Gustavo Perednik, *Matar sin que se note: El ataque de los ayatolas en Argentina, el encubrimiento del caso AMIA y el fiscal* (Buenos Aires: Planeta, 2009). For information about the young Jewry who 'rescued the memory,' see Rodolfo Compte, *Atentado a la AMIA. Crónica de los jovenes que rescataron la memoria* (Buenos Aires: Editorial Generación Joven, 2006).

4. On this elective affinity, see Bernardo Kliksberg, "El Judaismo Latinoamericano y Albert Memmi," *Pensamiento Judío Contemporaneo* 2 (1984): 34–36.

5. Marcos Aguinis, *La cuestión Judía vista desde la izquierda* (Buenos Aires: MILA/AMIA, 2004), 4, 22.

6. This will be one of the central topics of chapter five. See Gary Wilder and Albert Memmi, "Irreconcilable Differences: A Conversation with Albert Memmi," *Transitions* 71 (1996): 174.

7. I will explain in the next chapters the connection between this oscillation and the legacy of classical colonial strategies. I start from a reading of "predominant" and "normative" intellectual discourses on the portrayal of Jews in order to contest them throughout this book.

8. See an anthropological exploration of this conversion in Karen Brodkin, *How Jews Became White Folks and What That Says about Race in America* (New Brunswick: Rutgers University Press, 1994).

9. I will explore this case further in chapter seven. See, for example, Alain Finkielkraut, "Vers une Société Pluriculturelle?," in *La Défaite de la Pensée* (Paris: Gallimard 1987), 121–133. Judith Friedlander, trans., "Toward a Multicultural Society?" in *The Defeat of a Mind* (New York: Columbia University Press, 1995), 89–108 and Bernard-Henry Levy, *Left in Dark Times: A Stand Against the New Barbarism* (New York: Random House, 2008).

10. Theodor Herzl, *Der Judenstaat* (Berlin: Jüdischer Verlag, 1920), 24. Jacob Alkow, trans., *The Jewish State* (New York: Dover Publications, 1988), 96. In chapter six, I will explore the luck of "Fourth World" *Mizrahi* Jews.

11. In chapter five we will analyze the colonial attempt to divide native populations. Though Algeria is the most illustrative case, this tendency can be perceived in other colonies of the Middle East. This strategy cannot, however, be generalized to all Jewries in the Maghreb/Middle East and is not exceptionally a Jewish case. Gil Anidjar persuasively compares this maneuver to other colonial African experiences such as Tutsis' in Rwanda, placing them within a colonized paradigm. See *The Jew, The Arab: A History of the Enemy* (Stanford: Stanford University Press, 2003), xv–xvi.

12. We will further explain this situation in chapter six. This was one of the paradoxes of this experience. While some Arab-Jews left their homelands because of their association with civilization, for material and ideological reasons they became re-barbarized in Israel and their history was reinterpreted to justify the Orientalist portrayal of timeless Muslim hatred and irrationality. Just to add to the paradox, this racialization was usually conducted by Eastern European Jews that had already been racialized by Western European Jews.

13. The critique of the political implications of the post-war inter-religious dialogue between Jews and Christians can be found in Marc Ellis, *Unholy Alliance* (Minneapolis: Fortress Press, 1997), 45–108.

14. In recent years the deconstruction of Jewish history had led some scholars to challenge the existence of an essential/essentialized Jewish people and history. These authors argue that this was largely a construction of a "Zionist historiography" that understood Judaism in a framework that justified nationalist objectives. Several scholars, especially Arab Jews, preceded this work, but see the already iconic text of Shlomo Sand, *Matai ve'ekh humtza ha'am hyedhudi* (Tel Aviv: Resling, 2008). Yael Lotan, trans., *The Invention of the Jewish People* (London: Verso, 2009).

15. See Santiago Slabodsky, "A Latin@ Jewish Disruption of an Only US-Centric Neo-Constellation of Suffering," in *Latin@s in the World System: Decolonization Struggles in the 21st century US Empire*, Ramon Grosfoguel, et al., ed. (Boulder: Paradigm Publishers, 2006), 141–156.

16. Edward Said, *Orientalism* (New York: Vintage Books, 1978) and Homi Bhabha, *The Location of Culture* (London: Routledge, 1994).

17. In the 2012 annual meeting of the American Academy of Religion I organized a panel entitled "Religion and Barbarism." Nancy Bedford presented a paper entitled "Waiting for the Barbarians? Caliban's Sisters and Christian Hope," which identified the risks attendant upon the reappropriation of barbaric identities from a Christian Latin American Feminist perspective. Much further below, I will explain how she is able (much more persuasively than me!) to question the implications of this phenomenon. For this reason I consider it necessary to trace the history of Jewish reappropriation of barbarism and, toward the end of this book, analyze whether this is one of the reasons for their ultimate failure.

18. On the historical possibilities of re appropriation, see G. N. Giladi *Discord in Zion: Conflict between Ashkenasi and Sepharadi Jews* (London: Scorpion Publishing London, 1990), 252–312. For the most articulate problematization of these categories and contemporary retrieval of early twentieth century conception of "Arab Jews" (in moments of pejorative use of "the Arab") see Ella Shohat, "The Invention of the Mizrahim," *Journal of Palestine Studies* 29.1 (1999): 5–20 and "Dislocated Identities: Reflection of an Arab Jew," *Movement Research: Performance Journal* 5 (Fall-Winter 1992): 8.

1 Jewish Thought, Postcolonialism, and Decoloniality: The Geo-Politics of a Barbaric Encounter

1. Edward Said, "Zionism from the Standpoint of its Victims," in *The Question of Palestine* (New York: Random House, 1992), 77–78 and *Orientalism* (New York: Vintage Books, 1978), xxiv.

2. A revision of Orientalism in a framework of Jewish studies can be found in Ivan Kalmar and Derek Penslar, eds., *Orientalism and the Jews* (Hanover: University Press of New England, 2004). Other works in the field of Jewish Postcolonial studies that pay special attention to the racialization

of Jews and the Jewish racialization of others in literature, anthropology, history, and sociology include Brian Cheyette and Laura Marcus, eds., *Modernity, Culture and the Jew* (Cambridge: Polity Press, 1998); Rebecca Stein, *Israel, Palestine and the Politics of Popular Culture* (Durham: Duke University Press, 2005); Ilan Pappe, *A History of Modern Palestine: One Land, Two People* (Cambridge: Cambridge University Press, 2006); and Aziza Khazzom, "The Great Chain of Orientalism: Jewish Identity, Stigma Management and Ethnic Exclusion in Israel," *American Sociological Review* 68.4 (2003): 481–510.

3. Ella Shohat, "Sephardim in Israel: Zionism from the Standpoint of Its Jewish Victims," *Social Text* 19/20 (1988): 1–35. Another complementary trend in the field is Yehuda Shenhav, *The Arab Jews: A Postcolonial Reading of Nationalism, Religion and Ethnicity* (Stanford: Stanford University Press, 2006).

4. Ammiel Alcalay, *After Jews and Arabs: Remaking Levantine Culture* (Minneapolis: University of Minessota Press, 1992) and Gil Anidjar, *The Arab, the Jew: History of an Enemy* (Stanford: Stanford University Press, 2003).

5. Susannah Heschel, *Abraham Geiger and the Jewish Jesus* (Chicago: University of Chicago Press, 1998), 19–21. See also Jonathan Hess, *Germans, Jews, and the Claims of Modernity* (New Heaven: Yale University Press, 2002), 13–15. This later trend have gone beyond intellectual history and included philosophers who understand European Jewish thought as an opportunity to challenge the relation between global Jewry and Israel. One of these examples (but in contraposition to the trend questioning Said) is Judith Butler, *Parting Ways: Jewishness and the Critique of Zionism* (New York: Columbia University Press, 2012).

6. Daniel Boyarin, *Unheroic Conduct: The Rise of Heterosexuality and the Invention of the Jewish Man* (Berkeley and Los Angeles: University of California Press, 1997) and Sander Gilman, *Jewish Frontiers: Essays on Bodies, Histories and Identities* (New York: Palgrave Macmillan, 2003). In collaboration with the Center for Jewish Studies at the University of Cape Town, Gilman has extended his superb critique to other locations. See Sander Gilman and Milton Shain, eds., *Jewries at the Frontier: Accomodation, Identity, Conflict* (Campaign: University of Illinois Press: 1999). I would like to thank a lively conversation I shared with Prof. Shain about this topic when his center and the department of religious studies hosted me during a visit to UCT in 2009.

7. Ella Shohat, "Notes on the Post-Colonial," *Social Texts* 31/32 (1992): 99–113.

8. I would like to clarify that my alternative is to illuminate decolonial Jewish thought with a particular interconnection between French/Spanish decolonialisms. English-Speaking Postcolonialists has had a long history of drawing from their interconnection with French (and to lesser extent Spanish) theory.

9. Walter Mignolo, *Local Histories/Global Designs: Coloniality, Subaltern Knowledges, and Border Thinking* (Princeton: Princeton University Press, 2000), 209–303. This tradition, in Latin America and the Caribbean, includes works such as Rodolfo Kutsch, *La seducción de la barbarie* (Buenos Aires: Raigal, 1953); Leopoldo Zea, *Discurso desde la* marginación *y la barbarie* (Barcelona: Anthopos, 1987); and Roberto Fernandez Retamar, *Algunos usos de civilización y barbarie* (La Habana: Letras Cubanas, 2003).

10. There is a provocative trend within Jewish studies pursing an alternative retrieval of rabbinical sources with categories of Anglophone Postcolonialism. See Boyarin in note 6.

11. See also Enrique Dussel, "Autopercepción Intelectual de un Procesor Histórico," *Anthropos* 3 (1998): 13–36.

12. Albert Memmi, *La statue de sel* (Paris: Gallimard, 1966), 145. Edouard Roditti, trans., *The Pillar of Salt* (New York: Beacon Press, 1992), 165.

13. Aime Cesaire, *Discours sur le colonialisme* (Paris: Presence Africaine, 1955), 31. John Pinkham, trans., *Discourse on Colonialism* (New York: Monthly Review Press, 2001), 36.

14. Frantz Fanon, *Peau noire, masques blancs* (Paris: Éditions du Seuil, 1952), 98. Charles Markmann, trans., *Black Skin/White Masks* (New York: Grove Press, 1991), 122.

15. For the first group, see Said, "Zionism from the Standpoint of its Victims," 66–67, 138 and the back-cover of Marc Ellis, *Out of the Ashes* (London: Pluto Press, 2002). For the second, *Freud and the non-European* (London and New York: Verso, 2003), the endorsement in the back-cover of Ella Shohat, *Israeli Cinema: East/West and the Politics of Representation* (London and New York: I. B. Tauris, 2010) and *Representations of the Intellectual* (New York: Vintage Books, 1996), 55–61.

16. Gayatri Chakravorty Spivak, "Subaltern Studies: Deconstructing Historiography," in *Selected Subaltern Studies*, Ranajit Guha, ed. (New York, Oxford University Press, 1988), 3–32 and Spivak, trans., *Of Gramatology* (Baltimore: Johns Hopkins University Press, 1974).

17. Homi Bhabha, "Joking Aside: The Idea of a Self-Critical Community," in *Modernity, Culture and the Jew*, Cheyette and Marcus, eds., xv.

18. See a description of the oscillation in Ella Shohat and Robert Stam, *Unthinking Eurocentrism: Multiculturalism and the Media* (London and New York: Routledge, 1994), 143.

19. See Immanuel Wallerstein, "The Three Instances of Hegemony in the History of the Capitalist World-System," *International Journal of Comparative Sociology* XXIV (1983): 100–107.

20. This reflection is based on Enrique Dussel, "La colonialidad del saber," *Eurocentrismo y ciencias sociales. Perspectivas Latinoamericanas*, in Edgardo Lander, ed. (Buenos Aires: Clacso 2000), 41–53.

21. It is important to notice that this history, "from Spain to Germany," could be employed to justify a common history of suffering, centered in Europe,

that justifies the need for a postwar civilizational stage. In this work, in the contrary, I will use it to follow the authors of some of the counter-narratives to re-imagine a solidarity of Jews with other barbarians. Even though it is acknowledged that no general history can include all the variety of Jewish experiences.

22. Yosef Yerushalmi has been a pioneer identifying the sixteenth century as a turning point. See *Assimilation and Racial Anti-Semitism: The Iberian and the German Models* (New York: Leo Baeck Institute, 1982). A contemporary overview of the end of the Augustinian dominance can be found in Adam Suttclife, *Judaism and Enlightenment* (Cambridge: Cambridge University Press, 2003), 23–57.

23. An alternative reading of this assertion that associates Christian supressionism with Jewish irremidibility can be seen in Jonathan Boyarin, *The Uncoverted Self: Jews, Indians and the identity of Christian Europe* (Chicago: The University of Chicago Press, 2009), 137–138.

24. A wonderful analysis of the plot can be read in Irene Silverblatt, *Modern Inquisitions* (Durham: Duke University Press, 2004), 150–154.

25. Bhabha's conception of hybridity has had a long-term impact in English-speaking Postcolonial studies. See the explanatory introduction to *The Location of Culture* (London: Routledge, 1994), 4.

26. Gilman is at the forefront of the theoretical analysis of Jewish culture and thought. See "'We're not Jews': Imagining Jewish History and Jewish Bodies in Contemporary Multicultural Literature," in *Orientalism and the Jews*, Kalmar and Penslar, eds., 201–204.

27. See the collective sustaining this narrative in Mabel Moraña, et al., *Coloniality at Large: Latin America and the Postcolonial Debate* (Durham: Duke University Press, 2008). One of the few exceptions within Anglophone Postcolonialism who sets an early beginning of modernity is Jamaican cultural theorist Stuart Hall. See Hall, *Modernity: An Introduction to Modern Societies* (New York: Blackwell, 1996), 7–10. I would suggest the same may be inferred reading the Arab Jewish challenge to Jewish history offered by Ella Shohat in "Taboo Memories, Diasporic Visions: Columbus, Palestine and, Arab-Jews," in *Taboo, Memories, Diasporic Voices* (Durham: Duke University Press, 2006): 201–206.

28. A deep understanding of the generation of the laws in Spain and the extension beyond the metropolis can be found in Maria Elena Martinez, *Genealogical Fictions: Limpieza de Sangre, Religion, and Gender in Colonial Mexico* (Stanford: Stanford University Press, 2008), 25–41 and 173–199.

29. Mignolo, *Local Histories/Global Designs*, 28–30.

30. For the return of identity see the work of Benzion Netanyahu, *The Origins of the Inquisition in the Fifteen Century* (New York: Random House, 1995), 975–980 and *The Marranos of Spain: From the Late 14th to the Early 16th Century* (Ithaca: Cornell University Press, 1999), 1–4. I must confess I feel uncomfortable employing a "Zionist revisionist" political

historiographer (and father of two national Israeli figures including a current prime minister) to justify a decolonial reading of Judaism. I would like to think this is one of the few times that the polar critiques of mainstream readings help in the construction of a new perspective. But I believe it is fair to acknowledge this ideological tension of my work and return to this problem in my epilogue.

31. See Mignolo, *Local Histories/Global Designs*, 30–31, for Mignolo analytical distinction between racializations.

32. Ibid., 29.

33. Mignolo, "Dispensable and Bare Lives: Coloniality and the Hidden Political/Economy Agenda of Modernity," *Human Architecture* 2.7 (2009): 77.

34. Ibid., 78.

35. Ibid., 77.

36. Anibal Quijano, "Coloniality of Power, Eurocentrism, and Latin America" *Nepantla: Views from the South* 1.3 (2000): 533–580.

37. Enrique Dussel, "Para una fundamentación filosófica de la liberación Latinoamericana," in *Liberación latinoamericana y Emmanuel Levinas*, Enrique Dussel and Daniel E. Guillot, eds. (Buenos Aires: Bonum, 1975), 8.

38. We will explore this reading in chapter four.

39. Mignolo, *Local Histories/Global Designs*, 108–109 and 146.

40. Ibid.

41. A previous employment of conceptual Jewish counter-narratives can be found in Michael Mack, *German Idealism and the Jew: The Inner Anti-Semitism of Philosophy and German Jewish Responses* (Chicago: Chicago University Press, 2003).

42. The sociology of Jewish knowledge was explored for pre-Holocaust intellectuals by Michael Lowy, *Redemption et Utopie: Le Judaisme libertarie en Europe central* (Paris: Presses Universitaires de France, 1988), 7–9. Hope Heaney, trans., *Redemption and Utopia: Jewish Libertarian Thought in Central Europe: A Study in Elective Affinity* (Stanford: Stanford University Press, 1992), 2–3.

2   The Narrative of Barbarism: Western Designs for a Globalized North

1. J. M. Coetzee, *Waiting for the Barbarians* (New York: Vintage, 1976).

2. Walter Benjamin, "Über den Begriff der Geschichte," in *Walter Benjamin Erzählen* (Frankfurt Au Main: Shurkamp, 2007), 132. Hannah Arendt, ed., "Thesis on the Philosophy of History," in *Illuminations* (New York: Schocken Books, 1969), 256.

3. See Enrique Dussel, "Europe, Modernity and Eurocentrism," *Nepantla* 1.3 (2000): 465–468.

4. Homer, *Iliad*, Robert Fagles, trans. (New York: Penguin Classics, 1998), 2, 867.

5. Herodotus, *The Histories*, George Rawlinson, trans. (Lawrence: Digireads, 1987), 4, 168. See a critical reflection in James Redfield, "Herodotus the

Tourist," in *Greeks and Barbarians*, Thomas Harrisson, ed. (New York: Routledge, 2002), 24–49.

6. Aeschylus, *Persae*, A. E. F. Garvie, trans. (Oxford and New York: Oxford University Press, 2009), 27–3, 422, 608, 544.

7. Euripides, *Iphigenia at Aulis*, trans. n/a (Whitefish: MT Kessinger Publishing, 2004), 57–58. See a critical reflection in Andromache Suzane Said, "Greek and Euripides Tragedies: The End of Differences," in *Greeks and Barbarians*, Harrisson, ed. (New York: Routledge, 2002), 24–49, 72–73.

8. Aristotle, *The Politics and the Constitution*, Stephen Everson, trans. (Cambridge and New York: Cambridge University Press, 1996), 1252b. See critical engagement in Edith Hall, *Inventing the Barbarian: Greek Self-definition Through Tragedy* (Oxford and New York: Oxford University Press, 1991), 164–165.

9. Hall, *Inventing the Barbarian*, 101.

10. Marcus Tullius Cicero, *The Republics and the Law*, Nial Rudd, trans. (New York and Oxford: Oxford University Press, 2009), 1, 57–59.

11. Livy, *Ab Urbe Condita*, B. O. Foster, trans. (Cambridge: Harvard University Press, 1967), IX. 86 and XXI. 29, 15–16. For critical analysis see W. R. Jones, "The Image of the Barbarian in Medieval Europe," *Comparative Studies in Society and History* 13.4 (1971): 379.

12. Jones, "The Image of the Barbarian in Medieval Europe," 381.

13. Augustine of Hippo, *The City of God Against Pagans*, R. W. Dyson, trans. (Cambridge: Cambridge University Press, 1998), I, 5–23.

14. H. J. Thomson, ed., *Prudentius* (Harvard University Press, 1961), II, 70. For a critical assessment see Jones, "The Image of the Barbarian in Medieval Europe," 381–384.

15. Julia Kristeva, *Strangers to Ourselves*, Leon Roudiez, trans. (New York and Oxford: Columbia University Press, 1991), 88–90.

16. As cited in Jones, "The Image of the Barbarian in Medieval Europe," 391.

17. An alternative reading of this assertion that associates Christian supressionism with Jewish irremidibility can be seen in Jonathan Boyarin, *The Uncoverted Self: Jews, Indians, and the Identity of Christian Europe* (Chicago: The University of Chicago Press, 2009), 137–138.

18. Ivan Hannaford, *Race: The History of an Idea in the West* (Baltimore: Johns Hopkins University Press, 1996), 87–126.

19. Dante Alighieri, *The Divine Comedy*, Mark Musa, trans. (New York: Penguin Classics, 2003), 97–108 and 325–327. See critical comments in Edward Said, *Orientalism* (New York: Vintage Books, 1978), 68–72. The origin of the word Saracen is object of scholarly disagreements. Some versions argue it is a Greco-Roman term, but others radically dismiss it. If this were true, it would argue for an earlier retrieval of Greco-Roman conceptions of otherness.

20. Nancy Bisaha, "New Barbarian or Worthy Adversary? Humanist Constructs of the Ottoman Turks in the Fifteen-Century Italy," in *Western Views of*

Islam in Medieval and Early Modern Europe: Perception of Other, Michael Frassetto and David Blanks, eds. (New York: St. Martin's Press, 1999), 191.

21. Ibid., 192–193.
22. Ibid., 194.
23. Ibid., 188–189.
24. Tudor Parfitt, "The Use of the Jew in Colonial Discourse," in *Orientalism and the Jews*, Ivan Kalmar and Derek Penslar, eds. (Waltham: Brandeis University Press, 2005), 51–67.
25. Lewis Hanke, *All Mankind Is One: A Study of the Disputation between Bartolomé de las Casas and Juan Ginés de Sepulveda in 1550 on the Intellectual and Religious Capacity of the American Indians* (De Kalb: Northern Ilinois University Press, 1959), 57–71.
26. Immanuel Wallerstein, *European Universalism: The Rhetoric of Power* (New York: The New Press, 2006), 5–14.
27. Juan Ginés de Sepúlveda, *Democrates Segundo; o De Las justas causas de la guerra contra los indios* (Madrid: CSIC, 1951), 35.
28. Ibid., 87–88. See critical engagement in Hebert Frey, "La Mirada de Europa y el 'otro' indoamericano," *Revista Mexicana de Sociología* 58.2. (1996): 61–62.
29. Sepúlveda, *Democrates Segundo; o De Las justas causas de la guerra contra los indios*, 122. See critical engagement in Luis Rivera-Pagan, *A Violent Evangelism* (Louisville: Westminster/John Knox Press, 1992), 135.
30. Sepúlveda, *Democrates Segundo; o De las justas causas de la guerra contra los indios*, 93.
31. For a decolonial critique of the typology presented by *Bartolomé* de las Casas see Walter Mignolo, *The Darker Side of the Renaissance* (Ann Harbor: Michigan University Press, 1995), 441–443.
32. As cited in Sue Peabody "'A Nation Born to Slavery': Missionaries and Racial Discourse in Seventeen-Century French Antilles," *Social History* 38.1 (2004): 117.
33. Peter Mack, "Perceptions of Black Africans in the Renaissance," in *Africa and the Renaissance*, Ezio Bassani and William Fagg, eds. (New York: Center for African Art, 1989), 21–26.
34. As cited in Andrew Curran, *The Anatomy of Blackness: Science and Slavery in an Age of the Enlightenment* (Baltimore: Johns Hopkins University Press, 2011), 32–41.
35. Emmanuel Eze has done a superb groundwork collecting these voices. See Denis Diderot, "Negre," and David Hume, "On National Characters," in *Race and Enlightenment: A Reader*, Emmanuel Chukwudi Eze, ed. (Malden: Blackwell, 1997), 29 and 30–34.
36. Kant, "Physical Geography," in *Race and Enlightenment,* Eze, ed., 58–64. For a critical engagement see also Eze, "The Color of Reason: The Idea of "Race in Kant's Anthropology," in *Postcolonial African Philosophy* (Cambridge: Blackwell, 1997), 103–140.

37. Susan Back-Morss, "Hegel and Haiti," *Critical Inquiry* 26.4 (2000): 863–864.
38. Achille Mbembe, *On the Postcolony* (Berkeley and Los Angeles: University of California Press, 2001), 175.
39. Georg W. F. Hegel, *Vorlesungen über die Philosophie der Geschichte* (Berlin: Dunker and Humbolt, 1840), 116. Hugh Barr Nisbet, trans., *Lectures on the Philosophy of World History* (Cambridge: Cambridge University Press, 1975), 176.
40. Ibid.
41. Ibid.
42. Ibid., 101–102/163.
43. Said, *Orientalism*, 59.
44. As quoted in Richard Swedberg, *Toqueville's Political Economy* (Princeton: Princeton University Press, 2009), 49–53.
45. Alexis de Toqueville, *Travail sur l'Algérie (Octobre 1841)* (Quebec: University of Quebec, 2001), 4. Jenniffer Pitts, ed. and trans., "Essay on Algeria (October, 1841)," in *Writings on Empire and Slavery* (Baltimore: Johns Hopkins University Press, 2003), 59.
46. Ibid., 17/70.
47. Ibid., 87/130.
48. Ibid., 87/130.
49. Said, *Orientalism*, 39.
50. Mark Salter, *Barbarians and Civilization in International Relations* (London: Pluto Press, 2002), 25–27.
51. Anthony Collins, *A Discourse of Free Thinking* (London: n/a, 1713), 123–124. It is important to notice that the use of the Biblical text was not a novelty among champions of Oriental secularism. The text, however, was not interpreted as a truth but as a source of "Oriental history and literature." See Ivan Kalmar, "Race by the Grace of God: Race, Religion, and the Construction of 'Jew' and 'Arab,'" in *Race, Color, Identity*, Efraim Sicher, ed. (New York/Oxford: Berghan Books, 2013), 501–503. I thank Dr. Kalmar for generously share a draft of the article.
52. Henry St Jones Bolingbroke, "Fragments or Minutes of Essay," and "A Letter on One of Archbishop Tillotson's Sermons," in *The Works of Lord Bolingbroke* (Philadelphia: Carey and Hart, 1841), vol. 4, 241 and vol. 3, 22. An analysis of both deists can be found in Anthony Julius, *Trials of Diaspora: A History of English Anti-Semitism* (Oxford: Oxford University Press, 2010), 388–390.
53. Voltaire, *Oeuvres completes XXVIII* (Paris: Garnier frères, 1879), 549. Arthur Hertzberg, trans., *The French Enlightenment and the Jews: The Origins of Modern Anti-Semitism* (New York: Columbia University Press, 1990), 301.
54. Walter Mignolo, *Local Histories/Global Designs: Coloniality, Subaltern Knowledges, and Border Thinking* (Princeton: Princeton University Press, 2000), 21–35.

55. In chapters three and five, I will explain the role of the extension of citizenship in Prussia and Algeria in the development of this narrative of barbarism. The reasons that preceded this decision and the political consequences were different. Yet, both of them will confirm this reading of Judaism.

56. Parfitt, "The Use of the Jew in Colonial Discourses," 61.

57. Irene Silverblatt, *Modern Inquisitions: Peru and the Colonial Origins of the Civilized World* (Durham: Duke University Press, 2004), 107, 143–153.

58. Gustavo Martínez Zuviría, *Cuentos de Oro* (Buenos Aires: Tor, 1923), *El Kahal* (Buenos Aires: Editores de Hugo Wast, 1935), and *666* (Buenos Aires: Editores de Buenos Aires, 1942).

59. Henry Ford, *The International Jew: The World's Foremost Problem* (York, SC: Liberty Bell Publishing, 1920).

60. Victor Mardsen, *The Protocols of the Learned Elders of Zion* (San Diego: The Book Trees, 1999), 96.

61. Ibid., 276. For the influence of the protocols, see the classic Norman Cohn, *Warrant for Genocide: The Myth of the Jewish World Conspiracy and the Protocols of the Wise of Zion* (New York: Harper and Row, 1967); and a more contemporary interpretation Esther Webman, *The Global Impact of the Protocols of the Elders of Zion: A Century Old Myth* (London and New York: Routledge, 2011).

62. Sander Gilman, *Jewish Self-Hatred: Anti-Semitism and the Hidden Language of the Jews* (Baltimore, Johns Hopkins, 1986), 8 and 311.

63. Ibid., 7.

64. Ibid.

65. Ibid.

66. Jonathan Schorsch, *Jews and Blacks in the Early Modern World* (Cambridge: Cambridge University Press, 2004).

67. Rabson Wuriga, "Role and Impact of Intellectual Factor in the 18th-20th century 'European conception of' Jews as Jews': A Revisition," *Human Architecture* 7.2. (2009): 53–68.

68. In chapter five, we will explore these cases further.

69. Kalmar and Penslar, *Orientalism and the Jews*, xiv.

70. Ivan Kalmar, "Jesus Did Not Wear Turban: Orientalism, the Jews and Christian Art," in *Orientalism and the Jews*, Kalmar and Penslar, eds., 3–31.

71. Adam Sutcliffe, *Judaism and Enlightenment* (Cambridge: Cambridge University Press, 2003) 7–12, 231–246.

72. John Efron, "Orientalism and the Jewish Historical Gaze," in *Orientalism and the Jews*, Kalmar and Penslar, eds., 80–93.

73. See Kalmar and Penslar, *Orientalism and the Jews*, xxvii and Cohn, *Warrant for Genocide,* 28–31, 24–49, and 232–248.

74. Narratives of the Muselmann can be found in multiple Holocaust survivors including Primo Levi and Elie Wiesel. A wonderful re-interpretation of this

role in the relation/split of Jews and Muslims can be found in Gill Anidjar, *The Jew, the Arab: A History of the Enem* (Stanford: Stanford University Press, 2003), 141 and 162.

3 Negative Barbarism: Marxist Counter-Narrative in the Provincial North

1. Isaac Deutscher, "Who is a Jew," in *The Non-Jewish Jew: The Non-Jewish Jew and Other Essays* (Oxford: Oxford University Press, 1968), 51. Deutscher became a leading voice of non-Zionist Jews. Lately there have been some voices critically re-evaluating this iconic figure. See Joseph Massad, "The 'Post-Colonial' Colony: Time, Space and Bodies in Palestine/Israel," in *The Pre-Occupation of Postcolonial Studies*, Fawzia Afzal-Khan, et al., eds. (Durham: Duke University Press, 2000), 319–332 and Norman Finkelstein, *Beyond Chutzpa: On the Misuse of Anti-Semitism and the Abuse of History* (Berkeley and Los Angeles: University of California Press, 2008), 11–12.
2. As cited in Robert Jackson Alexander, *International Trotskyism 1929–1885: A Documented Analysis of the Movement* (Durham: Duke University Press, 1991), 648.
3. Isaac Deutscher, "The Non-Jewish Jew," in *The Non-Jewish Jew and Other Essays*, 25–27.
4. Ibid., 26.
5. Ibid.
6. George Steiner, *Language and Silence* (New York: Atheneum, 1967), 5 and Hannah Arendt, *Eichmann in Jerusalem* (New York: Penguin, 1995), 56–58.
7. Ricardo Forster, *Notas sobre la barbarie y la esperanza: Del 11 de septiembre a la crisis Argentina* (Buenos Aires: Biblos, 2006). This will be one of the voices explored in the last chapter.
8. Michael Lowy, "Modern Barbarism: Notes on the Fiftieth Anniversaries of Auschwitz and Hiroshima," *Monthly Review* 47 (1995): 4–26.
9. Jonathan Hess, *Germans, Jews, and the Claims of Modernity* (New Haven: Yale University Press, 2002), 4 and 15 and Susannah Heschel, "Revolt of the Colonized: Abraham Geiger's Wissenschaft des Judentums as a Challenge to Christian Hegemony in the Academy," *New German Critique* 77 (1999): 62–64.
10. As cited in Paul Lawrence Rose, *Revolutionary Anti-Semitism in Germany from Kant to Wagner* (Princeton: Princeton University Press, 1990), 8 and 92.
11. See Hess, *Germans, Jews, and the Claims of Modernity*, 82–84.
12. Ibid., 68–84.
13. The anti-Semitism of German idealism has been discussed in a variety of Jewish sources. For an excellent engagement with the authors I engage

here, see Rose, *Revolutionary Anti-Semitism in Germany*, 91–116 and for a re-reading in the context of counter-narratives see Michael Mack, *German Idealism and the Jew: The Inner Anti-Semitism of Philosophy and German Jewish Responses* (Chicago: University of Chicago Press, 2003), 23–68.

14. Rose, *Revolutionary Anti-Semitism in Germany*, 15–22 and Hess, *Germans, Jews, and the Claims of Modernity*, 5–6.

15. Paul Mendes-Flohr, *German Jews: A Dual Identity* (New Heaven: Yale University Press, 1999), 16–17.

16. Heinrich Heine, "A Ticket of Admission to European Culture," in *The Jew in the Modern World: A Documentary History*, Mendes-Flohr and Jehuda Reinharz, eds. (Oxford and New York: Oxford University Press, 1995), 258–259.

17. See Steven Aschheim, *Brothers and Strangers: The East European Jew in German and German Jewish Consciousness 1800–1923* (Madison: University of Winsconsin Press, 1982), 3–31.

18. Michael Lowy, *Redemption et Utopie: Le Judaisme libertarie en Europe central* (Paris: Presses Universitaries de France, 1988), 28–30 and Mendes-Flohr, *German Jews*, 25.

19. As cited in Mendes-Flohr, *German Jews*, 46.

20. Ibid., 47.

21. This is the description that Susanna Heschel makes of Abraham Geiger's revolutionary religious reformation in *Abraham Geiger and the Jewish Jesus* (Chicago: University of Chicago Press), 4.

22. For the conception of "avant-garde" of the "decolonized people" see John Cuddihy, *The Ordeal of Civility: Freud, Marx, Lévi-Strauss, and the Jewish Struggle with Modernity* (Boston: Beacon Press, 1987), 4–7, 21–26. I would like to point out that reactions to colonization is not a product of post-1940s struggle but is simultaneous to colonization.

23. Charles Fourier, *The Theory of the Four Movements*, Ian Patterson, trans. (Cambridge: Cambridge University Press, 1996), 104.

24. See critical reading of Fourier in Jonathan Beecher, *Charles Fourier: The Visionary and His World* (Berkeley and Los Angeles: University of California Press, 1986), 196–204.

25. See an excellent source for the discussion of these topics in Sander Gilman, *Jewish Self-Hatred: Anti-Semitism and the Hidden Language of the Jews* (Baltimore: Johns Hopkins University Press, 1986), 188–208.

26. Karl Marx and Friedrich Engels, *Manifest der kommunistischen* (London: J. E. Burghard, 1848) 4. Eugene Kamenka, trans.,"Manifesto of the Communist Party," in *The Portable Karl Marx* (New York: Viking Press, 1981), 204. While my analysis has a different direction, Lowy's analysis was crucial to build this genealogy. See note number 8 of this chapter.

27. Ibid.

28. Ibid., 6/206.

29. Marx, "The Future Results of the British Rule in India," in *Karl Marx on Colonialism and Modernization*, Shlomo Avineri, ed. (Garden City: New York, 1968), 126.

30. Marx, *Das Kapital* (Berlin: Dietz Verlag, 1961), I, 791. Ben Folken, trans., *The Capital* (Penguin Books: London, 1976), I, 916.

31. Karl Marx, "*Ökonomische-philosophische Manuskript*," in *Marx/Engels Gesamtausgabe* (Berlin: Dietz Verlag, 1982), 353. Rodney Livingstone and Gregor Benton, trans., "Economic and Philosophical Manuscripts (1844)," in *Early Writings* (London: Penguin Books, 1981), 359–360.

32. Ibid., 322/74.

33. Ibid., 336/86–87.

34. Karl Marx, "Zur Judenfrage," in *Marx/Engels Gesamtausgabe*, 168. Lloyd D. Easton and Kurt H. Guddat, trans., "On the Jewish Question," in *Writings of the Young Marx on Philosophy and Society* (New York: Anchor Books, 1967), 247.

35. Ibid., 163/242.

36. Karl Marx, "Zur kritik der hegelschen rechtsphilosophie," in *Marx/Engels Gesamtausgabe*, 6–8. David Easton and Guddat trans., "Toward a Critique of Hegel's Philosophy of Law," in *Writings of the Young Marx on Philosophy and Society*, 249–250.

37. Marx, "Zur Judenfrage," in *Marx/Engels Gesamtausgabe*, 148, 150. Easton and Guddat, trans., "On the Jewish Question," in *Writings of the Young Marx on Philosophy and Society*, 225, 227.

38. A good introduction to the debates can be found in James Joll, *The Second International 1898–1914* (New York: Harper and Row, 1966).

39. Rosa Luxemburg, "Die Krise der Sozialdemokratie," in *Politische Schriten* (Frankfurt: Europaische Verlagsanstalt, 1966), 29–30. Dick Howard, trans. and ed., "The Crisis of the German Social Democracy," in *Rosa Luxemburg, Selected Political Writings* (New York: Monthly Review Press, 1971), 332–333.

40. Ibid., 31–32/334–335.

41. Ibid. 31/334.

42. Ibid., 34/335

43. Luxemburg's letter to Mathilda Wurm, dated February 16, 1916, in Mendes-Flohr and Reinharz, eds. *The Jew in the Modern World: A Documentary History*, 261–262.

44. Discussion about the collaborative/conflictive nature of the first generation of the school can be found in the following texts: Martin Jay, *The Dialectical Imagination: A History of the Frankfurt School and the Institute of Social Research 1923–1950* (Berkeley and Los Angeles: University of California, 1996) and Rolf Wiggershaus, *The Frankfurt School: Its History, Theories and Political Significance*, Michael Roberton, trans. (Cambridge: MIT Press, 1995).

45. Walter Benjamin, "Über den Begriff der Geschichte," in *Walter Benjamin Erzählen* (Frankfurt Au Main: Shurkamp, 2007), 129. Hannah Arendt, ed., "Thesis on the Philosophy of History," in *Illuminations* (New York: Harcourt, Brace & World, 1968), 253.

46. Ibid., 135–136/260.

47. Ibid., 133/257.

48. Ibid.

49. Ibid.

50. Ibid., 139–140/264.

51. Ibid.

52. It is necessary to point out that in one text Benjamin does once mention a "positive barbarism." But his reading of positive barbarism serves to confirm our thesis. He understands that in a world devoid of culture, the only remaining possibility is to collaborate with the process of destruction. This does not represent an alternative but the positive barbarism of the destruction/deconstruction. See Walter Benjamin, "Die Welt im Wort," in *Gesammelte Schriften*, II (Frankfurt am Main: Shurkamp, 1972–1989), 213–219. Benjamin, "Experience and Poverty," in Walter Benjamin, *Selected Writings V. 2 1927–1934*, Rodney Livingstone and Michael W. Jennings, trans. and ed. (Cambridge: Harvard University Press, 2005), 731–736. I appreciate early discussions with Paula Schwebel about this issue.

53. Sigmund Freud is another "heretical" Jew cited by Deutscher, who is deeply influential in the Frankfurt School, and usually employs the term barbarism. While his readings are also negative, he reproduces the scientific taxonomies existent in the early twentieth century. His engagement with this narrative as well as his placement outside the Marxist tradition makes his participation in the negative counter-narrative dubious. For this reason I did not include him in this chapter.

54. Max Horkheimer and Theodor Adorno, *Dialectic of Enlightenment*, *Dialectic of Enlightenment: Philosophical Fragments*, Edmund Jephcott, trans. (Stanford: Stanford University Press, 2002), xii–xiii. (This is the preface to the English edition and not the original.)

55. Max Horkheimer and Theodor Adorno, *Dialektik der Aufklärung* (Amsterdam: Querido Verlag N.V., 1947), 11., in *Dialectic of Enlightenment*, xix.

56. Ibid., 13/1.

57. Ibid., 16–18/4–5.

58. Ibid., 16/4.

59. Ibid., 27/15.

60. Ibid., 21/9.

61. Ibid., 199–244/137–172. Also see Horkheimer "The Jews and Europe," in *The Frankfurt School on Religion,* Eduardo Mendieta, ed. (New York: Routledge, 2005), 225–241.

62. Horkheimer and Adorno, *Dialektik der Aufklärung*, 201/139.
63. Ibid., 199, 214/137, 152.
64. Ibid., 29/17.
65. Ibid.
66. See the "fraud" of Hitler's retrieval of the term barbarism in Hermann Rauschning's collection of private conversations with him: *Hitler Speaks: A Series of Political Conversations* (Whitefish: Kessinger Publishing, 2006), 87 and discussions about its role as a propaganda ally in Richard Steigmann-Gall, *The Holy Reich: Nazi Conceptions of Christianity* (Cambridge: Cambridge University Press, 2003), 29.

4 Transitional Barbarism: Levinas's Counter-Narrative and the Global South

1. A previous and shorter version of this chapter was published in Santiago Slabodsky, "Emmanuel Levinas' Geopolitics: Overlooked Conversations between Rabbinical and Third World Decolonialisms," *Journal of Jewish Thought and Philosophy* 28.2 (2010): 147–165.
2. Voltaire, "Juifs" *Oeuvres complètes de Voltaire 8: Dictionnaire philosophique* (Paris: Chez Furne, 1835), 36–42. E. R. Dumont, trans., "Jews," in *A Philosophical Dictionary* (New York: Coventry House, 1932), 99–116. For further exploration read Harvey Mitchel, *Voltaire's Jews and Modern Jewish Identity* (Oxford and New York: Routledge, 2008), 38–61.
3. Several scholars have researched the figure of the Jew in contemporary French discourse. Among recent works on the subject, I strongly recommend Jonathan Judaken, *Jean-Paul Sartre and the Jewish Question: Anti-Semitism and the Politics of the French Intellectual* (Lincoln: University of Nebraska Press, 2006) and Sarah Hammerschlag, *The Figural Jew: Politics and Identity in Postwar French Thought* (Chicago: University of Chicago Press, 2010).
4. Achille Edmon-Halpen, *Recueil des lois: décrets, ordonnances, avis du conseil d'état, arrêtés et règlements concernant les israélites depuis la Révolution de 1789* (Paris: Bureaux des archives israélites, 1851), 184–189. J. Rubin trans., "The French National Assembly. Debate on the Eligibility of Jews for Citizenship," in *The Jew in the Modern World: A Documentary History,* Paul Mendes-Flohr and Jehuda Reinharz, eds. (New York: Oxford University Press, 1995), 115. For more information, see the canonical work on the subject in Anglophone academia Paula Hyman, "The French Revolution and the Emancipation of Jews," in *The Jews of Modern France* (Berkeley and Los Angeles: University of California Press, 1998), 17–36.
5. Emile Zola, "J'accuse…! Lettre Au President De La Republique," in *L'Aurore* (January 13, 1898), 1–2. L. F. Austin, trans., *Emile Zola, The Dreyfus Case: Four Letters to France* (London and New York: John Lane, 1898), 22. To understand the context within which the case unfolded

see Michael Graetz, *The Jews in the Nineteenth-Century France: From the French Revolution to the Alliance Israelite Universale* (Stanford: Stanford University Press, 1996), 194–287.

6. An excellent exploration of the role of Jews, Judaism, the Holocaust, and decolonization in the context of the 1968 revolt can be found in Yair Auron, *Les juifs d'extrême-gauche en mai 68: une génération révolutionnaire marquée par la Shoah* (Paris: Albin Michel, 1996). A brief summary of this book was published in English under the title of *Tikkun Olam: The Phenomenon of the Jewish Radicals in France During the 1960s and '70s* (Jerusalem: Institute of the World Jewish Congress, 2000).

7. An superb sociological analysis of these changing demographics can be found in Dominique Schnapper, *Jewish Identities in France* (Chicago: University of Chicago Press, 1983).

8. For this study, see Auron, *Les juifs d'extrême-gauche*, 71–87.

9. Cited in Ibid., 181.

10. Claude Lévi-Strauss, *Race et Historie* (Paris: Denoel, 1987), 22. Lévi-Strauss, *Race and History* (Paris: UNESCO, 1952), 11.

11. For the multiple sources see the role of re-reading Marx in, for example, the work of Louis Alhusser and his students: Althusser, Étienne Balibar, Roger Establet, Pierre Macherey, and Jacques Rancière, *Lire le Capital, Tome 1 & 2* (Paris: Maspero, 1965). Ben Brewster, trans., *Reading Capital* (London: Verso 1997). In addition, for an analysis of the role of the journal of Cornelius Castoriadis see Philipe Gottraux, *Socialisme ou Barbarie? Un engagement politique et intellectual dans la France de l'apres-guerre* (Lausanne: Payot, 1997). Lastly, for Levi-Strauss' influence, see *Anthropologie structurale deuz* (Paris: Plon, 1973), 383–384. Monique Layton, trans., *Structural Anthropology* v. 2 (Garmondsworth: Penguin, 1978), 329–330.

12. Judith Friedlander, *Vilna on the Seine: Jewish Intellectuals in France since 1968* (New Heaven: Yale University Press, 1990), 5–23 and 80–106.

13. Salomon Malka, *Emmanuel Levinas: His Life and Legacy* (Pittsburgh: Duquesne University Press, 2006), 86–92.

14. Short biographies of the founders of the institute can be read in the http://www.levinas.fr/institut/institut.asp. In chapter seven, we will explore this "failed" legacy.

15. Jill Robbins, trans. and ed., "Interview with Francois Poire, 1986," in *Is it Righteous to Be?: Interviews with Emmanuel Levinas* (Stanford: Stanford University Press, 2001), 27.

16. It is important to clarify that this may not have been the only influence of Levinas option to employ a negative conception of barbarism and apply it to civilization. Other decolonial scholars who analyzed Levinas before myself showed the extension of the negative counter-narrative of barbarism beyond Marxism in, for example, Levinas's teacher Edmund Husserl. See Maldonado-Torres, *Against War*, 43–46.

17. Levinas is widely understood an iconic philosopher of otherness. The canonical work in North America portraying this important and predominant interpretation is Adriaan Peperzak, *To the Other: An Introduction to the Philosophy of Emmanuel Levinas* (West Lafayette: Purdue University Press, 1996).

18. Emmanuel Levinas, *A l'heure des nations* (Paris: Minuit, 1988), 9. Michael Smith, trans., *In Times of the Nations* (London: Athlone, 1994), 1.

19. The most interesting texts that practice this suspicion of Levinas's politics at different levels are Howard Caygill, *Levinas and the Political* (London: Routledge, 2002) and George Salemohamed, "Levinas: From Ethics to Political Theology," *Economy and Society* 21 (1992): 78–94.

20. Emmanuel Levinas, "The Actuality of Maimonides," cited in Caygill, *Levinas and the Political*, 45–46.

21. Emmanuel Levinas, "La pensée juive aujourd'hui," in *Difficile liberté* (Paris: Albin Michel, 2006), 210. Sean Hand, trans., "Jewish Thought Today," in *Difficult Freedom* (Baltimore: Johns Hopkins University Press, 1997), 160.

22. Raoul Mortley, *French Philosophers in Conversation* (London: Routledge, 1991), 18.

23. Emmanuel Levinas, "Jacob Gordin," in *Difficile liberté*, 224. Hand, trans., "Jacob Gordin," in *Difficult Freedom*, 171.

24. Emmanuel Levinas, *Entre Nous* (Paris: Bernard Grasset et Fasquelle, 1991). Michael Smith, trans., "Useless Suffering," in *Entre Nous* (London and New York: Continuum, 2006), 83.

25. Emmanuel Levinas, "Une religion d'adultes," in *Difficile liberté*, 26. Sean Hand, trans., "A Religion for Adults," in *Difficult Freedom*, 11–12.

26. Emmanuel Levinas, *Autrement qu'être, ou au-delà de l'essence* (La Haye: Martin Nijhoff, 1974), 273. Alphonse Lingis, trans., *Otherwise Than Being, or Beyond Essence* (Pittsburgh: Duquesne University Press, 2002), 178.

27. Ibid.

28. Emmanuel Levinas, "Les Nations et la presence d'Israël," 114. Michael Smith, trans., "The Nations and the Presence of Israel," 99.

29. Ibid. Levinas writes that Ethiopia stands for a loose conception of the Third World. In his own words, it represents all the "countries doubtless similar to it" that comprise "between a third and a fourth of mankind."

30. Ibid., 108/93.

31. Ibid., 122–123/107.

32. Ibid., 113–115/100–102.

33. Ibid., 116/103.

34. Ibid.

35. Ibid., 74/106.

36. Ibid., 113/104.

37. I explored these interpretations in a previous article entitled "Talmudic Terrorism in Bethlehem," in *Biblical Texts, UR-Contexts and Contemporary*

Realities in Israel and Palestine, Mitri Raheb, ed. (Bethlehem: Dyar Publisher, 2011), 181–198.

38. I would like to thank Nelson Maldonado-Torres for the discussions about this particular limitation of Levinas.

39. It is important to notice this change was never complete. While Levinas does recognize the dualism colonizer/colonized and the role of the history of Rome, Israel, and Egypt, his comments on the historical role of Ethiopia are highly problematic and still reproduce the Humanist stratification of peoples with no history.

40. Emmanuel Levinas, "Philosophie, Justice et Amour," in *Entre Nous* (Paris: Bernard Grasset, 1991), 138. Jill Robbins, trans., "Philosophy, Justice and Love," in *Is It Righteous to Be?*, 179.

41. The original text was published in Enrique Dussel, "El Método Analéctico y la Filosofía Latinoamericana," in *America Latina, Dependencia y Liberación* (Buenos Aires: Garcia Cambeiro, 1973), 111–113, and later expanded into an article published years later: Enrique Dussel, "Sensibility and Otherness in Emmanuel Levinas," *Philosophy Today* 37 (1999): 123–127.

42. Enrique Dussel, "Para una Fundamentación Filosófica de la Liberación Latinoamericana," in *Liberación Latinoamericana y Emmanuel Levinas* (Buenos Aires: Bonum, 1975), 8. This encounter has not been studied outside Latino/a social theory. See some of the critical appraisals in Linda Martin Alcoff and Eduardo Mendieta, eds., *Thinking from the Underside of History* (Lanham: Rowman and Littlefield Publishers, 2000). Of particular importance are the Introduction, written by the editors (18–21), Walter Mignolo's "Dussel's Philosophy of Liberation: Ethics and Geopolitics of Knowledge" (28–30), and Michael Barber's "Dussel's Marx and Marion on Idolatry" (204–210). The only reference to this encounter I could find within Jewish thought is Robert Gibbs' acknowledgment of the existence of this influence. See Gibbs, *Correlations in Rosenzweig and Levinas* (Princeton: Princeton University Press, 1992), 229. There was a superb late re-evaluation of the encounter in philosophical terms in the already-cited Maldonado-Torres, *Against War.*

43. This work, *Emmanuel Levinas and Latinoamerican Liberation*, has not been translated into English.

44. Dussel, *"El Método Analéctico y la Filosofía Latinoamericana,"* 112.

45. Levinas, *Autrement qu'être,* 273. Lingis, trans., *Otherwise than Being,* 178.

46. Levinas, "Une religion d'adultes," 26. Hand, trans., "A Religion for Adults," 26/11–12. In private conversations I had with Dussel, he repeated that he was unaware of the Jewish writings of Levinas at the time he asked him the question (Berkeley 2004 and San Antonio and Amherst 2005). He said it was a mere *pálpito* (a hunch) that later he was able to overcome in one of his most celebrated works: *Filosofía de Liberación* (Mexico D. F.: Edicol, 1977). Aquilina Martinez, trans., *Philosophy of Liberation* (Maryknoll: Orbis Books, 1985).

47. Dussel, "Sensibility and Otherness in Emmanuel Levinas," 126.
48. Dussel wrote his first dissertation on the topic of Natives, the Church, and Colonial Latin America at the Complutense University of Madrid in 1959. His work was particularly important in commemorating the discovery of the Americas in 1492. See Enrique Dussel, *El encubrimiento del otro: Hacia el origen del mito de la modernidad* (La Paz: Plural Editores, 1994). Michael Barber, trans., *Eclipse of "The Other" and the Myth of Modernity* (New York: Continuum, 1995).
49. Caygill, *Levinas and the Political*, 60, 159–161. The reference to Israeli historiography is of the leading historian of Fascism and long-time head of the department of political science at the Hebrew University of Jerusalem Zeev Sternhell. See *The Founding Myths of Israel: Nationalism, Socialism and the Making of the Jewish State* (Princeton: Princeton University Press, 1999).
50. Emmanuel Levinas, "Etat d'Israël et religion d'Israël," in *Difficile liberté*, 282. Hand, trans., "The State of Isael, The Religion of Israel," in *Difficult Freedom*, 218.
51. Emmanuel Levinas, "Qui joue le dernier?," in *L'Au-delà du verset* (Paris: Minuit, 1982), 72. Gary Mole, trans., "Who Plays last?," in *Beyond the Verse* (London: Athlone Press, 1994), 54.

5 Positive Barbarism: Memmi's Counter-Narrative in a Southern Network

1. Albert Memmi, *La statue de Sel* (Paris: Gallimard, 1966), 109 and 145. Edouard Roditti, trans., *The Pillar of Salt* (New York: Beacon Press, 1992), 96 and 165. While the works that analyze life and work of Memmi in the English-speaking academia are scarce, they open interesting doors of analysis. See, for example, Judith Roumani, *Albert Memmi* (Philadelphia: Celfan/Temple, 1987), Kelly McBride, "Albert Memmi in the Era of Decolonization," *Journal of French and Francophone Philosophy* 19.2 (2011): 50–66, and Lawrence R. Schehr, "Albert Memmi's Tricultural Tikkun," *French Forum* 28.3 (2003): 59–83.
2. The connection between the original events and the influential imagery can be found in Nicholas Robins, *Native Insurgencies and the Genocidial Impulse in the Americas* (Bloomington: Indiana University Press, 2005); Carolyn Hamilton, *Terrific Majesty: The Powers of Shaka Zulu and the Limits of Historical Imagination* (Cambridge: Harvard University Press, 1998); and Sybille Fischer, *Modernity Disvowed: Haiti and the Cultures of Slavery in the Age of Revolution* (Duke: Duke University Press, 2004).
3. Marc Ferro, *Colonialism: A Global History*, K. D. Prithipaul, trans. (London: Routledge, 1997), 211–230. The best theoretical contribution to differentiate between native and settler revolution (subaltern vs bourgeois nationalist elitism) can be found in the analysis of the South-Asian sub-continent. See Ranajit Guha, "On Some Aspects of the Historiography of Colonial

India," in *Selected Subaltern Studies* (New York: Oxford University Press, 1988), 37–44.

4. Marc Ferro, *Colonialism: A Global History*, 239–261.

5. An excellent introduction to these terms can be found in Robert Young, *Postcolonialism: An Historical Introduction* (Malden: Blackwell, 2001), 113–334.

6. The influence of Lenin and Mao for the movement can be found in Young, *Postcolonialism*, 116–126 and 183–188. The path that led to this movement was preceded by solidarity meetings between 1954 and 1957 in Bogor, Bandung, Cairo, and Belgrade.

7. Robert Young, *Postcolonialism*, 167–181.

8. A good introduction to the power of epistemological decolonization can be found in Bill Ashcroft et al, *The Empire Writes Back: Theory and Practice of Post-colonial Literatures* (London and New York: Routledge, 1994).

9. The relation between the Harlem Renascence and the Negritude Movement is superbly explained in Gary Wilder, *The French Imperial Nation State: Negritude and the Colonial Humanism between the Two World Wars* (Chicago: University of Chicago Press, 2005), 201–255.

10. Richard Watts, "Negritude, Presence Africaine, Race," in *Post-colonial Thought in the French Speaking World*, Charles Fordsdick and David Murphy, eds. (Liverpool: Liverpool University Press, 2009), 227–237.

11. Michael Lambert, "From Citizenship to Negritude: 'Making a Difference' in Elite Ideologies of Colonized Francophone West Africa," *Comparative Studies in Society and History* 35.2 (1993): 249.

12. Mary Gallagher, "Aime Cesaire and Francophone Postcolonial Thought," in *Postcolonial Thought in the French Speaking World*, 31–41.

13. Aime Cesaire, *Cahier d'un retour au pays natal* (Paris: Presence Africaine, 1983). Clayton Eshleman and Annette Smith, trans., *Notebook of a Return to the Native Land* (Middletown: Wesleyan University Press, 2001).

14. Ibid. 7–14/2–7.

15. Ibid., 24/19.

16. Ibid., 43–48/38–41.

17. Ibid., 63–65/55–57. An excellent interpretation of the text that inspired mine can be found in Wilder, *The French Imperial Nation State*, 278–292.

18. Cesaire, *Cahier*, 20. Eshleman and Smith, trans., *Notebook*, 15. Cesaire recognizes that if he were to leave his land, he would be like each one of them.

19. See Jean-Paul Sartre, "Orphée noir," in *Anthologie de la nouvelle poésie négre et malgache de langue française*, Leopold Sédar-Senghor, ed. (Paris: Presses Universitaries de France, 1948), ix–xlivl. S. W. Allen, trans., "Black Orpheus," in *What is Literature* (Cambridge: Harvard University Press, 1988), 289–331 and Jean-Paul Sartre, *Réflexions sur la question juive* (Paris: Paul Morihien, 1946). George J. Baker, trans., *Anti-Semite and Jew* (New York: Schoken, 1995).

20. Aime Cesaire, *Discurs sur le Colonialisme* (Paris and Dakar: Presence Africaine, 1955), 11–15, 53. Joan Pinkham, trans., *Discourse of Colonialism* (New York: Monthly Review, 2000), 35–39, 72.
21. G. R. Coulthard, "Rejection of European Culture as a Theme in Caribbean Literature," *Caribbean Quaterly* 5.4. (1959): 238.
22. Aime Cesaire, "Barbare," in *Soleil cou-coupe* (Paris: ed. K; 1948), 73. Emile Snyder and Sanford Upson, trans., "Babare," in *Cadastre* (New York: The Third Press, 1973), 81.
23. Cesaire, *Discurs,*11. Pinkhman, trans., *Discourses*, 35.
24. Frantz Fanon, *Peau noire, masques blancs* (Paris: Éditions du Seuil, 1952), 98. Charles Markmann trans., *Black Skin, White Masks* (New York: Grove Press, 1991), 122.
25. Ibid., 93/115. It is important to note that Fanon did have personal experience with non-European Maghrebi Jews and even partnered with some of them in professional activities.
26. Memmi, *La statue de Sel*, 109. Roditti, trans., *The Pillar of Salt*, 96.
27. Albert Memmi, "'Questions au colonel Kadhafi,'" in *Juifs et arabes* (Paris: Gallimard, 1974), 64. Eleonor Levieux, trans.,"Questions for Colonel Kadhafy," in *Jews and Arabs* (Chicago: O'Hara, 1975), 34.
28. Albert Memmi, *Portrait du colonise. Prcecede du Portrait du colonisateur* (Paris: Buchet/Chastel, 1957), 51. Howard Greenfeld, trans., *The Colonizer and the Colonized* (New York: Beacon Press, 1991), 13.
29. Michael M. Laskier, *North African Jewry in The Twentieth Century: The Jews of Morocco, Tunisia and Algeria* (New York and London: New York University Press, 1994), 24 and 85.
30. Ibid., 25, 288–289.
31. Ibid., 57–58.
32. Memmi, "Qu'est-ce qu'un Juif-Arabe," in *Juifs et arabes*, 53. Levieux, trans., "What is in an Arab Jew," in *Arabs and Jews*, 23.
33. Memmi, *La statue de salt*, 213–217, 230–240. Roditti, trans., *The Pilar of Salt*, 263–268, 283–295.
34. Victor Malka and Albert Memmi, *La terre intérieure* (Paris: Gallimard, 1976), 80. Patricia Nirimberk, trans., *Conversaciones con Albert Memmi* (Buenos Aires: Timerman Editores, 1976), 66.
35. Ibid., 125–126/103.
36. Memmi, *La statue de Sel*, 136–137. Roditi, trans., *The Pillar of Salt,*160.
37. It is important to notice that Memmi never renounces his interest in the Magrheb. During this period he edits two collections and compiles a bibliography of writers of the area. But he emphasizes the Francophone nature defying the imposition of Arab language that excluded Jews. See *Anthologie des ecrivains maghrebins d'expression francaise* (Paris: Presence Africaine, 1965), *Bibliographie de la littérature nord-africaine d'expression française* (Paris: Mouton, 1965), and *Anthologie des écrivains francais du Mahgreb* (Paris: Presence Africaine, 1969).

38. It is not a surprise that Memmi prefers Senghor over Cesaire when analyzing the political implications of Negritude. While the Caribbean always had difficulties with a national break from France, the Senegalese supported a wide African Socialist commonwealth.

39. Albert Memmi, "Negritude et Judeite," in *L' Homme Dominé* (Paris: Gallimard, 1968), 35–49. n.d. trans., "Negritude and Jewishness," in *Dominated Man* (New York: Orion Press, 1968), 27–39. While he acknowledges the existence of "Black Jews" he does not follow this line of inquiry.

40. Ibid.

41. See note 16. Critics, especially Jonathan Judaken, have identified Sartre's project with the replication of supresessionism found not only in Christian but also in modern enlightened projects. See, Jonathan Judaken, *Jean Paul Sartre and the Jewish Question Anti-Semitism and the Politics of the French Intellectual* (Lincoln: University of Nebraska Press, 2006), 139–146.

42. Albert Memmi, "La vie impossible de Frantz Fanon," *Esprit* 39 (1971): 267–269. Thomas Cassirer and Michael Twomey, trans., "The Impossible Life of Frantz Fanon," *The Massachusetts Review* 14.1 (1973): 32–34.

43. Memmi, "Les Chemins de la révolte," in *L'Homme dominé*; n.d trans., "The Paths of Revolt," in *Dominated Man*, 12–13.

44. Ibid.

45. Albert Memmi, *Portrait d'un Juif* (Paris: Gallimard, 1962), 29. Elisabeth Abbott, trans., *Portrait of a Jew* (New York: The Orion Press, 1962), 21.

46. Ibid., 92/83. It is important to notice that Memmi uses the narrative of barbarism to describe Jewish portray throughout the book. Sometimes he employs the term barbarians and some of their characteristics (sedition, incorregibility, etc).

47. Ibid., 104–105/106–107.

48. Albert Memmi, *La libération du juif* (Paris: Gallimard, 1966), 48–59. Judy Hyun, trans., *The Liberation of the Jew* (New York: Orion Press, 1966), 55–68.

49. Ibid., 118/137.

50. Ibid., 107–193/125–224.

51. Ibid, 227–262/ and 263–303.

52. Albert Memmi, *Agar* (Paris: Correa, 1955), 184–185. Brian Rhys, trans., *Strangers* (New York: Orion Press, 1960), 128–129.

53. Memmi, *La libération du juif,* 197–212. Abbott, trans., *Portrait of a Jew,* 227–245.

54. Ibid., 211/244–245.

55. Memmi, "Israël, les Arabes et le Tiers-Monde," in *Juifs et Arabes,* 144. Levieux, trans., "Israel, The Arabs and the Third World," in *Jews and Arabs,* 144/144.

56. Ibid., 144–149/144–149.

57. Ibid. Memmi, "Qu'est-ce qu'un Juif-Arabe," in *Juifs et Arabes,* 58–59. Levieux, trans., "What is an Arab Jew," in *Jews and Arabs,* 28–29.

58. Memmi, "Questions au colonel Kadhafi," in *Juifs et Arabes*, 62–63. Levieux, trans., "Questions for Colonel Kadhafi," in *Jews and Arabs*, 33.
59. Memmi, "Justice et Nation," in *Juifs et Arabes*, 137. Levieux, trans., "Justice and Nation," in *Jews and Arabs*, 137.
60. Memmi, "Pour une solution socialiste," in *Juifs et Arabes*, 216. Levieux, trans., "In Favor of a Socialist Solution," in *Jews and Arabs*, 217.
61. Memmi, "Justice et Nation," and "Israël, les Arabes et le Tiers-Monde," in *Juifs et Arabes*, 152 and 163. Levieux, trans., "Justice and Nation," and "Israel, The Arabs and the Third World," in *Jews and Arabs*, 152 and 163.
62. Memmi, "Qu'est-ce q'un sioniste?," in *Juifs et Arabes*, 45–46. Levieux, "What is a Zionist?," in *Jews and Arabs*, 96.
63. Memmi, *Portrait du colonise*, 162. Greenfeld, trans., *Portrait of Colonized*, 151.
64. Memmi, "La vie impossible de Frantz Fanon," 270–271. Cassirer and Michael Twomey, trans., "The Impossible Life of Frantz Fanon," 36–37.
65. Ibid. Memmi, "Pour une solution socialiste," 215. Levieux, trans., "In Favor of a Socialist Solution," 216.
66. Gary Wilder and Albert Memmi, "Irreconcilable Differences: A Conversation with Albert Memmi," *Transitions* 71 (1996): 174.
67. Robert Stam and Ella Shohat, *Race in Translation: Culture Wars Around the Postcolonial Atlantic* (New York: New York University Press, 2012), 162–163.
68. Memmi, *Portrait du décolonisé*, 40–41. Roberto Bnonnono, trans., *Decolonization and the Decolonized* (Minneapolis: University of Minnesota Press, 2006), 24.
69. Ibid., 3–39/3–40.

6 Barbaric Paradoxes: Zionism from the Standpoint of the Borderlands

1. Theodor Herzl, *Der Judenstaat* (Berlin: Jüdischer Verlag, 1920), 24. Trans. n.d., *The Jewish State* (New York: Dover Publications, 1988), 96
2. See Homi Bhabha, *The Location of Culture* (London: Routledge, 1994), 4, a general critique in Bill Ashcroft et al., *Post-colonial Studies: The Key Concepts*, 108–110 and a critique from Jewish studies in Sander Gilman, "'We're not Jews,'" in *Orientalism and the Jews*, Ivan Kalmar and Derek Penslar eds. (Waltham: Brandeis University Press, 2005), 201–204.
3. It is important to clarify I am emphasizing an interpretation of Border Thinker that privileges the common matrix of coloniality since the sixteenth century over the distinction between external and internal borders.
4. Walter Mignolo, "Delinking," *Cultural Studies* 21.2 (2007): 449–514. While Mignolo acknowledges the need to go beyond the school to "de-link" from the standpoint of the wretched of earth, he acknowledges that the Jewishness of the Frankukters make them "barbarian theorizing."

5. Walter Mignolo, *Local Histories/Global Designs: Coloniality, Subaltern Knowledges, and Border Thinking* (Princeton: Princeton University Press, 2000), 108–109 and 146.

6. Walter Mignolo, *Capitalismo y geopolítica del conocimiento* (Buenos Aires: Editorial Del Signo y Duke University, 2001), 28–29.

7. Memmi is an excellent example of this trend. See the analysis of this early school in Elia Zureik, *The Palestineans in Israel: A Study in Internal Colonialism* (London and Boston: Routledge and K. Paul, 1979), 76–82.

8. One of the most articulate scholars who presents this option by analyzing Israel employing Anglophone Postcolonial theory is Derek Penslar, "Is Zionism a Colonial Movement?" in *Israel in History: The Jewish State in Comparative Perspective* (Oxford and New York: Routledge, 2007), 90–111.

9. In this section, I will be quoting a variety of sources that support this trend.

10. Zeev Sternhell, *The Founding Myths of Israel: Nationalism, Socialism and the Making of the Jewish State* (Princeton: Princeton University Press, 1988), 6. It is important to notice that the early political Zionism derived in "nominally" mainstream socialist Zionism. To understand this reduction to "nominal" standing, see also 16–19.

11. Shlomo Avineri, *The Making of Modern Zionism: The Intellectuals Origins of the Jewish State* (New York: Basic Books, 1981), 88–90.

12. This comment is based on Joseph Massad, "The Post-Colonial: Time, Space, and Bodies in Israel/Palestine," in *The Pre-Occupation of Postcolonial Studies*, Fawzia Afzal-Khan et al., eds. (Durham: Duke University Press, 2000), 313–314.

13. It is interesting to notice, however, that one of the forerunners of Western Zionism, Moses Hess, elaborates his program allegedly affected by a development in the Middle East and not Western Europe. This could be interpreted in multiple ways and may require further reflection. See Ken Koltun-Fromm, *Moses Hess and Modern Jewish Identity* (Bloomington: Indiana University Press, 2001), 42–56.

14. Herzl, *Der Judenstaat* 24. N.d. *The Jewish State*, 96.

15. Theodor Herzl, "letter 6/12/1985," in *The Complete Diaries of Theodor Herzl*, Raphael Patai, ed., Harry Zohn, trans. (New York: Herzl Press, 1960), 88–89.

16. Herzl, *Altneuland: Roman* (Berlin: H. Seeman 1900). Lotta Levenshon, trans., *The Old-New-Land* (New York: Bloch Publishing, 1941).

17. Sternhell rightly points out that "Zionism was not blind to the presence of Arabs in Palestine" but still "could not frame a policy toward the Palestinian national movement." See Sternhell, *The Founding Myths of Israel*, 43.

18. Avineri, *The Making of Modern Zionism*, 98–99.

19. Zureik, *The Palestinians in Israel*, 9–10.

20. Edward Said, *The Question of Palestine* (New York: Times Books, 1979), 66–69.
21. Ibid., 13.
22. See Ilan Pappe, *The Ethnic Cleansing of Palestine* (Oxford: One World, 2006).
23. Zureik, *The Palestinians in Israel*, 18–28.
24. Said, *The Question of Palestine*, 81–84.
25. Ibid., 7.
26. Ibid., 111–112.
27. Ibid., 89.
28. Ibid., 24–26.
29. As cited in Ibid., 91.
30. Ibid., 69.
31. Ella Shohat, "Sepharadim in Israel: Zionism from the Standpoint of Its Jewish Victims," *Social Text* 19/20 (1988): 17–23.
32. Ibid., 7–10. This gap has been only wided today. See, for example, Meyrav Wurmser, "Post-Zionism and the Sepharadi Question," *The Middle East Quarterly* 12.2 (2005): 21–30.
33. As cited in G. N. Giladei, *Discord in Zion: Conflict between Ashkenasi & Sepharadi Jews in Israel* (Essex: Scorpion Publishing, 1990), 209.
34. Ibid., 254–276.
35. Shohat, "Sepharadim in Israel," 23.
36. Giladei, *Discord in Zion*, 209–210.
37. Ibid., 211.
38. Massad, "Zionism's Internal Others," 62.
39. Ibid., 62–63.
40. Shohat, "Sephardim in Israel," 7–9.
41. Ibid., 5. It is important to notice Aloni employs the term barbarous and savage at the same time perhaps differentiating between good savage and barbaric savage.
42. Ibid., 30–32. Also see Shlomo Swirski, *Israel: The Oriental Majority* (London: Zed Books, 1989), 45–49 and Massad, "Zionism's Internal Others," 57–65.
43. I would like to mention that a case can be made for the reproduction of the narrative of barbarism after the immigration of Ethiopian Jews from sub-Saharan Africa that, already in 1989 Shohat is already alerting (see page 5). Since these discourses start when the counter-narratives were finishing, however, I will leave this exploration for a future project when I analyze a post-1980s situation. It is interesting to read a self-referential "Afrocentric" interpretation of it in Durrenda Ojanuga, "The Ethiopian Jewish Experience as Blacks in Israel," *Journal of Black Studies* 24.2 (December 1993): 147–158. Of special interest is the discussion of Sephardic Jewry as antecedent in 156–157.

44. As seen in chapter five, Memmi does recognize the situation of Arab Jews and Palestinians. But argues these are internal social problems that can be solved within the logic of a Zionist state.

45. Nathalie Debrauwere-Miller very well points out that since the 1960s there has been a change of attitudes toward the Israel-Palestine conflict in the Francophone world that reached its pinnacle only after the Intifada in 1987. See the periodization in "Introduction: France and the Israeli-Palestinean Conflict," in *Israeli-Palestinian Conflict in the Francophone World* (New York and London: Routledge, 2010), 1–22.

46. Edward Said, "Diary," *London Review of Books* 22.11 (June 2000): 42–43.

47. A superb critical analysis of Sartre's relation with Judaism can be found in Judaken, "On Ambivalent Commitments. Sartre, Israel, and the Politics of the Intellectual," in *Jean-Paul Sartre and the Jewish Question Anti-Semitism and the Politics of the French Intellectual* (Lincoln: University of Nebraska Press, 2006), 184–207.

48. Enrique Dussel, "Transmodernity and Interculturality: An Interpretation from the Perspective of Philosophy of Liberation," n/a, 16–26.

7   After 9/11: New Barbarism and the Legacies in the Global South

1. Marcos Aguinis, *La cuestión Judía vista desde la izquierda* (Buenos Aires: Centro Peretz, 1986), 32.

2. Ibid.

3. Daniel Pipes (February 1, 2007) "Radical Islam vs Civilization," http://www.danielpipes.org/4254/radical-islam-vs-civD\ilization

4. Bernard-Henry Levy, *Left in Dark Times: A Stand Against the New Barbarism* (New York: Random House, 2008).

5. Ricardo Forster, *Notas sobre la barbarie y la esperanza: Del 11 de septiembre a la crisis Argentina* (Buenos Aires: Editorial Biblos, 2006).

6. See the competition between Francis Fukuyama, *The End of History and the Last Man* (New York: Free Press, 1992) and Samuel Huntington, *Clash of Civilizations* (New York: Simon and Schuster, 1996).

7. See an excellent explanation of the return of the dualism in Mark Salter, *Barbarians and Civilization in International Relations* (London: Pluto Press, 2002), 163–167.

8. George W. Bush (October 7, 2001), "Presidential Address to the Nation," http://georgewbush-whitehouse.archives.gov/news/releases/2001/10/20011007-8.html

9. Cited in Kathleen Rhem (May 2, 2003), "Bush: Americans Have Security for the Next Generations," http://www.defense.gov/News/NewsArticle.aspx?ID=29027

10. Greg Burke, (September 28, 2001), "Berlusconi War of Words," http://www.time.com/time/magazine/article/0,9171,176876,00.html
11. cited in Roni Sofer, (March 7, 2008), "Bush Condemns Barbaric and Vicious Attack," http://www.ynetnews.com/articles/0,7340,L-3516063,00.html
12. See his official website and the list of top global thinkers in the following websites: http://www.robertdkaplan.com/robert_d_kaplan_bio.htm and http://blog.foreignpolicy.com/posts/2011/11/28/the_fp_top_100_global_thinkers_of_2011
13. See note number 6.
14. Robert Kaplan, "The Coming Anarchy" *Atlantic Magazine* (1994). http://www.theatlantic.com/magazine/print/1994/02/the-coming-anarchy/304670/
15. Ibid. See also Brett Bowden, *The Empire of Civilization: The Evolution of an Imperial Idea* (Chicago and London: The University of Chicago Press, 2009), 164–167.
16.. Kaplan, "The Coming Anarchy"; Bowden, *The Empire of Civilization;* See a critique in Dag Tuastad, "Neo-Orientalism and the new barbarism thesis: Aspects of the Symbolic Violence in the Middle East conflict(s)," *Third World Quarterly* 24.4 (2004), 591–599.
17. Huntington, *Who Are We? The Challenge to America's National Identity* (New York: Simon and Schuster, 2004), 99–100.
18. Kaplan, "The Coming Anarchy."
19. Alain Finkielkraut, "Vers une Société Pluriculturelle?," in *La Défaite de la Pensée* (Paris: Gallimard, 1987), 121–133. Judith Friedlander, trans., "Toward a Multicultural Society?," in *The Defeat of a Mind* (New York: Columbia University Press, 1995), 89–108.
20. Pipes, "Radical Islam vs Civilization."
21. Abe Foxman, *Never Again? The Threat of New Anti-Semitism* (New York: Harper Collins, 2003), 7–12.
22. Pierre-Andre Taguieff, *Rising from the Muck* (Chicago: Ivan R. Dee, 2004), 54–56, 200.
23. Fortunately the forerunners have been developing these ideas for a long time. See some examples in Marc Ellis, *Judaism Does not Equal Israel* (New York: The New Press, 2009) and Norman Finkelstein, *Beyond Chutzpa: On the Misuse of Anti-Semitism and the Abuse of History* (Berkeley and Los Angeles: University of California Press, 2008).
24. It is important to realize that one could relate his position to the assimilation of settlers with Jews in Algeria since the 1870s. Yet, it is important to realize that BHL and many other Maghrebis did join in the Left in the 1960s Paris. This creates an epistemological break between the colonial policy and the actual lives of Jews in Paris in the post-Holocaust and post-colonial world.

25. Bernard-Henry Levy, *La Barbarie* à *visage humain* (Paris: Bernard Grasset, 1977), 133–140, 178. George Holoch, trans., *Barbarism with a Human Face* (New York, NY: Harper and Row, 1979), 111–119, 152.
26. Ibid.
27. Ibid.
28. Levy, *Left in Dark Times*, 44–46.
29. Ibid., 33.
30. Ibid., 33–36, 187.
31. Ibid., 167–170.
32. Ibid., 154.
33. Ibid., 125.
34. Ibid., 194–195.
35. See Bernardo Kliksberg, "El Judaismo Latinoamericano y Albert Memmi," *Pensamiento Judío Contemporaneo* 2 (1984): 34–36.
36. Marcos Aguinis, *La Gesta del Marrano* (Buenos Aires: Planeta, 1991).
37. Please see his official website in English following this link: http://www.aguinis.net/eng/enindex.htm
38. Marcos Aguinis. *La cuestión judía vista desde el tercer mundo* (Buenos Aires: Centro Peretz, 1986).
39. Aguinis, *La cuestión judía vista desde la izquierda*, 22.
40. Ibid., 4–6.
41. Ibid., 14–15.
42. Ibid., 24–26.
43. Ibid.
44. Ibid, 26–28.
45. Marcos Aguinis, (January 2011), "La Invención del Pueblo Palestino," http://congresojudio.org.ar/coloquio_nota.php?np=9
46. Ibid.
47. Ibid.
48. Marcos Aguinis, *Las redes del odio: recursos para desactivar la violencia* (Buenos Aires: Planeta, 2003), 85–88.
49. http://www.cartaabierta.org.ar/
50. Forster, *Notas sobre la barbarie y la esperanza*, 13–17 and 43–44.
51. Ibid., 16–21, 45–46.
52. Ibid., 17, 53–54.
53. Ibid., 30–34, 50–51.
54. Ibid., 47, 50–53.
55. See in the same volume the welcome to, for example, Jose Carlos Mariategui or Frantz Fanon that he lists sharing the space with European (largely Jewish) radicals, Ibid., 201–204.
56. Ibid., 55.
57. Ibid., 56–60.

58. Ricardo Forster, "Lo Judío, lo Palestino y los dilemas de la historia" *Pagina/12* (November 23, 2012), http://www.pagina12.com.ar/diario/elmundo/4-208389-2012-11-23.html

Epilogue Duped by Jewish Suffering
(Analectical Interjections)

1. Shlomo Sand, *Matai, ve'ekh humtza ha'am hyedhudi* (Tel Aviv: Resling, 2008). Yael Lotan, trans., *The Invention of the Jewish People* (London: Verso, 2009).
2. Ammiel Alcalay, *After Jews and Arabs: Remaking Levantine Culture* (Minneapolis: University of Minnesota Press, 1993), 1–4.
3. Ella Shohat, "Dislocated Identities: Reflection of an Arab Jew," *Movement Research: Performance Journal* 5 (1992): 8.
4. Juan Gelman, "Del estado del Estado de Israel" *Pagina/12* (March 18, 2001): 32.

Bibliography

Adorno, Theodor. *Prismen; Kulturkritik und Gesellschaft Prisms*. Bèerlin: Suhrkamp Verlag, 1955. Translated by Samuel and Shierry Weber as *Prisms: Reflections from a Damaged Life* (Cambridge: MIT Press, 1986).

———. *Negative Dialektik*. Frankfurt au main: Shurkamp, 1966. Translated by E. B. Ashton as *Negative Dialectics* (New York: Continuum, 2003).

Aguinis, Marcos. *La cuestión Judía vista desde el tercer mundo*. Buenos Aires: Centro Peretz, 1986.

———. *La gesta del marrano: novela*. Buenos Aires: Planeta, 1991.

———. *Las redes del odio: recursos para desactivar la violencia*. Buenos Aires: Planeta, 2003.

———. *La cuestión Judía vista desde la izquierda*. Buenos Aires: MILA/AMIA, 2004.

———. "La invención del pueblo Palestino," *Congreso Judio Mundial*, January 2011. http://congresojudio.org.ar/coloquio_nota.php?np=9

Aizenberg, Edna. *Books and Bombs in Buenos Aires: Borges, Gerchunoff, and Argentine-Jewish Writing*. Hanover: University Press of New England, 2002.

Alcalay, Ammiel. *After Jews and Arabs: Remaking Levantine Culture*. Minneapolis: University of Minnesota Press, 1993.

Alcoff, Linda, and Eduardo Mendieta. *Thinking from the Underside of History: Enrique Dussel's Philosophy of Liberation*. Lanham: Rowman & Littlefield Publishers, 2000.

Alexander, Robert. *International Trotskyism, 1929–1985: A Documented Analysis of the Movement*. Durham: Duke University Press, 1991.

Althusser, Louis, and Etienne Balibar. *Lire le Capital*. Paris: F. Maspero, 1965. Translated by Bren Brewster as *Reading Capital* (London: Verso, 1997).

Anidjar, Gil. *The Jew, the Arab: A History of the Enemy*. Stanford: Stanford University Press, 2003.

———. *Semites: Race, Religion, Literature*. Stanford: Stanford University Press, 2008.

Anzaldua, Gloria. *Borderlands. La Frontera: The New Mestiza*. San Francisco: Aun Lute Books, 1987.

Arendt, Hannah. *The Origins of Totalitarianism*. San Diego and New York: Harvest Books, 1973.

———. *Eichmann in Jerusalem: A Report on the Banality of Evil*. London: Penguin Books, 1995.

Aschheim, Steven. *Brothers and Strangers: The East European Jew in German and German Jewish Consciousness, 1800–1923*. Madison: University of Wisconsin Press, 1982.

Ashcroft, Bill, Gareth Griffiths, and Helen Tiffin. *The Empire Writes Back: Theory and Practice in Post-Colonial Literatures*. London: Routledge, 1989.

Auron, Yair. *Les juifs d'extrême-gauche en mai 68: une génération révolutionnaire marquée par la Shoah*. Paris: Albin Michel, 1998.

———. *Tikkun olam: The Phenomenon of the Jewish Radicals in France During the 1960s and '70s*. Jerusalem: Institute of the World Jewish Congress, 2000.

Avineri, Shlomo, ed. *Marx on Colonialism and Modernization*. Garden City: New York, 1968.

———. *The Making of Modern Zionism: Intellectual Origins of the Jewish State*. New York: Basic Books, 1981.

Back-Morss, Susan. "Hegel and Haiti." *Critical Inquiry* 26.4 (2000): 821–865.

Bedford, Nancy. "Waiting for the Barbarians? Caliban's Sisters and Christian Hope," (paper presented at the annual meeting of the American Academy of Religion, Chicago, Il. November 2012).

Beecher, Jonathan. *Charles Fourier: The Visionary and His World*. Berkeley: University of California Press, 1986.

Benjamin, Walter. *Illuminations*. New York: Harcourt, Brace & World, 1968.

———. *Selected Writings*. Edited by Rodney Livingstone and Michael W. Jennings. Cambridge: Harvard University Press, 2005.

Benjamin, Walter, and Rolf Tiedemann. *Gesammelte Schriften*. Frankfurt am Main: Suhrkamp, 1977.

Benjamin, Walter, Rolf Tiedemann, and Alexander Honold. *Erzählen: Schriften zur Theorie der Narration und zur literarischen Prosa*. 1. Aufl. ed. Frankfurt am Main: Suhrkamp, 2007.

Berensztein, Sergio. *AMIA: doce años despues; jornadas de reflexion*. 1. ed. Buenos Aires: Ed. Mila, 2006.

Bernal, Mario. *Black Athena: The Afro-Asiatic Roots of Classical Civilization*. London: Free Association Books, 1987.

Bhabha, Homi K. *The Location of Culture*. London: Routledge, 1994.

Biale, David. *Power and Powerlessness in Jewish History*. New York: Schocken Books, 1986.

Bisaha, Nancy. "New Barbarian or Worthy Adversary? Humanist Constructs of the Ottoman Turks in the Fifteen-Century Italy." In *Western Views of Islam in Medieval and Early Modern Europe: Perception of Other*, Michael Frassetto and David Blanks, eds., 185–205. New York: St. Martin's Press, 1999.

Benbassa, Esther and Jean-Christophe Attias. *Israël imaginaire*. Paris: Flammarion, 1998.

———. *Le Juif et l'Autre*. Gordes: La Raile, 2001. Translated by G. M. Goshgarian (Ithaca: Cornell University Press, 2004).

Boyarin, Daniel. *Unheroic the Rise of Heterosexuality and the Invention of the Jewish Man*. Berkeley: University of California Press, 1997.

———. *Socrates and the Fat Rabbis*. Chicago: University of Chicago Press, 2012.

Boyarin, Jonathan. *The Unconverted Self: Jews, Indians, and the Identity of Christian Europe*. Chicago: University of Chicago Press, 2009.

Brodkin, Karen. *How Jews Became White Folks and What That Says about Race in America*. New Brunswick: Rutgers University Press, 1998.

Burke, Greg. "Berlusconi War of Words," Time.com, September 28, 2001. http://www.time.com/time/magazine/article/0,9171,176876,00.html

Bush, George W. "Presidential Address to the Nation" (2001, October 7), whitehouse.gov http://georgewbush-whitehouse.archives.gov/news/releases/2001/10/20011007-8.html

Butler, Judith. *Parting Ways: Jewishness and the Critique of Zionism*. New York: Columbia University Press, 2012.

Castoriadis, Cornelius, and Philipe Gottraux. *Socialisme ou Barbarie? Un engagement politique et intellectual dans la France de l'apres-guerre*. Lausanne: Payot, 1997.

Caygill, Howard. *Levinas and the Political*. London: Routledge, 2002.

Cesaire, Aime. "Barbare." In *Soleil cou-coupe*. Paris: ed. K, 1948, 73. Translated by Emile Snyder and Sanford Upson as "Babare." In *Cadastre*. New York: The Third Press, 1973, 81.

———. *Discurs sur le Colonialisme*. Paris/Dakar: Presence Africaine, 1955. Translated by Joan Pinkham as *Discourse of Colonialism* (New York: Monthly Review, 2000).

———. *Cahier d'un retour au pays natal*. Paris: Presence Africaine, 1983. Translated by Clayton Eshleman and Annette Smith as *Notebook of a Return to the Native Land* (Middletown: Wesleyan University Press, 2001).

Cheyette, Bryan, and Laura Marcus. *Modernity, Culture, and 'the Jew'*. Stanford: Stanford University Press, 1998.

Cicero, Marcus Tullius, Niall Rudd, and J. G. F. Powell. *The Republic and the Laws*. Oxford: Oxford University Press, 1998.

Clemens, Aurelius. *Prudentius*. Repr. ed. Cambridge: Harvard University Press, 1961.

Coetzee, J. M. *Waiting for the Barbarians*. New York: Penguin Books, 1999.

Cohen, Joseph, and Raphael Zagury-Orli. *Judéités: questions pour Jacques Derrida*. Paris: Galilée, 2003. Translated by Bettina Bergo and Michael B. Smith as *Judeities: Questions for Jacques Derrida* (New York: Fordham University Press, 2007).

Cohn, Norman. *Warrant for Genocide: The Myth of the Jewish World-Conspiracy and the Protocols of the Elders of Zion*. New York: Harper & Row, 1967.

Cohn-Bendit, Daniel. *Le Gauchisme, remède à la maladie sénile du communisme*. Paris: Éditions du Seuil, 1968.

———. *Nous l'avons tant aimée, la revolution*. Paris: Barrault, 1986.

———. *1968, die Revolte*. Frankfurt Au Main: S. Fischer, 2007.

Collins, Anthony. *A Discourse of Free Thinking*. London: n/a, 1713.

Compte, Rodolfo. *Atentado a la AMIA: Crónica de los jóvenes que rescataron la memoria*. Buenos Aires: Editorial Generación Joven, 2006.

Coulthard, G. R. "Rejection of European Culture as a Theme in Caribbean Literature." *Caribbean Quaterly* 5.4. (1959): 231–244.

Cuddihy, John Murray. *Freud, Marx, Levi-Strauss, and the Jewish Struggle with Modernity*. New York: Basic Books, 1974.

Curran, Andrew S. *The Anatomy of Blackness: Science & Slavery in an Age of Enlightenment*. Baltimore: Johns Hopkins University Press, 2011.

Dante. *The Divine Comedy*. Translated by Mark Musa. London: Penguin Books, 2003.

Debrauwere-Miller, Nathalie ed. *Israeli-Palestinian Conflict in the Francophone World*. New York: Routledge, 2010.

Della-Pergola, Sergio, and Leah Cohen eds., *World Jewish population: Trends and Policies*. Jerusalem: HUJI, 1992.

Derrida, Jacques. *Circonfession*. Paris: Seuil, 1991. Translated by Geoffrey Benington as *Circumfession* (Chicago: University of Chicago Press, 1993).

———. *Adieu à Emmanuel Lévinas*. Paris: Galilée, 1997. Translated by Pascale-Anne Brault and Michael Naas as *Adieu to Emmanuel Levinas* (Stanford: Stanford University Press, 1999).

Deutscher, Isaac. *The Non-Jewish Jew and Other Essays*. Edited by Tamara Deutscher. London: Oxford University Press, 1968.

Diop, Cheikh Anta. *Civilisation ou barbarie: anthropologie sans complaisance*. Paris: Présence africaine, 1981. Translated by Yaa-Lengi Meema Ngemi as *Civilization and Barbarism: An Authentic Anthropology* (New York: Lawrence Hill Books, 1991).

Drabinski, John. *Levinas and the Postcolonial: Race, Nation, Other*. Edinburgh: Edinburgh University Press, 2011.

Dussel, Enrique. *El Humanismo Semita*. Buenos Aires: Eudeba, 1969.

———. *Filosofía de Liberación*. Mexico DF: Edicol, 1977. Translated by Aquilina Martinez as *Philosophy of Liberation* (Maryknoll: Orbis Books, 1985).

———. *1492: El encubrimiento del otro: Hacia el origen del "mito de la modernidad": conferencias de Frankfurt, octubre de 1992*. La Paz: Plural Editores, 1994. Translated by Michael D. Barber as *The Invention of the Americas: Eclipse of "the other" and the Myth of Modernity* (New York: Continuum, 1995).

———. "Sensibility and Otherness in Emmanuel Levinas." *Philosophy Today* 37 (1999): 125–133.

———. *Política de la liberación. Historia mundial y crítica*. Madrid: Trotta, 2007. Translated by Thia Cooper as *Politics of Liberation. A Critical Global History* (London: SCM Press, 2011).

———. *Ética de la liberación en la edad de la globalización y de la exclusión*. Madrid: Trotta, 1998. Translated and edited by Alejandro Villega, Eduardo Mendieta et al. as *Ethics of Liberation in the Age of Globalization and Exclusion* (Durham: Duke University Press, 2013).

Dussel, Enrique, and Daniel E. Guillot. *Liberación Latinoamericana y Emmanuel Levinas*. Buenos Aires: Editorial Bonum, 1975.

Dussel, Enrique, et al. *Coloniality at Large: Latin America and the Postcolonial Debate*. Durham: Duke University Press, 2008.

Dyson, R. W. ed. *The City of God Against the Pagans*. Cambridge: Cambridge University Press, 1998.

Efron, John. "Orientalism and the Jewish Historical Gaze." In *Orientalism and the Jews*, Ivan Kalmar and Derek Penslar, eds., 80–93. Waltham: Brandeis University Press, 2005

Elias, Norbert. *The Civilizing Process.* Oxford: Blackwell, 1994.

Ellis, Marc. *Unholy Alliance: Religion and Atrocity in Our Time.* Minneapolis: Fortress Press, 1997.

———. *Israel and Palestine: Out of the Ashes the Search for Jewish Identity in the Twenty-First Century.* London: Pluto Press, 2002.

———. *Judaism Does Not Equal Israel.* New York: New Press, 2009.

Ertur, Basak, et al. eds. *Waiting for the Barbarians: A Tribute to Edward W. Said.* London: Verso, 2008.

Everson, Stephen, Raymond Geuss, Quentin Skinner, and Richard Tuck. *Aristotle: The Politics and The Constitution of Athens.* 2nd ed. Cambridge: Cambridge University Press, 1996.

Eze, Emmanuel Chukwudi. *Postcolonial African philosophy: A Critical Reader.* Cambridge: Blackwell, 1997.

———. *Race and the Enlightenment: A Reader.* Cambridge: Blackwell, 1997.

———. *Achieving Our Humanity: The Idea of a Postracial Future.* New York: Routledge, 2001.

Fagles, Robert, and Bernard Knox. *The Iliad.* New York: Penguin Books, 1998.

Fanon, Frantz. *Peau noire, masques blancs.* Paris: Éditions du Seuil, 1952. Translated by Charles Markmann as *Black Skin/White Masks* (New York: Grove Press, 1991).

———. *Les damnés de la terre.* Paris: F. Maspero, 1961. Translated by Richard Philcox as *The Wretched of the Earth* (New York: Grove Press, 2004).

Fernandez Retamar, Roberto. *Algunos usos de civilización y barbarie.* La Habana: Letras Cubanas, 2003.

Ferro, Marc. *Colonization a Global History.* London: Routledge, 1997.

Finkelstein, Norman G. *Beyond Chutzpah: On the Misuse of Anti-Semitism and the Abuse of History.* Berkeley: University of California Press, 2005.

Finkielkraut, Alain. *Défaite de la Pensée.* Paris: Gallimard, 1987. Translated by Judith Friedlander as *The Defeat of the Mind* (New York: Columbia University Press, 1995).

Fischer, Sibylle. *Modernity Disavowed: Haiti and the Cultures of Slavery in the Age of Revolution.* Durham: Duke University Press, 2004.

Flohr, Paul. *German Jews a Dual Identity.* New Haven: Yale University Press, 1999.

Flohr, Paul, and Jehuda Reinharz. *The Jew in the Modern World: A Documentary History.* 2nd ed. New York: Oxford University Press, 1995.

Forsdick, Charles. *Postcolonial Thought in the French-Speaking World.* Liverpool: Liverpool University Press, 2009.

Foster, Benjamin, Alfred Cary Schlesinger, and Russel Geer. *Livy: With an English translation.* Revised. ed. Cambridge: Harvard University Press, 1967.

Forster, Ricardo. *Notas sobre la barbarie y la esperanza: del 11 de septiembre a la crisis Argentina.* Buenos Aires: Editorial Biblos, 2006.

———. *Los hermeneutas de la noche. De Walter Benjamin a Paul Celan.* Madrid: Trotta, 2009.

———. *"Lo Judio, Lo Palestino y los Dilemas de la Historia." Pagina/12.* November 23, 2012.

Forster, Ricardo, and Diego Tatián. *Mesianismo, nihilismo y redención*. Buenos Aires: Altamira, 2005.

Fourier, Charles. *The Theory of the Four Movements*. Translated by Ian Patterson. Cambridge: Cambridge University Press, 1996.

Foxman, Abraham H. *Never Again?: The Threat of the New Anti-Semitism*. San Francisco: HarperSanFrancisco, 2003.

Frey, Hebert. "La Mirada de Europa y el 'otro' indoamericano." *Revista Mexicana de Sociología* 58.2 (1996): 61–62.

Friedlander, Judith. *Vilna on the Seine: Jewish Intellectuals in France Since 1968*. New Haven: Yale University Press, 1990.

Fromm, Ken. *Moses Hess and Modern Jewish Identity*. Bloomington: Indiana University Press, 2001.

Fukuyama, Francis. *The End of History and the Last Man*. New York: Free Press: 1992.

Gall, Richard. *The Holy Reich: Nazi Conceptions of Christianity, 1919–1945*. New York: Cambridge University Press, 2003.

Garvie, A. F. *Persae*. New ed. Oxford: Oxford University Press, 2009.

Gibbs, Robert. *Correlations in Rosenzweig and Levinas*. Princeton: Princeton University Press, 1992.

Giladi, G. N. *Discord in Zion: Conflict between Ashkenazi & Sephardi Jews in Israel*. London: Scorpion, 1990.

Gilman, Sander. *Jewish Self-hatred: Anti-Semitism and the Hidden Language of the Jews*. Baltimore: Johns Hopkins University Press, 1986.

———. *Jewish Frontiers: Essays on Bodies, Histories, and Identities*. New York: Palgrave Macmillan, 2003.

Gilman, Sander, and Milton Shain. *Jewries at the Frontier: Accommodation, Identity, Conflict*. Urbana: University of Illinois Press, 1999.

Gelman, Juan. "Del estado del Estado de Israel." *Pagina/12*. March 18, 2001, 32.

Gordon, Lewis. *Existentia Africana: Understanding Africana Existential Thought*. New York: Routledge, 2000.

———. *Disciplinary Decadence*. Boulder: Paradigm Publishers, 2006.

Guha, Ranajit, and Gayatri Chakravorty Spivak. *Selected Subaltern Studies*. New York: Oxford University Press, 1988.

Hall, Edith. *Inventing the Barbarian: Greek Self-definition Through Tragedy*. Oxford: Clarendon Press, 1989.

Hall, Stuart. *Modernity: An Introduction to Modern Societies*. Cambridge: Blackwell, 1996.

Hamilton, Carolyn. *Terrific Majesty: The Power of Shaka Zulu and the Limits of Historical Invention*. Cambridge: Harvard University Press, 1998.

Hammerschlag, Sarah. *The Figural Jew: Politics and Identity in Postwar French Thought*. Chicago: University of Chicago Press, 2010.

Hanke, Lewis. *All Mankind Is One: A Study on the Disputation . . .* DeKalb: Northern Illinois University Press, 1974.

Hannaford, Ivan. *Race: The History of an Idea in the West*. Washington, DC: Woodrow Wilson Center Press, 1996.

Hertzberg, Arthur. *The French Enlightenment and the Jews: The Origins of Modern Anti-Semitism*. New York: Columbia University Press, 1990.

Herzl, Theodor. *Altneuland: Roman*. Berlin: H. Seeman, 1900. Translated by Lotta Levenshon as *The Old-New-Land* (New York: Bloch Publishing, 1941).

———. *Der Judenstaat*. Berlin: Jüdischer Verlag, 1920. Translated by Jacob Alkow as *The Jewish State* (New York: Dover Publications, 1988).

———. *The Complete Diaries of Theodor Herzl*. Edited by Rapahel Patai. New York: Herzl Press and T. Yoseloff, 1960.

Heschel, Sussanah. *Abraham Geiger and the Jewish Jesus*. Chicago: University of Chicago Press, 1998.

———. "Revolt of the Colonized: Abraham Geiger's Wissenschaft des Judentums as a Challenge to Christian Hegemony in the Academy." *New German Critique* 77 (1999): 61–85.

Hess, Jonathan. *Germans, Jews, and the Claims of Modernity*. New Haven: Yale University Press, 2002.

Horkheimer, Max, and Theodor W. Adorno. *Dialektik der Aufklärung: philosophische Fragmente*. Amsterdam: Querido, 1947. Translated by Gunzelin Noerr as *Dialectic of Enlightenment: Philosophical Fragments* (Stanford: Stanford University Press, 2002).

———. "The Jews and Europe." In *The Frankfurt School on Religion*, Eduardo Mendieta ed. New York: Routledge, 2005.

Huntington, Samuel. *The Clash of Civilizations and the Remaking of World Order*. New York: Simon & Schuster, 1996.

———. *Who Are We?: The Challenges to America's National Identity*. New York: Simon & Schuster, 2004.

Hyman, Paula. *The Jews of Modern France*. Berkeley: University of California Press, 1998.

Jay, Martin. *The Dialectical Imagination A History of the Frankfurt School and the Institute of Social Research, 1923–1950*. Berkeley: University of California Press, 1996.

Joll, James. *The Second International, 1889–1914*. New York: Harper & Row, 1966.

Jones, W. R. "The image of the Barbarian in Medieval Europe." *Comparative Studies in Society and History* 13.4 (1971): 376–407.

Judaken, Jonathan. *Jean-Paul Sartre and the Jewish Question: Anti-Semitism and the Politics of the French Intellectual*. Lincoln: University of Nebraska Press, 2006.

Julius, Anthony. *Trials of the Diaspora: A History of Anti-Semitism in England*. Oxford: Oxford University Press, 2010.

Kalmar, Ivan. *The Trotskys, Freuds and Woody Allens: Portrait of a Culture*. Toronto: Viking, 1993.

———. *Early Orientalism: Imagined Islam and the Notion of Sublime Power*. London: Routledge, 2012.

Kalmar, Ivan, and Derek Penslar. *Orientalism and the Jews*. Waltham: Brandeis University Press, 2005.

Kamenka, Eugene. *The Portable Karl Marx*. Middlesex: Viking Penguin, 1981.

Kaplan, Robert. "The Coming Anarchy" *Atlantic Magazine*, 1994. http://www.theatlantic.com/magazine/print/1994/02/the-coming-anarchy/304670/

Khazzom, Aziza. "The Great Chain of Orientalism: Jewish Identity, Stigma Management and Ethnic Exclusion in Israel." *American Sociological Review* 68.4 (2003): 481–510.

Kliksberg, Bernardo. "El Judaismo Latinoamericano y Albert Memmi." *Pensamiento Judío Contemporaneo* 2 (1984): 34–36.

Kristeva, Julia. *Strangers to Ourselves*. Translated by Leon Roudiez. New York: Columbia University Press, 1991.

Kutsch, Rodolfo. *La seducción de la barbarie*. Buenos Aires: Raigal, 1953.

Lambert, Michael. "From Citizenship to Negritude: 'Making a Difference' in Elite Ideologies of Colonized Francophone West Africa." *Comparative Studies in Society and History* 35.2 (1993): 239–262.

Lander, Edgardo. *La colonialidad del saber: eurocentrismo y ciencias sociales: perspectivas latinoamericanas*. Buenos Aires: CLACSO, 2000.

Laskier, Michael M. *North African Jewry in the twentieth Century: the Jews of Morocco, Tunisia, and Algeria*. New York: New York University Press, 1994.

Levinas, Emmanuel. *Totalité et Infini: essai sur l'extériorité*. The Hague: M. Nijhoff, 1961. Translated by Alphonso Lingis as *Totality and Infinity: An Essay on Exteriority* (Pittsburgh: Duquesne University Press, 1969).

———. *Quatre lectures talmudiques*. Paris: Minuit, 1968 and *Du sacré au saint: Cinq nouvelles lectures talmudiques*. Paris: Minuit, 1977. Translated by Annette Aronowicz as *Nine Talmudic Readings* (Bloomington: Indiana University Press, 1990).

———. *Autrement qu'être, ou au-delà de l'essence*. La Haye: Martin Nijhoff, 1974. Translated by Alphonse Lingis as *Otherwise Than Being, or Beyond Essence* (Pittsburgh: Duquesne University Press, 2002).

———. *L'Au-delà du verset*. Paris: Minuit, 1982. Translated by Gary Mole as *Beyond the Verse* (London: Athlone Press, 1994).

———. *A l'heure des nations*. Paris: Minuit, 1988. Translated by Michael Smith as *In Times of the Nations* (London: Athlone Press, 1994).

———. *Entre Nous*. Paris: Bernard Grasset et Fasquelle, 1991. Translated by Michael Smith as *Entre Nous* (London/New York: Continuum, 2006).

———. *Difficile liberté*. Paris: Albin Michel, 2006. Translated by Sean Hand as *Difficult Freedom* (Baltimore: Johns Hopkins University Press, 1997).

Levi-Strauss, Claude. *Race et histoire*. 1. udg. ed. Paris: Denoël, 1987. Translated by n.a as *Race and History*. Paris: UNESCO, 1952.

Levy, Bernard-Henry. *La Barbarie à visage humain*. Paris: Bernard Grasset, 1977. Translated by George Holoch as *Barbarism with a Human Face* (New York: Harper and Row, 1979).

———. *Left in Dark times: A Stand Against the New Barbarism*. New York: Random House, 2008.

Lincoln, Bruce. *Holy Terrors: Thinking about Religion After September 11* (Chicago: The University of Chicago Press, 2002).

Lowy, Michael. *Redemption et Utopie: Le Judaisme libertarie en Europe central.* Paris: Presses Universitaries de France, 1988. Translated by Hope Heaney as *Redemption and Utopia: Jewish Libertarian Thought in Central Europe: A Study in Elective Affinity* (Stanford: Stanford University Press, 1992).

———. "Modern Barbarism: Notes on the Fiftieth Anniversaries of Auschwitz and Hiroshima." *Monthly Review* 47 (1995): 4–26.

———. *Fire Alarm: Reading Walter Benjamin's on the Concept of History.* Translated by Chris Turner. London: Verso, 2005.

Luxemburg, Rosa. *Politische Schriften.* Frankfurt: Europäische Verlagsanstall, 1966. Selections translated by Dick Howard as *Selected Political Writings of Rosa Luxemburg* (New York: Monthly Review Press, 1971).

Lyotard, Jean Francoise. *Heidegger et "les juifs."* Paris: Galilée, 1988, Translated by Andreas Michel and Mark Robertsy as *Heidegger and "the jews"* (Minneapolis: University of Minessota Press, 1990).

Mack, Michael. *German Idealism and the Jew: The Inner Anti-Semitism of Philosophy and German Jewish Responses.* Chicago: University of Chicago Press, 2003.

Maldonado-Torres, Nelson. *Against War: Views from the Underside of Modernity.* Durham: Duke University Press, 2008.

Malka, Salomon. *Emmanuel Levinas: La vie et la trace.* Paris: Albin Michel, 2002. Translated by Sonja Embree as *Emmanuel Levinas: His Life and Legacy* (Pittsburgh: Duquesne University Press, 2006).

Mannheim, Karl. *Ideologie und Utopie.* Bonn: F. Cohen, 1929. Translated by Louis Wirth as *Ideology and Utopia* (New York: Hartcourt, 1954).

Marcuse, Herbert. *Reason and Revolution: Hegel and the Rise of Social Theory.* Atlantic Highlands: Humanities Press, 1983.

Martinez, Maria Elena. *Genealogical Fictions: Limpieza de Sangre, Religion, and Gender in Colonial Mexico.* Stanford: Stanford University Press, 2008.

Martínez Zuviría, Gustavo. *Cuentos de Oro.* Buenos Aires: Tor, 1923.

———. *El Kahal.* Buenos Aires: Editores de Hugo Wast, 1935.

———. *666.* Buenos Aires: Editores de Buenos Aires, 1942.

Marx, Karl. *Werke, Artikel, Entwürfe, März 1843 bis August 1844.* Berlin: Dietz Verlag, 1982.

Marx, Karl, and Ernest Mandel. *Capital: a critique of political economy.* New York, N.Y.: Penguin Books, 1976.

Marx, Karl, and Friedrich Engels. *Manifest der Kommunistischen Partei veröffentlicht im Februar 1848.* London: Gedruckt in der Office der "Bildungs-Gesellschaft für Arbeiter" von J. E. Burghard, 1848.

———. *Buch II. Der Zirkulationsprozess des Kapitals.* 8. Aufl. ed. Berlin: Dietz, 1961.

———. *Karl Marx Friedrich Engels Gesamtausgabw.* Berlin: Dietz Verlag, 1982.

Marx, Karl, and Shlomo Avineri. *Karl Marx on Colonialism and Modernization; His Despatches [sic] and Other Writings on China, India, Mexico, the Middle East and North Africa.* Garden City: Doubleday, 1968.

Marx, Karl, Loyd David Easton, and Kurt H. Guddat. *Writings of the Young Marx on Philosophy and Society.* Garden City: Doubleday, 1967.

Massad, Joseph. "The 'Post-Colonial' Colony: Time, Space and Bodies in Palestine/ Israel." In *The Pre-Occupation of Postcolonial Studies*, Fawzia Afzal-Khan et al., ed., 319–332. Durham: Duke University Press, 2000.

Mate, Reyes. *Memoria de Occidente. Actualidad de Pensadores Judios Olvidados*. Barcelona: Anthropos, 1997.

———. *De Atenas a Jerusalem: pensadores judios de la modernidad*. Torrejon Ardaz: Akal, 1999.

Mbembe, Achille. *On the Postcolony*. Berkeley: University of California Press, 2001.

McBride, Kelly. "Albert Memmi in the Era of Decolonization." *Journal of French and Francophone Philosophy* 19.2 (2011): 50–66.

Memmi, Albert. *Agar: Roman*. Paris: Correa, 1955. Translated by Brian Rhys as *Strangers* (New York: Orion Pres, 1960).

———. *Portrait du colonise. Prcecede du Portrait du colonisateur*. Paris: Buchet/ Chastel, 1957. Translated by Howard Greenfeld as *The Colonizer and the Colonized* (New York: Beacon Press, 1991).

———. *Portrait d'un Juif*. Paris: Gallimard, 1962. Translated by Elisabeth Abbott as *Portrait of a Jew* (New York: The Orion Press, 1962).

———. *Anthologie des ecrivains maghrebins d'expression francaise: sous la direction de A. Memmi. Choix et presentation de J. Arnaud et al*. Paris: Presence Africaine, 1965.

———. *La libération du juif*. Paris: Gallimard, 1966. Translated by Judy Hyun as *The Liberation of the Jew* (New York: Orion Press, 1966).

———. *La statue de sel*. Paris: Gallimard, 1966. Translated by Edouard Roditti as *The Pillar of Salt* (New York: Beacon Press, 1992).

———. *L' Homme Dominé*. Paris: Gallimard, 1968. Translated by n.d. as *The Dominated Man* (New York: Orion Press, 1968).

———. "La vie impossible de Frantz Fanon."*Esprit* 39 (1971): 267–269. Translated by Thomas Cassirer and Michael Twomey as "The Impossible Life of Frantz Fanon." *The Massachusetts Review* 14.1 (1973): 32–34.

———. *Juifs et Arabes*. Paris: Gallimard, 1974. Translated by Eleonor Levieux as *Jews and Arabs* (Chicago: J Philip O'Hara, 1975).

———. *Portrait du décolonisé arabo-musulman et de quelques autres*. Paris: Gallimard, 2004. Translated by Roberto Bnonnono as *Decolonization and the Decolonized* (Minneapolis: University of Minnesota Press, 2006).

Memmi, Albert, and Victor Malka. *La terre interieure: Entretiens d'Albert Memmi avec Victor Malka*. Paris: Gallimard, 1976.

Mendieta, Eduardo. *The Frankfurt School on Religion: Key Writings by the Major Thinkers*. New York: Routledge, 2005.

Mignolo, Walter. *The Darker Side of the Renaissance: Literacy, Territoriality, and Colonization*. Ann Arbor: University of Michigan Press, 1995.

———. *Local Histories/Global Designs: Coloniality, Subaltern Knowledges, and Border Thinking*. Princeton: Princeton University Press, 2000.

———. *Capitalismo y geopolítica del conocimiento*. Buenos Aires: Ediciones del Signo, 2001.

———. "Delinking." *Cultural Studies* 21:2 (2007): 449–514.

———. "Dispensable and Bare Lives: Coloniality and the Hidden Political/ Economy Agenda of Modernity." *Human Architecture* 2.7 (2009): 69–87.

———. *The Darker Side of Western Modernity: Global Futures, Decolonial Options.* Durham: Duke University Press, 2011.

Mitchell, Harvey. *Voltaire's Jews and Modern Jewish Identity: Rethinking the Enlightenment.* Oxon: Routledge, 2008.

Morshead, E. D. A. et al. *Nine Greek Dramas by Aeschylus, Sophocles, Euripides and Aristophanes.* Whitefish: Kessinger Publishing, 2004.

Mortley, Raoul. *French Philosophers in Conversation: Levinas, Schneider, Serres, Irigaray, Le Doeuff, Derrida.* London: Routledge, 1991.

Myers, David. *Resisting History: Historicism and Its Discontents in German-Jewish Thought.* Princeton: Princeton University Press, 2003.

Netanyahu, Benzion. *The Origins of the Inquisition in Fifteenth Century Spain.* New York: Random House, 1995.

———. *The Marranos of Spain: From the Late 14th to the Early 16th Century.* Ithaca: Cornell University Press, 1999.

Ojanuga, Durrenda. "The Ethiopian Jewish Experience as Blacks in Israel." *Journal of Black Studies* 24.2 (December 1993): 147–158.

Rivera-Pagan, Luis. *A Violent Evangelism: The Political and Religious Conquest of the Americas.* Louisville: Westminster/John Knox Press, 1992.

Pagden, Anthony. *The Fall of Natural Man: The American Indian and the Origins of Comparative Ethnology.* Cambridge: Cambridge University Press, 1982.

Pappe, Ilan. *A History of Modern Palestine: One Land, Two Peoples.* Cambridge, UK: Cambridge University Press, 2004.

———. *The Ethnic Cleansing of Palestine.* Oxford: Oneworld, 2006.

Parfitt, Tudor. "The Use of the Jew in Colonial Discourses." In *Orientalism and the Jews*, Ivan Kalmar and Derek Penslar, eds., 51–67. Waltham: Brandeis University Press, 2005.

Peabody, Sue. "'A Nation Born to Slavery': Missionaries and Racial Discourse in Seventeen-Century French Antilles." *Social History* 38.1 (2004): 113–126.

Penslar, Derek. *Israel in History the Jewish State in Comparative Perspective.* London: Routledge, 2007.

Peperzak Adriaan. *To the Other: An Introduction to the Philosophy of Emmanuel Levinas.* West Lafayette: Purdue University Press, 1993.

Perednik, Gustavo. *Matar sin que se note. El ataque de los ayatolás a la Argentina...* Buenos Aires: Planeta, 2009.

Pipes, Daniel. "Radicalism Islam vs Civilization." Danielpipes.org, http://www. danielpipes.org/4254/radical-islam-vs-civD\ilization

Rhem, Kathleen. "Bush: Americans Have Security for the Next Generations," defense.gov, May 2, 2003, http://www.defense.gov/News/NewsArticle. aspx?ID=29027

Robins, Nicholas. *Native Insurgencies and the Genocidal Impulse in the Americas.* Bloomington: Indiana University Press, 2005.

Rock, David. *Authoritarian Argentina the Nationalist Movement, Its History, and Its Impact.* Berkeley: University of California Press, 1993.

Rose, Paul Lawrence. *Revolutionary Anti-Semitism in Germany from Kant to Wagner.* Princeton: Princeton University Press, 1990.

Roumani, Judith. *Albert Memmi.* Edited by Celfan. Philadelphia: Dept. of Fren.& It. – Temple U, 1987.

Said, Edward. *Orientalism.* New York: Vintage Books, 1978.

———. *The Question of Palestine.* New York: Times Books, 1979.

———. *Culture and Imperialism.* New York: Knopf, 1993.

———. *Representations of the Intellectual.* New York: Vintage Books, 1996.

———. "Diary: An Encounter with Jean-Paul Sartre." *London Review of Books* 22.11 (June 1, 2000): 42–43.

———. *Freud and the Non-European.* London and New York: Verso, 2003.

Salemohamed, George. "Levinas: From Ethics to Political Theology." *Economy and Society* 21 (1992): 78–94.

Salter, Mark. *Barbarians and Civilization in International Relations.* London: Pluto Press, 2002.

Sand, Shlomo. *Matai ve'ekh humtza ha'am hyedhudi.* Tel Aviv: Resling, 2008. Translated by Yael Lotan as *The Invention of the Jewish People* (London: Verso, 2009).

Sartre, Jean-Paul. *Réflexions sur la question juive.* Paris: Paul Morihien, 1946. Translated by George J. Baker as *Anti-Semite and Jew* (New York: Schoken, 1995).

Schehr, Lawrence. "Albert Memmi's Tricultural Tikkun." *French Forum* 28.3 (2003): 59–83.

Schnapper, Dominique. *Jewish Identities in France: An Analysis of Contemporary French Jewry.* Chicago: University of Chicago Press, 1983.

Schorsch, Jonathan. *Jews and Blacks in the Early Modern World.* New York: Cambridge University Press, 2004.

Sepúlveda, Juan Ginés de. *Democrates segundo; o, De las justas causas de la guerra contra los indios.* 1951.

Shenhav, Yehouda. *The Arab Jews: A Postcolonial Reading of Nationalism, Religion, and Ethnicity.* Stanford: Stanford University Press, 2006.

Shohat, Ella. "Sephardim in Israel: Zionism from the Standpoint of Its Jewish Victims." *Social Text* 19/20 (1988): 1–35.

———. "Dislocated Identities: Reflection of an Arab Jew." *Movement Research: Performance Journal* 5 (1992): 8.

———. "Notes on the Post-Colonial." *Social Texts* 31/32 (1992): 99–113.

———. "The Invention of the Mizrahim." *Journal of Palestine Studies* 29.1 (1999): 5–20.

———. *Taboo, Memories, Diasporic Voices.* Durham: Duke University Press, 2006.

———. *Israeli Cinema: East/West and the Politics of Representation.* London and New York: I.B. Tauris, 2010.

Shohat, Ella, and Robert Stam. *Unthinking Eurocentrism: Multiculturalism and the Media*. London and New York: Routledge, 1994.

Sicher, Efraim. *Race, Color, Identity: Rethinking Discourses about "Jews" in the Twenty-first Century*. New York: Berghahn Books, 2013.

Silverblatt, Irene. *Modern Inquisitions: Peru and the Colonial Origins of the Civilized World*. Durham: Duke University Press, 2004.

Slabodsky, Santiago. "De-Colonial Jewish Thought and the Americas." In *Post-Colonial Philosophy of Religion*, Purshumottama Bilimoria and Andrew Irvine eds., 251–272. Dordrecht, The Netherlands: Springer, 2010.

———. "Emmanuel Levinas' Geopolitics: Overlooked Conversations between Rabbinical and Third World Decolonialisms." *Journal of Jewish Thought and Philosophy* 28.2 (2010): 147–165.

———. Talmudic Terrorism in Bethlehem." In *Biblical Texts, UR-Contexts and Contemporary Realities in Israel and Palestine*, Mitri Raheb, ed., 181–198. Bethlehem: Dyar Publisher, 2011.

Sofer, Roni. "Bush Condemns Barbaric and Vicious Attack," ynetnews.com, March 7, 2008, http://www.ynetnews.com/articles/0,7340,L-3516063,00.html

Stam, Robert, and Ella Shohat. *Race in Translation: Culture Wars Around the Postcolonial Atlantic*. New York: New York University Press, 2012.

Stein, Rebecca, and Ted Swedenburg. *Palestine, Israel, and the Politics of Popular Culture*. Durham: Duke University Press, 2005.

Steiner, George. *Language and Silence; Essays on Language, Literature, and the Inhuman*. New York: Atheneum, 1967.

Sternhell, Zeev. *The Founding Myths of Israel: Nationalism, Socialism, and the Making of the Jewish State*. Princeton: Princeton University Press, 1998.

Suttclife, Adam. *Judaism and Enlightenment*. Cambridge: Cambridge University Press, 2003.

Swedberg, Richard. *Tocqueville's Political Economy*. Princeton: Princeton University Press, 2009.

Swirski, Shlomo. *Israel: The Oriental Majority*. Translated by Barbara Swirski. London: Zed Books, 1989.

Taguieff, Pierre. *Rising from the Muck: The New Anti-Semitism in Europe*. Translated by Patrick Camiller. Chicago: Ivan R. Dee, 2004.

Tocqueville, Alexis de. *Writings on Empire and Slavery*. Translated and edited by Jenniffer Pitts. Baltimore: Johns Hopkins University Press, 2001.

Tuastad, Dag. "Neo-Orientalism and the New Barbarism Thesis: Aspects of the Symbolic Violence in the Middle East conflict(s)." *Third World Quarterly* 24.4 (2004): 591–599.

Voltaire, *Oeuvres completes XXVIII*. Paris: Garnier frères, 1879.

Wallerstein, Immanuel. "The Three Instances of Hegemony in the History of the Capitalist World-System." *International Journal of Comparative Sociology* XXIV (1983): 100–107.

———. *European Universalism: The Rhetoric of Power*. New York: New Press, 2006.

Wiggershaus, Rolf. *The Frankfurt School: Its History, Theories, and Political Significance.* Translated by Michael Robertson. Cambridge: MIT Press, 1995.

Wilder, Gary. *The French Imperial Nation-State: Negritude & Colonial Humanism Between the Two World Wars.* Chicago: University of Chicago Press, 2005.

Wilder, Gary, and Albert Memmi. "Irreconcilable Differences: A Conversation with Albert Memmi." *Transitions* 71 (1996): 158–177.

Wuriga, Rabson. "Role and Impact of Intellectual Factor in the 18th-20th century 'European conception of' Jews as Jews': A Revisition." *Human Architecture* 7.2 (2009): 53–68.

Wurmser, Meyrav. "Post-Zionism and the Sepharadi Question." *The Middle East Quarterly* 12.2 (2005): 21–30.

Yerushalmi, Yosef. *Assimilation and Racial Anti-Semitism: The Iberian and the German Models.* New York: Leo Baeck Institute, 1982.

Young, Robert. *Postcolonialism: An Historical Introduction.* Oxford, UK: Blackwell Publishers, 2001.

Zea, Leopoldo. *Discurso desde la* marginación *y la barbarie.* Barcelona: Anthopos, 1987.

Zola, Emile. "J'accuse…! Lettre Au President De La Republique." In *L' Aurore* (January 13, 1898), 1–2. Translated by L. F. Austin as *Emile Zola, The Dreyfus Case: Four Letters to France* (London and New York: John Lane, 1898), 22.

Zureik, Elia. *The Palestinians in Israel: A Study in Internal Colonialism.* London: Routledge & K. Paul, 1979.

Index

CPSIA information can be obtained at www.ICGtesting.com
Printed in the USA
LVOW04s2042210915

455093LV00014B/152/P